MW00913828

Working with Students with Disabilities

Working with Students with Disabilities

Utilizing Resources in the Helping Profession

First Edition

Edited by Cassandra Sligh Conway, David Staten, and Mable Scott

cognella
SAN DIEGO

Bassim Hamadeh, CEO and Publisher
Amy Smith, Senior Project Editor
Alia Bales, Production Editor
Jess Estrella, Senior Graphic Designer
Stephanie Kohl, Licensing Coordinator
Natalie Piccotti, Director of Marketing
Kassie Graves, Vice President of Editorial
Jamie Giganti, Director of Academic Publishing

Copyright © 2021 by Cognella, Inc. All rights reserved. No part of this publication may be reprinted, reproduced, transmitted, or utilized in any form or by any electronic, mechanical, or other means, now known or hereafter invented, including photocopying, microfilming, and recording, or in any information retrieval system without the written permission of Cognella, Inc. For inquiries regarding permissions, translations, foreign rights, audio rights, and any other forms of reproduction, please contact the Cognella Licensing Department at rights@cognella.com.

Trademark Notice: Product or corporate names may be trademarks or registered trademarks and are used only for identification and explanation without intent to infringe.

Cover image copyright © 2011 Depositphotos/cienpies.

Printed in the United States of America.

ACADEMIC PUBLISHING
3970 Sorrento Valley Blvd., Ste. 500, San Diego, CA 92121

Contents

Foreword

W*ORKING WITH STUDENTS WITH DISABILITIES: UTILIZING Resources in the Helping Profession* is a dynamic and engaging text that introduces us to individuals who are diverse with similarities and differences that are common to all of us, yet they have disabilities that impair the quality of their educational lives. To help these individuals, an understanding of their disabilities is of paramount importance. Professionals need to communicate with other professionals who are working with the same individual with disabilities to be able to effectively incorporate strategies that will assist the whole human being. Professionals who are members of a multidisciplinary team work together to assist individuals who are disabled. When professionals are not aware of what other professionals are cognizant of in disabilities, students will not achieve their maximum potential. In addition, to effectively work with students with disabilities, the most current and empirical research needs to be employed to enable these individuals to maximize their academic, behavioral, social and emotional needs. Students need competent experts in the helping profession to assist them in achieving their academic goals. Specific content and strategies are introduced to learn practical methods to work with students to reach their goals.

This contemporary book has been designed to provide basic information that includes relevant research and resources that professionals need to know. The text presents several broad areas of services and components to be considered. The text includes contemporary services that work with students with disabilities. This content stresses the importance of working with students with disabilities. Empirical and conceptual research is presented such as: multiple resources to utilize in working with students with disabilities based on different perspectives; factors to consider when working with students who are culturally diverse; Americans with Disabilities Act (ADA) and student services; working with students with learning disabilities, developmental disabilities, mental disabilities, physical disabilities, and recommendations and suggestions in future global pandemics (Covid 19 and other pandemic situations).

Working with Students with Disabilities: Utilizing Resources in the Helping Professions is written for general educators, counselors, special educators, students, agencies, researchers and administrators. It is also written for lay persons who interact with individuals with disabilities.

The diversity of contributors from different disciplines for this text exemplifies how Dr. Cassandra Slight Conway was able to bring a group of professionals together to produce a phenomenal text with a broad range of topics that include strategies for working with students with disabilities, research, resources, techniques and current content to the readers. Society will always have individuals who need the support of the helping professions. This text provides the best resources that professionals can utilize to work with students.

Dr. Cynthia Bryant

Preface

PROVIDING REASONABLE ACCOMMODATION SERVICES TO UNDERGRADUATE and graduate students can be a challenge at times, especially when there may be less resources due to budget cuts at universities. I had to learn how to be creative and be expeditious in providing quality resources to students. Over the years, my roles have fluctuated from administrator to professor, and I have observed the delivery of resources from both sides. I have taught undergraduate and graduate students at Predominantly White Institutions (PWIs) and Historically Black Colleges and Universities (HBCUS). Essentially, most of my teaching experiences have been in the area of graduate level education. Most of my success in delivering quality resources to graduate students has been in networks and organization contacts I have developed over the years. I developed a vast list of networks with persons in agencies and corporations internal and external to the community that I teach. Ultimately, the more resources a person (faculty member) has to offer students, the more opportunities or exposure the students may have while matriculating in a program of study.

The ideas behind this book effort began about three years ago while I taught a graduate class. As I was analyzing case scenario examples with several of my graduate students, I began thinking, "we need a textbook that is interactive and reviews vital areas in utilizing resources with students with disabilities in the helping professions." To accomplish this task, I approached two colleagues in the helping professions to join this endeavor. Dr. David Staten and Dr. Mable Scott joined this project and through joint collaborations, we have found others to write chapters on select topics. I applaud Dr. Staten and Dr. Scott for their dedication and their due diligence in bringing others to this project. This project is successful because of the many helping professions identified within the chapters. Professionals from many agencies, colleges, and universities joined this book effort.

Why Is This Area Important?

Over the last years, I have taught in a rural setting where some graduate students with disabilities have a lack of resources. The university in which the student attended were faced with insurmountable budget issues placed on them by state systems and at times were faced with some tough decisions. In many instances, one cannot blame the university for the situation. If one examines the situation closely, there are many variables that are at the heart of these issues and the main reasons are systemic and historical in nature. Considering the recent 2020 pandemic, the tragic deaths of people due to brutal methods, and other current situations that have affected our educational system, there are useful recommendations addressed in this textbook that can be applied across many global systems.

While reading this textbook, I hope that each person is open to the purpose. This textbook is meant to serve its purpose, promote a positive change in the lives of students with disabilities. I hope a global message from this textbook is one of love and peace. "I think the best lesson we all learn in life is to give back to others and when we help one another, our lives are not lived in vain."

Dr. Cassandra Sligh Conway

Chapter 1

Working with Students with Disabilities
A Holistic View

Cassandra Sligh Conway and Cherilyn T. Minniefield

Abstract

This chapter provides essential information on understanding the needs of undergraduate and graduate students with disabilities. It notes several terms that are essential in understanding the history of the word *disability* and other key terms. The chapter provides the reader with empirical and conceptual literature, essential statistics, model programs, valued resources, and recommendations to work with students with disabilities.

Introduction

What services will I need to be successful? Who can work with me as I matriculate through the university? Will I be "different" if I disclose my disability? Who can I turn to receive services? These may be some of the questions that undergraduate and graduate students with disabilities have, as there are many things to consider when a student plans to seek a degree. In order to examine the resources to assist students with disabilities in undergraduate and graduate programs one must review the background research (empirical and conceptual) and statistical information on the groups and discuss the importance of the group in the helping professions. As faculty who have worked at HBCUS and PWIs, there seems to be an observational finding (e.g., students with disabilities who transition from high school to the college level very often were followed throughout the secondary experience with a 504 plan or IDEA (individualized disability education plan)). Therefore, if a college/university does not have resources to effectively work with these students with disabilities, what happens? Do the students leave the setting after 1 year? What can the college provide to enhance the students' matriculation and success? How do the faculty, administrators, and staff continue to provide resources that are effective throughout the college or graduate years? These same questions can be reviewed with graduate students.

For example, if there are no valuable resources provided to graduate students with disabilities, then how are these students supposed to be successful? For purposes of these types of discussions, one can acknowledge the helping professions as these professions provide direct or indirect services to students with disabilities, for example, counseling, medical fields, health sciences, social sciences, physical education, rehabilitation counseling, and others. To further understand the emphasis on this area in higher education, *Working With Students With Disabilities: Utilizing Resources in the Helping Professions,* the information provided in this effort includes those studies, ideas, and concepts that best fit the area reviewed.

There are interesting findings related to students with disabilities. For instance, a U.S. Department of Education, National Center for Education Statistics Report (2018) noted the following results:

> The Individuals with Disabilities Education Act (IDEA), enacted in 1975, mandates that children and youth ages 3–21 with disabilities be provided a free and appropriate public-school education. The percentage of total public-school enrollment that represents children served by federally supported special education programs increased from 8.3 percent to 13.8 percent between 1976–77 and 2004–05. Much of this overall increase can be attributed to a rise in the percentage of students identified as having specific learning disabilities from 1976–77 (1.8 percent) to 2004–05 (5.7 percent). The overall percentage of students being served in programs for those with disabilities decreased between 2004–05 (13.8 percent) and 2014–15 (13.0 percent). However, there were different patterns of change in the percentages served with some specific conditions between 2004–05 and 2014–15. The percentage of children identified as having other health impairments (limited strength, vitality, or alertness due to chronic or acute health problems such as a heart condition, tuberculosis, rheumatic fever, nephritis, asthma, sickle cell anemia, hemophilia, epilepsy, lead poisoning, leukemia, or diabetes) rose from 1.1 to 1.7 percent of total public school enrollment, the percentage with autism rose from 0.4 to 1.1 percent, and the percentage with developmental delay rose from 0.7 to 0.8 percent. The percentage of children with specific learning disabilities declined from 5.7 percent to 4.5 percent of total public-school enrollment during this period. (p. xx)

Students with disabilities who are enrolled in undergraduate and graduate programs must understand the culture of the university/college attended. This is also important to have access to certain services. Dobies (2018) recommended some remarkable aspects of successful planning:

It is important for individuals to have a clear understanding of their own disability and how it impacts them daily. Students should work with their school counselors to determine the right fit; search the web and explore all the different options that are available; attend college fairs and community events to discuss majors, academic program, and resources; and visit with the service providers at different colleges to determine if you can find academic success. It comes down to academic programs and if the college is the right fit for you. The laws shift after graduation of high school, so it is important that individuals know how academic and non-academic accommodations are accessed at the postsecondary level. Self-advocacy is the foundation to knowing your rights and responsibilities, and students should not be afraid to ask questions and seek assistance. BE THE EXPERT. Look at the accommodations that have worked for you in the past and make sure that the college or university that you choose can address these needs. BE THE CHEERLEADER. Know that you have great strengths. Seek out opportunities to help build upon these strengths. BE PART OF THE TEAM. Remember that you are not alone. There are great support systems in place at many colleges that can help guide you and support you along your journey."

BE A SPOKESPERSON. Remember that effective communication with support service providers and faculty is key to your success. BE FLEXIBLE. Organization and time management are two skills not developed overnight and are continually changing depending on class schedules, extracurriculars, busy semesters, and myriad other factors.

In researching the background information related to the needs of students with disabilities, there are other important and valuable articles in the literature based on 30–40 years of work (Barnard-Brak & Sulak, 2010; Barnard-Brak, et al., 2009; Burgstahler et al., 2004; Collopy & Arnold, 2009). Other aspects that were discovered in researching this area included the differences in student learning, specifically the learning for students with disabilities in face-to-face, online, hybrid learning environments. Research in those areas pointed to several convincing discoveries such as (a) the universities must have ways to meet the needs of students with disabilities online, as this type of learning will possibly require more resources that are readily available or accessible; (b) faculty and staff need trainings on the latest ways to meet the needs of students with disabilities. In other words, old foundational pedagogical principles will not be effective with working with millennials and nontraditional students with disabilities; and (c) move toward using theoretical models that are current and base pedagogical and practical application on the latest research and practice (Barnard-Brak & Sulak, 2010; Barnard-Brak et al., 2009; Burgstahler et al., 2004; Collopy & Arnold 2009; Getzel & Thoma, 2008). There were certain articles chosen for this research as background information; moreover, certain research leaned more toward the information that students may need to know immediately in order to matriculate through the higher education environment successfully. Thus, the research provided sheds light on the rationale to provide contemporary resources to undergraduate and graduate students in higher education programs.

The next section reviews some empirical and conceptual literature related to students with disabilities in higher education, services, and groundbreaking strategies. In understanding the experience of students with disabilities in postsecondary education, it is important to involve students in a dialogue to determine the best resources that are available to students. Equally important is the fact that the best resources be chosen in the helping profession to provide students with access to a quality education.

Background

Working with students with disabilities is an important aspect in higher education. Some students already come from different backgrounds. For instance, some students may come from backgrounds in which schools had advocates and many resources to assist them throughout secondary school. As the student progresses to the postsecondary area, some resources may still be needed in order to have a fair chance at receiving a quality education. It is the responsibility of those in higher education to ensure that an equal playing field is provided to those students with disabilities. In order to ensure that there is an equal playing field to receive a quality education, the university officials, faculty, staff, and students must be involved in a dialogue and a sharing of information. According to Hampton and Godsden (2007),

> Universities provide a competitive environment that in some ways resembles the sporting field. But unlike the arrangements made for disabled athletes, for whom separated fields of competition are available, disabled students are required to enter into open competition with non-disabled students. To make this open competition fair, students with disability are provided with a range of accommodations to compensate. The availability of these compensatory measures gives rise to some difficult decision making for university administrators. These difficulties are mostly concerned with two questions of fairness: who is eligible for the accommodation, and how much accommodation is appropriate? (pp. 225–238)

Past dissertations on students with disabilities have impacted this area tremendously. For instance, Duggan (2010) noted,

> Students with disabilities in higher education are a growing population throughout the United States. The most recent statistics from the U.S. Department of Education's National Center for Education Statistics show that 12.4 % of students in community colleges during academic year 2003 to 2004 had a disability; this evidences an increasing trend from the 8% reported for 1992. The U.S Department of Education determined there are over 1,400,000 students with disabilities in American higher education today. This increase shows there are even more students who never disclose their disability, or in the case of learning and cognitive disabilities, may not even realize they have one. Clearly this is a large group of students, yet data tracking and research on students with disabilities in higher education, and more specifically students with disabilities in community colleges, are both limited and outdated. This lack of data and research on students with disabilities is a serious issue that needs to be addressed. There are many remarkable persons with disabilities who have made major contributions to the United States and the world. Some of the country's most famous people have had some type of disability. Steven Hawking, a physicist with Amyotrophic Lateral Sclerosis (ALS), was one of the first individuals to apply complex mathematics to explain astronomical phenomena such as black holes and the Big Bang Theory. (pp. 1, internal citations omitted)

Colleges and universities should ensure that there is an office for students with disabilities on campus that houses information and resources for students with disabilities. With this type of office, the students are aware of where to go to sign up for services or to obtain reasonable accommodations in the classroom and on campus. There is great value in having these types of offices at any campus. This office not only provide these resources but can be a valuable aid in providing workshops and seminars to students, faculty, and staff related to reasonable accommodations. As noted by the American Psychological Association (2008),

> Reasonable accommodations are modifications or adjustments to the tasks, environment or to the way things are usually done that enable individuals with disabilities to have an equal opportunity to participate in an academic program or a job. Broad categories of accommodations include changes to the application process to ensure an equal opportunity to apply for program enrollment,

changes that enable a student with a disability to perform the essential functions of the academic program, and changes that enable a student with a disability to enjoy equal benefits and privileges of the program (e.g., access to training). The Americans with Disabilities Act (1990) stipulates that postsecondary institutions are responsible for providing necessary accommodations when a student discloses a disability. ... Providing accommodations do not compromise the essential elements of a course or curriculum; nor do they weaken the academic standards or integrity of a course. Accommodations simply provide an alternative way to accomplish the course requirements by eliminating or reducing disability-related barriers. They provide a level playing field, not an unfair advantage. (para. 1–3, internal citations omitted)

Colleges and universities have a responsibility to provide individuals with physical and mental health disabilities an opportunity to participate fully in educational programs and services, granting them the capability of participating in activities of daily living and ensuring equality in daily life (Staglin, 2019). With the rising number of suicides, alcohol-related incidents, and other serious emotional and mental health problems students experience, it is imperative that faculty and support staff at institutions of higher education recognize the warning signs and symptoms that characterize common mental health challenges among college students, respond immediately and effectively, and assist with creating a sustainable environment for this growing segment of the student population.

College students face a number of developmental challenges by virtue of their age at the traditional time of entry, the novelty of an inherently more rigorous educational process than the one they have typically just completed, and the potentially daunting task of managing all of the pressures that inevitably accompany the college experience. In addition to the academic pressures, stresses, and demands students face in and outside the classroom, many will bring with them and develop their own set of personal, or even psychological, difficulties that serve to compound an already complex journey with built-in twist and turns.

Often at the heart of the battle is the juggling act that forces students to strike a balance between the values and expectations communicated by parents before they head off to college and the spoken and unspoken influence they perceive from peers and professors throughout their matriculation. Add to the mix the learning curve, risky alternative methods of coping, and extracurricular activities and you have a formula for potential crisis. It is through this exploration of struggles that the mental health dilemma begins. Awareness of the major challenges facing students is the first step toward responding appropriately to individuals with mental health disabilities. In the wake of a host of campus shootings and threats to safety across the United States in the past couple of decades, institutions of higher learning—much like government, school, and public transportation systems in the United States—are strengthening and enhancing their agency standards by requiring training, promoting mental health services, and imposing stricter policies in an effort to be more proactive versus reactive about public safety. Once constituents are aware, developing action plans for assisting students with achieving goals is the next step (Vidourek et al., 2014).

For students, tackling the crisis effectively will involve penetrating the barrier of stigma associated with mental health to seek the assistance they need. This is no easy task in an era dominated by social media. Teaching students to incorporate consistent self-care regimens into their everyday living and thinking is critical. Students must also learn to stay connected to parents, families, and communities no matter how much they may embrace their independence. Faculty and staff are key informants when it comes to stressing the importance of organization and management of the vast array of resources available to college students in confronting the campus mental health crisis (Vidourek et al., 2014).

Universities should offer a variety of services for students with documented disabilities in compliance with Section 504 of the American Disabilities Act of 1973 and with the Americans With Disabilities Act of 1990 (ADA). According to Section 504 and ADA, "A person with a disability is someone who has a disability that impairs a major life function, who has a history of having a disability, and or who is regarded as having a disability" (National Network: Information, Guidance, and Training on the Americans With Disabilities Act, n.d.b.).

Mentoring Students With Disabilities

Working with students with disabilities will involve a multiple array of services and advocacy on the college/university level. One of the ways to assist students with disabilities might be through using formal or informal mentoring interventions.

There is an abundance of literature on mentoring, mentoring functions, types of mentoring, and mentoring programs. For the most part, mentoring has been identified as a crucial element that can determine the failure or success in one's endeavors, whether they are academic, career related, or an adjustment to a new role in society. However, little has been written or said about mentoring at various stages of personal development. There are other models of mentoring that have shown that self-concept changes over time and develops as a result of experience. Self-concept and self-efficacy have shown to boost one's identity. Like career development, mentoring can be a lifelong phenomenon.

The mentor-mentee relationship is meaningful and valuable to both parties for attaining immediate goals and for deepening insights about performance and growth processes. Mentoring is important because any person who is motivated and concerned about achieving personal or professional growth faces the challenge of articulating a substantive direction or change in an area they do not completely understand. In addition, the person must plan and implement specific action steps that have the potential to lead to the desired growth. It is important to note that maturity and character count when choosing your mentor or mentee.

The mentoring relationship must be a kinesthetic shared experience between the mentor and the mentee. The mentor's role is to be an honest and open sounding board and a source of wisdom for assessing and planning (Leise, 2007). Leise outlined 10 effective principles that are essential to follow when choosing or practicing academic mentorship. These principles are presented in Table 1.1.

TABLE 1.1   The 10 Effective Principles of the Mentoring Process

1	Mentoring requires a trusting, confidential relationship based on mutual respect.
2	Mentoring involves a clearly bounded relationship that is close and not coerced (unlike friendship or parenting).
3	Mentoring involves a definite time commitment.
4	Mentoring relationship is planned for enhancing specific growth goals of a mentee, not for organizational requirements such as employee evaluation.
5	The purpose of mentoring must be mutually established by the mentor and mentee with clearly defined goals/outcomes.
6	Mentors should model performances for mentees thereby providing them with opportunities to observe and develop insights.
7	Mentors provide quality performance assessments, especially of a mentee's self-assessment.
8	Mentees must show progress by "raising the bar" for themselves as their insights and skills increase.
9	The mentoring relationship ends when the mentee is able to operate independently.
10	Mentors follow a servant leadership model by providing much value to another without receiving extrinsic rewards.

Mentoring in Table 1.1 is clearly illustrated and defined in a manner that is easy to observe and establishes the purpose and rationale for mentoring. This type of data validates the entire mentoring process in terms of efficiency and efficacy.

Types of Disabilities

There are many types of disabilities for which an undergraduate or graduate student may need access to services or resources while in college or attending a university. For this effort, there will be a focus on physical, mental and intellectual disabilities.

Programs/Students With Disabilities

For students with disabilities, the chances to receive some type of education are much more now. Some of the information mentioned about the model programs in research is essential in working with undergraduate and graduate students with disabilities. Burgstahler, Burgstahler & Cronheim (cited in Brown et al., 2010) encouraged educators to consider the benefits that online learning can have on working with students with disabilities if implemented based on best practices and necessary planning with reasonable accommodations. In reviewing this information, it seems that this model would be very instrumental in working with graduate students, as some graduate students may be working and taking care of families and need to have curricula designed at a distance. These authors say to "consider using the Internet to help create and support positive mentoring relationships ... [to] help students with disabilities achieve their social, academic, and career potential" (as cited in Brown et al., 2010 p. 108). Noonan et al. (as cited in Brown et al., 2010) "studied the successful career paths of 17 women with physical and sensory disabilities via in-depth semi structured interviews" (p. 108). From this study, it was noted that mentoring can serve as a great resource to work with students with disabilities who need career transitions, desire promotions, or need a career focus.

Purpose

This book provides essential information to students and educators related to resources for students with disabilities. The primary purpose of this contemporary text is to use the book in the classroom to provide students with useful information on the topic. Over 20 years of data in the disability area and from research conducted at different institutions note that students with disabilities request more services and resources. This effort gives more of a student focus as some of the resources that students need related to disability should come from those faculty and staff who are in direct interaction with undergraduate and graduate students. The helping profession is one that should consider the actual needs of the consumers and the market value of this exploration. The helping professions include counseling, psychology, sociology, physical education, health sciences, and other disciplines.

This book provides information to students and educators related to resources for students with disabilities.

1. Provide students' perceptions of disability resources to assist students with necessary services.
2. Provide information related to classroom management, online, hybrid, and face-to-face traditional classes.
3. Provide useful resources to assist students with disabilities.
4. Provide information related to reasonable accommodation services and students with disabilities.
5. Provide information related to different disabilities and students with disabilities.

6. Explore the usefulness of adding standards in curricula to add necessary information in working with students with disabilities.
7. Provide students with questions at the end of each chapter that can provide a more in-depth discussion and develop students' knowledge on areas such as types of disabilities, advocacy, services, resources, ADA, reasonable accommodations, technology, and library services, among other specialized topics in discipline specific area.

Definition of Terms

Several terms will be used throughout by authors and contributing authors. This current review of terms is to shed light on the aspects discussed by different authors, which may provide the reader with a conceptual review of the terms.

Disability

In the literature, the term *disability*, "in the context of the ADA, is a legal term rather than a medical one. Because it has a legal definition, the ADA's definition of disability is different from how disability is defined under some other laws, such as for Social Security disability–related benefits. The ADA defines a person with a disability as a person who has a physical or mental impairment that substantially limits one or more major life activities. This includes people who have a record of such impairment, even if they do not currently have a disability. It also includes individuals who do not have a disability but are regarded as having a disability. The ADA also makes it unlawful to discriminate against a person based on that person's association with a person with a disability" (National Network: Information, Guidance, and Training on the Americans With Disabilities Act, n.d.b.).

Helping Professions

According to Graf et al. (2014), a "helping profession is defined as a professional interaction between a helping expert and a client, initiated to nurture the growth of, or address the problems of a person's physical, psychological, intellectual or emotional constitution, including medicine, nursing, psychotherapy, psychological counseling, social work, education or coaching" (p .1).

ADA

The Americans With Disabilities Act (ADA) of 1990 gives civil rights protection to individuals with disabilities, similar to that provided to individuals on the basis of race, sex, national origin and religion. The ADA guarantees equal opportunity for individuals with disabilities in the areas of employment, state and local government services, public transportation, privately operated transportation available to the public, places of public accommodation and services operated by private entities, and telephone services offered to the general public. Many regard the ADA as the most sweeping piece of civil rights legislation since the Civil Rights Act of 1964 (APA, 2008).

Physical Disabilities

A physical disability is "a physical or mental condition that significantly limits a person's motor, sensory, or cognitive abilities" (The Free Dictionary, n.d.).

Intellectual Disabilities

According to the American Psychological Association (2017), "Intellectual disability involves problems with general mental abilities that affect functioning in two areas: intellectual functioning (such as learning, problem solving, judgement) adaptive functioning (activities of daily life such as communication and independent living)."

Mental Health Conditions

According to the Mayo Clinic (2019), these are "disorders that affect your mood, thinking and behavior. Examples of mental illness include depression, anxiety disorders, schizophrenia, eating disorders and addictive behaviors."

Responding to Students With Mental Health Disabilities

Data from the Association for the University and College Counseling Center Outreach (n.d.) indicates that today's students are primarily dealing with three major psychiatric conditions, including, "anxiety (48.2%), stress (39.1%), and depression (34.5%) (Lebron, 2018). The National Alliance on Mental Illness (NAMI, 2012) reports that "75 % of lifetime cases of mental health conditions begin by age 2." More than "40 % of college students have felt stressed" and some "(7%) have considered suicide within the past year. Additionally, more students than ever before are taking psychotropic medications to moderate the effects of mental illness."

Parents play a vital role in the process. There are a number of studies that seem to note the contribution of family support in the development of college students. Many authors, like Staglin (2019), Lebron (2018) and Vidourek et al. (2014), noted that support systems are important to consider in facilitating the adjustment process for students with disabilities.

The dual stress of leaving home and moving away from family presents a challenge to many new college students. For many adolescents in their teens, college is an experience that provides a unique opportunity for social, emotional, and intellectual growth and development (Baker & Bohdan, 1984). Secure parental attachment may foster self-confidence, a willingness to explore the environment, and the development of social competence during the leaving home period. When families cannot fulfill this support function because of distance, alternatives may need to be identified (Baker &Bohdan, 1984). For example, the campus support office could be viewed as reasonable family surrogates as these areas can provide support and a nonthreatening, trusting, sense of community.

In a survey conducted by the National Alliance on Mental Illness (NAMI, 2012), college students living with mental health conditions were queried about their experiences in school. The survey was designed to inquire about their perceptions of the campus resources and whether their needs were being met. Additionally, the survey inquired about whether improvements were needed. Based on the outcomes of the survey, university websites need to provide comprehensive, detailed, and updated information about services, symptoms, and risks associated with various mental health conditions. This allows many students to become acquainted with the signs and symptom, as well as the treatment options available to address challenges.

Alcohol usage is another challenge at colleges and other schools. Institutions both encourage and require students with alcohol or drug-related challenges to seek assistance, be it of their own volition or as a result of referrals by faculty, staff, or others. Campus counseling centers typically provide drug and alcohol education and information and referrals for substance abuse treatment. Community referrals are available to students who present with alcohol or drug issues. Additionally, campuses and agencies should provide crisis intervention options for after-hours and weekend emergencies.

The problem of substance abuse in college students is well documented and continues to receive considerable attention. Alcohol has been a drug of choice among college students and younger students, with marijuana usually being an equally as popular drug (Miller, n.d.). Substance abuse of any kind can be a contributor to many problems students experience (e.g., anxiety, depression, and suicidal ideation).

Responding to the Needs of Students With Disabilities (K–12)

The needs of students with disabilities on the K–12 level are much like the needs of college students. In the literature, there are many resources available on assisting students in K–12. By continuing to access these resources and by supporting the efforts of those in the helping professions, the needs of all students will be heard and reached in remarkable ways.

Value of Narratives/Students With Disabilities

Some authors, in chapters that follow, present narratives that are important in understanding the resources that assist students in undergraduate and graduate programs. In the chapters that choose to provide narratives, some helpful strategies and recommendations are provided. These narratives are defined as cases in which the author(s) tell a story or provide information on a case that the author(s) developed to promote an understanding of the concepts in the chapter. The grounding or foundational background to support this type of reflection is based on the need to give a voice to students with disabilities, which may provide a helpful way to apply resources that university personnel, and administrators can use to provide a better quality of life to the students served.

Future Directions

Future research should include empirically based studies that examine the value of utilizing effective resources for students with disabilities in higher education, and there must be an emphasis on developing comprehensive policies and continual dialogues based on student narratives (case-by-case situations), theories, and data. This same research must use a mixed process, including qualitative and quantitative measures. Student comments can greatly benefit from the resources and type of advocacy programs a university should institute.

After reviewing the literature, some points for administrators and faculty to consider are as follows:

1. Develop formalized programs that have a specific agenda. This agenda could introduce a formal program and the process of providing faculty and trainings or explain how to provide quality services and resources to students with disabilities. Orientation day would be part of this agenda.
2. Review polices on classroom management for students with disabilities.
3. Develop an environment based on faculty and student interactions. Provide workshops and seminars on this topic (Leise, 2007).

According to Leise (2007),

> Mentoring is an important strategy for enhancing specific areas of growth that are not yet required but that are likely to support future success in a mentee's career or personal life. In this overview module the basic principles, issues, processes, skills, and contexts of mentoring have been identified and described. The metacognitive insights gained during mentoring, and by using many processes and tools, will substantially improve transfer of learning both for the mentor and the mentee. Mentors benefit from servant-leadership experiences that can add meaning and purpose to their lives as experienced professionals. For mentees, the process opens a window on their futures and on themselves,

by making it possible to experience growth that may not have happened had they been left to their own devices. Mentoring is an essential process, especially in the fast-changing world of higher education. (p. 478).

Moreover, Leise understood the role and value of quality mentoring. One must take the role even further; the mentor must be available through the good and the not so popular experiences that the mentee may go through while in a faculty role. When the mentee values the mentor from a human side, it brings forth more trust and more authenticity.

Conclusion

If a university or an agency chooses to not provide quality resources to students with disabilities, it may add to some of the feelings noted in Duggan (2010):

> Conclusions drawn from the research suggest that administrators need to clarify the responsibilities both faculty and administrators have in working with students with disabilities. Moreover, faculty and administrators need to take greater responsibility in serving these students, and not rely solely on the college's Disability Services office or one particular office to provide all of the support. In order to accomplish this transition, more disability specific training for faculty and administrators is necessary. Finally, a pedagogical paradigm shift should be examined at the institution to better address the needs of students with disabilities, particularly in view of the current funding environment. Also, the needs of students should be included in short term operational and long-term strategic planning at the college.

Another report stated it plainly and can be utilized with undergraduate and graduate faculty, staff, and administrators in providing useful resources to students with disabilities:

> It is recommended that Congress support full funding for special education, and that any funding authorized by Congress emphasize the delivery of special education services in general education settings. Further, discretionary grants for research and development should establish expectations for inclusive school practices, particularly those that address personnel development and organizational changes to sustain effective education services that address the needs of all students in an equitable manner to achieve equitable outcomes. This report also recommends that the U.S. Department of Education (ED)

stand boldly in its support of inclusive education and maintain data collection on the amount of time students spend in general education and the location of student placements. Funding opportunities for national centers and significant projects should ensure that recipients plan to:

- prepare teachers, administrators, and related service providers to implement effective schoolwide, equity-based educational services; and
- build state and local capacity for sustainable inclusive education practices.

States should be expected to carefully analyze their placement data and consider it with respect to disproportionate placement practices for students by disability label and race, across their local jurisdictions. (National Council on Disability, 2018)

Questions/Considerations

1. In Chapter 1 there were many definitions of terms. Which definition of disability is defined by American Disabilities Act?
2. Define learning, physical, mental, and intellectual disabilities.
3. Why is the ADA important?
4. What are some valuable statistics on students with disabilities?
5. Based on the information in Chapter 1, what are some ways to provide resources to students with disabilities?

Next Steps

The chapters that follow this section are related to specific topic areas on students with disabilities:

Chapter 2: Culturally Responsive Teaching/Positive Insights in the Learning Process

Chapter 3: Disability Acts and ADA Standards: The Impact on Inclusion

Chapter 4: Cultural Considerations in School Disability Counseling

Chapter 5: Boots on the Ground: Meeting the Needs of VSD's in Higher Education

Chapter 6: Undiagnosed Post-Traumatic Stress Disorder: Implications for Counselor Education Programs at Historically Black Colleges and Universities

Chapter 7: Working With Students With Disabilities: College Students With Learning Disabilities

Chapter 8: Promoting Self-Advocacy in Students With Disabilities

Chapter 9: Library Resources: Working With Students With Disabilities

References

American Psychological Association. (2008). *Americans With Disabilities Act information*. https://www.apa.org/pi/disability/resources/ada/index.aspx

American Psychological Association (2017). *What is intellectual disability?* https://www.psychiatry.org/patients-families/intellectual-disability/what-is-intellectual-disability

Association for University and College Counseling Center Outreach (n.d.). *Home page*. https://www.aucco.com.

Baker, R., & Bohdan, S. (1984). Measuring adjustment to college. *Journal of Counseling Psychology, 31*(2), 179–189.

Barnard-Brak, L., Davis, T., Tate, A., & Sulak, T. (2009). Attitudes as a predictor of college students requesting accommodations. *Journal of Vocational Rehabilitation, 31*(3), 189–198.

Barnard-Brak, L., & Sulak, T. (2010). Online versus face-to-face accommodations among college students with disabilities. *The American Journal of Distance Education, 24*(2), 81–91.

Barnard-Brak, L., Sulak, T., Tate, A., & Lechtenberger, D. (2010). Measuring college students' attitudes toward requesting accommodations: A national multi-institutional study. *Assessment for Effective Intervention, 35*(3), 141–147.

Bourke, A. B., Strehorn, K. C., & Silver, P. (2000). Faculty members' provision of instructional accommodations to students with LD. *Journal of Learning Disabilities, 33*(1), 26–32.

Brown, S. E., Takahashi, K., & Roberts, K. D. (2010). Mentoring individuals with disabilities in postsecondary education: A review of the literature. *Journal of Postsecondary Education and Disability, 23*(2), 98–111.

Burgstahler, S., Corrigan, B., & McCarter, J. (2004). Making distance learning courses accessible to students and instructors with disabilities: A case study. *Internet and Higher Education, 7*(3), 233–246. https://doi.org/10.1016/j.iheduc.2004.06.004

Burgstahler, S., & Cory, R. (2010). *Universal design in higher education: From principles to practice.* Harvard Education Press.

Collopy, R. M. B., & Arnold, J. M. (2009). To blend or not to blend: Online and blended learning environments in undergraduate teacher education. *Issues in Teacher Education, 18*(2), 85–101.

Davis, B. G. (1993). *Tools for teaching.* Jossey-Bass.

Dobies (n.d.). *Disability resources for college students.* https://www.learnhowtobecome.org/college/resources-for-students-with-disabilities/

Duggan, M. W. (2010). *Improving services for students with disabilities at community colleges* [Dissertation, National Louis University]. https://digitalcommons.nl.edu/cgi/viewcontent.cgi?article=1028&context=diss

The Free Dictionary. (n.d.). *Disability.* https://medical-dictionary.thefreedictionary.com/
Physical+disability

Graf, E.-M., Sator, M., & Spranz-Fogasy, T. (Eds.). (2014). *Discourses of helping professions.* Benjamins.

Grigorenko, E. L., Compton, D. L., Fuchs, L. S., Wagner, R. K., Willcutt, E. G., & Fletcher, J. M. (2020).
Understanding, educating, and supporting children with specific learning disabilities: 50 years of
science and practice. *American Psychologist, 75*(1), 37– 51. https://doi.org/10.1037/amp0000452

Hodge, B. M., & Preston-Sabin, J. (1997). *Accommodations–or just good teaching?: Strategies for teaching
college students with disabilities.* Praeger.

Hampton, G., & Godsden, R. (2007). Fair play for students with disabilities. *Journal of Higher Education
and Policy Management, 26*(2), 225–238. https://doi.org/10.1080/1360080042000218276

Learning Rights Law Center & Dentons US. (2018, February 6). *ADA and 504 — When is an individual with a learning disability protected by these laws?* Learning Disabilities Association of America.
https://ldaamerica.org/info/ada-and-504/

Lebron, A. (2018). *The growing trends in college mental health statistics.* Rave. Mobile Safety. https://
www.ravemobilesafety.com/blog/the-growing-trends-in-college-mental-health-statistics.

Leise, C. (2007a). Becoming a self-grower. In S. W. Beyerlein, C. Holmes, & D. K. Apple, (Eds.), Faculty
guidebook: A comprehensive tool for improving faculty performance, (4th ed). Lise, IL: Pacific
Crest.

May, A. L., & Stone, C. A. (2010). Stereotypes of individuals with learning disabilities: views of college
students with and without learning disabilities. *Journal of Learning Disabilities, 43*(6), 483–499.
https://doi.org/10.1177/0022219409355483

Mayo Clinic. (2019). *Mental illness.* https://www.mayoclinic.org/diseases-conditions/mental-illness/
symptoms-causes/syc-20374968

Miller, A. (n.d.). *The effects of drugs and alcohol on college campuses.* Seattle Pi. https://education.seat-
tlepi.com/effects-drugs-alcohol-college-campuses-3031.html

National Alliance on Mental Illness. (2012). *College students speak: A report on mental health.* https://www.
nami.org/Blogs/NAMI-Blog/November-2012/Mental-Health-Survey-College-Students-Speak.

National Center for Learning Disabilities. (n.d.). *Home page.* http://www.ncld.org/

National Council on Disability. (2018, February 7). *The segregation of students with disabilities.* https://
eric.ed.gov/?q=source%3A%22National+Council+on+Disability%22&id=ED588494.

National Network: Information, Guidance, and Training on the Americans With Disabilities
Act. (n.d.a.). *What is the definition of disability under the ADA?* https://adata.org/faq/
what-definition-disability-under-ada

National Network: Information, Guidance, and Training on the Americans With Disabilities Act. (n.d.b.).
What does a "record" of disability mean? https://adata.org/faq/what-does-record-disability-mean

Paige, R., & Marcus, K. L. (2002). *Students with disabilities preparing for postsecondary education: Know
your rights and responsibilities.* http://purl.access.gpo.gov/GPO/LPS74685

Scorgie, K., Kildal, L., & Wilgosh, L. (2010). Post-secondary students with disabilities: Issues related to empowerment and self-determination. *Developmental Disabilities Bulletin, 38*(2010), 133–145.

Scott, S., Mcguire, J., & Shaw, S. (2003). Universal design for instruction. *Remedial and Special Education, 24*(6), 369–379.

Scott, S. S. (1998). Accommodating college students with learning disabilities: How much is enough? *Innovative Higher Education, 22*(2), 85–99.

Silver, P., Bourke, A., & Strehorn, K. C. (1998). Universal instruction design in higher education: An approach for inclusion. *Equity & Excellence in Education, 31*(2), 47–51.

Staglin, G. (2019). *Addressing mental health challenges on college campuses*. Forbes. https://www.forbes.com/sites/onemind/2019/10/04/addressing-mental-health-challenges-on-college-campuses/#-3f3077a7400d.

Walters, S. (2010). Toward an accessible pedagogy: Dis/ability, multimodality, and universal design in the technical communication classroom. *Technical Communication Quarterly, 19*(4), 427–454. https://doi.org/10.1080/10572252.2010.502090

Wolf, L. E., Brown, J. T., Bork, G. R. K., Volkmar, F. R., & Klin, A. (2009). *Students with Asperger syndrome: A guide for college personnel*. Autism Asperger .

U.S. Department of Education, National Center for Education Statistics. (2018). *Digest of education statistics, 2016* (NCES 2017-094), https://nces.ed.gov/pubsearch/pubsinfo.asp?pubid=2020009.

U.S. Legal. (n.d.). *Short-term disability law and legal definition.* https://definitions.uslegal.com/s/short-term-disability/

Vaccaro, A., Kimball, E. W., Wells, R. S., & Ostiguy, B. J. (2015). Researching students with disabilities: The importance of critical perspectives. *New Scholarship for Institutional Research, 2014*(163), 25–41. https://doi.org/10.1002/ir.20084.

Vidourek, R. A., King, K. A., Nabors, L. A., & Merianos, A. L. (2014). Students' benefits and barriers to mental health help-seeking. *Health Psychology and Behavioral Medicine, 2*(1), 1009–1022. https://doi.org/10.1080/21642850.2014.963586

Chapter 2

Culturally Responsive Teaching and the Positive Insights in the Learning Process

Rose Skepple, Cassandra Sligh Conway, and Wanda Copeland

Abstract

The classroom by far is the new lab for today's learning processes. The students with disabilities must experience a learning environment in which culture is infused in the learning process. Very often the cultural lens of teaching serves as an appendage. The purpose of this effort is threefold: (a) Provide a review of some literature in the area of culturally responsive teaching; (b) provide some recommendations, suggestions, and future directions to enhance the learning process; and (c) provide suggestions for future research in this area. When working with students with disabilities, a person must be open to unique styles of teaching and understand that students with disabilities learn in a variety of ways and that culture plays a part in the learning process.

Introduction

Culturally responsive teaching is essential in the learning process. In working with students in K–12 and undergraduate and graduate programs, it is essential to understand and try to reach them by the type of instruction one chooses. By the time some students enter college, they may have one or more disabilities. Depending on the disability, it is essential that faculty use techniques that are culturally responsive to reasonably accommodate students' academic needs. Receiving information is just as important as imparting information in the learning process. In fact, this reciprocal relationship is important in communicating ideas. According to Ladson-Billings (1994), Culture is central to learning. It plays a role not only in communicating and receiving information, but also in shaping the thinking process of groups and individuals. A pedagogy that acknowledges, responds to, and celebrates fundamental cultures offers full, equitable access to education for students from all cultures.

Purpose

The purpose of this effort is threefold: (a) Provide a review of some literature in the area of culturally responsive teaching; (b) provide some recommendations, suggestions, and future directions to enhance the learning process of students with disabilities; and (c) provide helpful resources to professionals who work with students with disabilities. The next section provides a literature review and an examination of several studies that define and establish the relationship between cultural diversity and student academic achievement.

Importance of Culture

While society has changed drastically over the past four decades, many teacher education programs and pre-K–12 school districts continued to frame and carry out their daily ritual within the traditional modernist model (Darling-Hammond, 2005). This current American system of education does not appear to be a viable option for educating culturally and linguistically diverse students. Several researchers believe that failure to acknowledge the role of culture in the teaching and learning process may explain why students from culturally diverse backgrounds do poorly in school (Gay, 2018, Irvine, 1991; Ladson-Billings, 1999). Proponents of a cultural mismatch perspective contend that students from diverse cultural backgrounds bring to school a set of cultural practices, norms, and preferences that are not valued, reinforced, or affirmed at school (Au, 2015, Gay, 2002, Irvine, 1991; Ladson-Billings, 1999).

Demographic trends indicate that the nation's school population is increasing in its percentage of children of color while preservice teacher candidates (PTCs) are largely European White women. Additionally, these PTCs have little experience with or knowledge of diverse cultures. The startling changes in student population have challenged schools and educators to find creative ways to work with culturally diverse students to ensure educational quality and equity for all. A rising tide of studies with statistical descriptions has inundated the multicultural literature by scholars in the past two decades. One wave of study strongly calls for the restructuring of teacher preparation programs to address the increasing cultural and ethnic diversity of public school student populations (Gay, 2002, 2018; Hodgkinson, 1996; Skepple, 2015). Due to changing racial and ethnic demographics in American schools more attention has been given in educational research to the disproportionate representation between diverse student body and developing culturally responsive teacher candidates (Gay, 2002; Skepple, 2015). Culturally responsive teaching is defined as using the cultural characteristics, experiences, and perspectives of ethnically diverse students as conduits for teaching them more effectively (Gay, 2018). As a result, the academic achievement of ethnically diverse students will improve when they are taught through their own cultural and experiential filters (Au, 2015; Au & Kawakami, 1994; Gay, 2002, 2018; Ladson-Billings, 1995).

Several other studies point out the disparity between a homogenous teaching population and increasing the heterogeneity of racial, ethnic, cultural, and social class in school student populations (Gay, 2013; Bennet, 2019). In many schools across the nation, racial and language minorities, African Americans and Latinos, usually attend schools with large concentrations of economically disadvantaged and/or low-achieving students (Foster, 2003). In the United States the challenge is encouraging preservice teachers to want to teach in urban schools and then educating them to respond to the cultural and ethnic characteristics and needs of the students who attend urban schools. As Wlodkowski and Ginsberg (1995) stated, "Any educational or training system that ignores the history or perspective of learners or does not attempt to adjust its teaching practices to benefit all its learners is contributing to inequality of opportunity" (p. 26).

Numerous studies have been conducted in an attempt to understand why preservice teachers typically do not regard equitable teaching as being a priority in the classroom. The call to action was headed by researchers who began to study the implications for teacher education programs to effectively develop culturally responsive preservice teachers for culturally and linguistically diverse students and often students with disabilities learners (Au, 2015; Gay, 2002, 2018; Ladson-Billings 1995, 1999; Skepple 2015).

One major finding was that teacher education programs struggled with converting formal curricula into culturally responsive curriculum designs and instructional strategies. Another finding included preservice teachers' limited knowledge about contributions of different ethnic groups across disciplines and a deeper understanding of multicultural education theory throughout their teacher education program. These major revelations highlight the need for teacher education programs to implement programmatic changes that will include five essential elements of culturally responsive teaching: a knowledge base of cultural diversity, culturally relevant curricula, cultural scaffolding instruction, cross-cultural communications skills, and cultural congruity in classroom instruction (Gay, 2002, Ladson-Billings, 1995).

Skepple (2015) identified two components of the preparation for and practice of developing culturally responsive preservice teachers: institutional and instructional. This expanded the findings of Gay (2002), Ladson-Billings (2001), and Villegas and Lucas (2002). The institutional component reflects the processes that have been put in place by university leadership (e.g., provosts, dean, chairs, and faculty) to facilitate conversations about developing culturally responsive preservice teachers. These conversations manifest themselves into policy, practices, and processes that support systemic culturally competent teacher education programs. How can we prepare culturally responsive preservice teachers to teach more effectively with students who are not part of the U.S. ethnic, racial ,and cultural mainstream? Researchers (Gay, 2002; Ladson-Billings,1995; Skepple, 2015) suggest restructuring the current instructional conceptual framework to include intercultural diversity thematic units across programs, content knowledge, curriculum, pedagogy, disposition, and technology, prior to internship. The author believes that an institution committed to intercultural diversity is the beginning of preparing faculty to develop culturally responsive preservice teachers regardless of their locale (Skepple, 2015).

Implications for Teacher Education Programs

Beginning in the 1970s, universities and colleges seeking accreditation of their professional programs had to demonstrate that their curricula addressed multiculturalism by educating teacher candidates to work with students from ethnically and culturally diverse backgrounds (Goodwin, 1997). Despite the existence of this requirement, the concept of multicultural teacher education has made little progress. In an investigation of 59 institutions, Gollnick (1992) found that only 56 percent of the professional education curricula sufficiently addressed cultural diversity by adequately preparing teacher candidates to work with culturally diverse students.

The field of teacher education, in general, has been slow in advancing and reimaging teacher education in both theory and practice within the existing paradigm (Banks, 2003). Thus, criticism of the traditional university curriculum is not new, but never before has there been such debate on the content of what is being taught in colleges and universities. The national standards movement provides teacher educators with a vision and a challenge that could strengthen their effort to prepare candidates to teach from multicultural and global perspectives that draw on the histories, experiences, and diverse cultural backgrounds of all people (Council for the Accreditation of Educator Preparation [CAEP], 2016). With an emphasis on cultural diversity perspectives, higher education institutions are faced with the challenge to find creative ways to prepare preservice teacher candidates to instruct culturally and linguistically diverse students.

In the 21st century, why are teacher education programs still struggling with preparing preservice teachers to work with culturally and linguistically diverse students? Scholars assert that most preservice teachers are European American middle-class females who speak one language and come from monocultural backgrounds with limited or no experiences with minorities (Florio-Ruane, 1994; Grant & Secada, 1990; Ladson-Billings, 2009; Zimpher & Ashburn, 1989). These preservice teacher candidates have unpleasant expectations regarding working with students from diverse cultures and ethnic groups (Aaronson et al., 1995; Habermant & Rickards, 1990).

Ladson-Billings (2009) suggests that most teachers have concerns about working with diverse student populations and need to examine their beliefs, expand their knowledge, and develop abilities related to students from diverse backgrounds. Research studies suggest that teachers treat racial and language minority students different from nonminority students and have lower expectations for them (Patton, 2015). Multiculturalist generally agree that preservice teacher candidates' paucity of culturally diversity knowledge base and beliefs is an implication for teacher education programs to design culturally relevant curricula as a reflection of the multiculturalism of our 21st-century schools.

While preparing preservice teachers to work in a multicultural society is important, most teacher education programs use a monocultural approach in their teacher preparation courses (Hinchman & LaLik, 2000). Swartz (2003) addresses the reality of how institutions have been producing generations of White teachers who typically use styles of pedagogy that fit with social dominance. These coercive teaching practices rely on transmission pedagogy (Delpit, 1992; Wink, 2010), rote learning, and behavior modification to control and track students as a precondition for teaching students of color (Darling-Hammond, 1997; Delpit, 1992; Ewing, 2001; Kohn, 2006; Oakes et al., 2018). Several researchers have provided evidence to explore, expand, and inform the knowledge base of preservice teachers in working with diverse populations while addressing the cultural discontinuity that exists between culturally diverse students and their White teachers (Banks, 2006; Gay, 2018; Ladson-Billings, 2001; Phuntsog, 1999; Villegas & Lucas, 2002).

In most colleges and universities, teacher preparation programs have responded to cultural difference studies and demographic imperatives in a variety of ways. For example, in many teacher education programs they have added multicultural education courses and provisions for cross-cultural teacher candidates' field experiences. How effective are multicultural education courses in teacher education programs?

According to Phuntsog (1999), a multicultural education course offered in teacher preparation programs is an attempt to provide preservice teachers with knowledge and skills to address the achievement gap between students of color and White students. This single-dose approach barely addresses deeply rooted cultural beliefs teacher candidates share about school teaching and the learning of students of color. Another related concern is that such holistic strategies and approaches don't necessarily work with all teacher candidates.

Defining Culturally Responsive Teaching

Within the last three decades, a group of scholars and researchers have been concerned about the serious academic achievement gap among low-income students and students of color (Au & Kawakami, 1994; Erickson, 1987; Gay, 2002; Jordan, 1985; Ladson-Billings, 1995). For more than a decade, these scholars and others have examined ways that teaching can better match the home and community cultures of students of color who have previously not had academic success in schools. Various scholars have constructed theoretical underpinnings for culturally responsive teaching, also called culturally relevant teaching.

Culturally responsive teaching has been used interchangeably with several terms, such as *cultural appropriate instruction* (Au & Jordan, 1981), *culturally congruent instruction* (Mohatt & Erickson, 1981), *culturally compatible instruction* (Jordan, 1985; Vogt et al., 1987), and *culturally relevant teaching* (Ladson-Billings, 1995).

Au and Jordan (1985) termed *culturally appropriate* the pedagogy of teachers in a Hawaiian school who incorporated aspects of students' cultural background into their reading instruction. By permitting students to use talk story, a language interaction style common among Native Hawaiian children, teachers were able to help students achieve at higher than predicted levels on standardized reading tests.

Mohatt and Erickson (1981) conducted a similar study with Native American students in the classroom. These researchers observed that teachers who used language spacing interaction patterns associated with students' home culture were more successful in improving students' academic performance. Odawa teachers were able to increase teacher-student interactions and participation by using a combination of Native American and Anglo language interaction patterns in their instructional conversation. They coined this language interaction style as *culturally congruent*.

Vogt et al. (1987) began using the term *culturally compatible* to explain the success of classroom teachers with Hawaiian children. By observing the students in their home/community environment, teachers were able to include aspects of the students' cultural environment in the organization and instruction of the classroom. Jordan (1985) discussed cultural compatibility in this way:

> Educational practices must match with the children's culture in ways which ensure the generation of academically important behaviors. It does not mean that all school practices need be completely congruent with cultural experiences, in the sense of exactly or even closely matching or agreeing with them. The point of cultural compatibility is that diverse students' cultures are used as a guide in the selection of educational program elements so that academically desired behaviors are produced and undesired behaviors are avoided. (p. 10)

Culturally relevant teaching is a term created by Gloria Ladson-Billings (1995) to describe a pedagogy that empowers students intellectually, socially, emotionally, and politically by using cultural referents to impart knowledge, skills, and attitudes. She argues that it urges collective action grounded in cultural understandings, experiences, and ways of knowing the world.

Ladson-Billings (1995) identified three components of culturally relevant teaching: (a) the teachers' conceptions of themselves and others, (b) the manner in which classroom social interactions are structured, and (c) teachers' conception of knowledge. Specifically, addressing the needs of African American students, she states that the primary aim of culturally relevant teaching is to assist in the development of a relevant "Black" personality that allows African American students to choose academic excellence yet still identify with Africana and African American culture. As this description implies, culturally relevant teachers must be observant and alert to the classroom behaviors and communications, verbal and nonverbal, of students. There is no "one-size-fits all" approach to culturally relevant teaching. Every student must be studied individually and stereotypes about a particular group discarded. Culturally relevant teaching occurs only when teachers are sensitive to cultural differences and when culture is naturally integrated into the curriculum, into instructional and assessment practices, and into classroom management. That is, culturally responsive teaching is based on the idea that culture is central to student learning.

In the 1980s and early 1990s interest in culturally responsive teaching grew as a result of concern over the lack of success of many ethnic/racial minority students despite years of education reform. Gay (2002) defines culturally responsive teaching as using the cultural knowledge, prior experiences, and performance styles of diverse students to make learning more appropriate and effective for them. That is, culturally responsive teaching teaches to and through the strengths of culturally and linguistically diverse students. Gay (2018) reported that part of the responsibility of teacher preparation programs is to prepare preservice teachers to work effectively with students from cultural and linguistically diverse (CLD) backgrounds.

Gay (2018) identified five important areas that need to be addressed when educating culturally responsive preservice teachers to work effectively with CLD students: (a) Develop a culturally diverse knowledge base, (b) design culturally relevant curricula, (c) demonstrate cultural caring and building a learning community, (d) build effective cross-cultural communications, and (e) deliver culturally responsive instruction. Gay (2002) asserts that culturally relevant teaching uses "the cultural characteristics, experiences, and perspectives of ethnically diverse students as conduits for teaching them more effectively" (p. 106). This sociocultural approach to teaching, based on the work of Russian psychologist Lev Vygotsky, provides instructional scaffolding that encourages students to learn by building on the experiences, knowledge, and skills they bring to the classroom. To do this effectively, teachers need to be open to learning about the cultural particularities of the ethnic groups within their classrooms and transform that sensitivity into effective classroom practice (McIntyre et al., 2001).

Villegas and Lucas (2002) identified six traits that are integral to becoming a culturally responsive teacher, expanding the works of Ladson-Billings (2001) and Gay (2002). The authors describe culturally responsive teachers as those who

1. are favorably disposed to diversity;
2. see themselves as cultural brokers in educational institutions;
3. understand and embrace constructivist views of knowledge, teaching and learning;
4. know about the lives of their students; and
5. design instruction to draw on students' strengths and addressing their needs (p. 121).

Most scholars agree that culturally responsive teachers who draw on students' cultural heritage in the classroom affect students' dispositions, attitudes, and approaches to learning.

Preparing Culturally Responsive Preservice Teachers

Studies have shown that the majority of teacher candidates who enter certification programs have little knowledge about diverse groups in the United States (Cochran-Smith, 1991; Evertson, 1990; Goodwin, 1997; Melnick & Zeichner, 1997). Overall, teacher candidates and beginning teachers know little about the histories and cultures of culturally diverse populations. Thus, in preparing teacher candidates to effectively teach diverse student populations, teacher education programs must (a) transform preservice teacher candidates' multicultural attitudes (Cabello & Burnstein, 1995; Gay, 2018; Pang & Sablan, 1998; Phuntsog, 2001; Ponterotto et al., 1998; Shade et al., 1997; Villegas & Lucas, 2002), (b) increase their culturally diverse knowledge base (Avery & Walker, 1993; Barry & Lechner, 1995; Guillaume et al., 1995; Hilliard, 1998), and (c) equip them with the skills needed to effectively teach culturally diverse students (Leavell et al., 1999).

Researchers believe that teacher education programs must assist preservice teacher candidates to critically examine their beliefs about diversity (Tatto & Coupland, 2003), expectations of diversity (Gay, 2018; Hilliard, 1998) and teaching in diverse educational settings (Cabello & Burnstein, 1995) and being responsive to student differences (Pang & Sablan, 1998; Phuntsog, 2001). Gay (2018), Shade et al. (1997), and Villegas and Lucas (2002) contend that tomorrow's teachers must develop an affirming attitude toward all students that is underscored by the belief that all students can learn. According to Weinstein et al. (2003), counterproductive beliefs held by teachers must be transformed before culturally responsive teaching can be implemented successfully. This is an important step as preservice teacher candidates begin to develop a culturally diverse knowledge base. Failure to transform counterproductive beliefs may contribute to teachers viewing culturally diverse differences through the lens of a counter-deficit perspective. Gay (2018) perhaps best summarizes this perspective by stating that it focuses on what "students do not have and cannot do" (p. 12).

Another component in the teacher education curriculum should assist students in developing a culturally diverse knowledge base (Avery & Walker, 1993; Barry & Lechner, 1995; Guillaume et al., 1995). The cultural content contained in this knowledge base includes but is not limited to the following: (a) communication preferences, (b) social interaction preferences, (c) response preferences, (d) linguistic preferences, (e) values, (f) tradition, (g) experiences, and (h) students' cultural contributions to civilization, history, science, math, literature, arts, and technology (Au & Kawakami, 1994; Hilliard, 1998; Irvine & Armento, 2001; King, 1994; Kunjufu, 2002; Shade, 1994; Villegas & Lucas, 2002). Developing this knowledge base is important because, according to Sleeter (2001), many preservice teacher candidates foresee working with culturally and linguistically diverse students but possess little knowledge about the cultural background of their potential students.

Preparing culturally responsive teachers to instruct culturally and linguistically diverse student populations involves assisting them in the ability to use their culturally diverse knowledge base to design culturally relevant curricula, instructional activities (Kunjufu, 2002), and compatible learning environments (Brown, 2003; Curran, 2003, Weinstein et al., 2003). As cited in Siwatu (2007), many scholars describe culturally responsive curriculum as the processes in which teachers (a) connect classroom activities to students' cultural and home experiences (Chion-Kenney, 1994; Dickerson, 1993); (b) modify instruction to maximize student learning (Hilliard, 1998; Villegas, 1991); (c) design culturally relevant curricula and instructional activities (Banks, 2003; Scherer, 1992; Spears et al., 1990); and (d) design instruction that is developmentally appropriate and meets students' affective, cognitive, and educational needs (Gay, 2018). Thus, preparing culturally responsive teachers involves equipping tomorrow's teachers with the necessary skills to use a variety of assessment procedures in their classrooms that provide students with multiple opportunities to demonstrate what they have learned (Irvine & Armento, 2001; Shade et al., 1997; Villegas & Lucas, 2002).

Recommendations/Future Directions

The literature on culturally responsive teaching strives to include efforts that are inclusive and that provide learning that goes beyond learning the basic concepts of a topic and how to apply it. A culturally sound classroom is one where the instructor strives to provide a culturally competent classroom where the lectures, activities, and units for assessment come together to explore concepts that free certain barriers. From the literature there are certain words that are not inclusive in the learning process. If an instructor plans to have a successful outcome in teaching students, one must strive to provide certain opportunities in the learning process. The main areas that are stressed in this section are as follows: (a) Provide students with an environment focused on mentoring, (b) use cultural experiences to teach key concepts through the use of narratives or cases, and (c) suggest ways to compliment students' processes by using materials that are as free-form cultural biases as possible.

Mentoring

A mentor is a person who provides another person with guidance or opportunities. Mentoring is an old concept dating back to the 1970s. Professors/instructors can serve as mentors in different ways. By mentoring students, a professor can teach the student many benefits of cultural aspects in the learning process. Concepts such as culture, diversity, glass ceiling, biases, and being culturally competent are some of the basic ones a professor can introduce to a learner. However, in order for the learner to benefit from the concepts, there must be a culturally sound way to apply the information. For example, in the time dedicated to introducing the meaning of the concept, the professor can choose to use cases that represent each ethnic group. Instead of focusing on only two ethnic groups, the professor can decide to represent each ethnic group in class. The instructor must be careful to not bring in too many stereotypes about a group. However, there can be an interesting dialogue about what stereotypes are and how this affects us when others have biases about the group. By placing students in several groups, each group can provide group interpretations of the cases by sharing narratives. When each student presents the narratives, students can review key concepts and gain feedback from the professor/instructor and other students. By using this type of learning style, students learn about what the concepts truly mean while at the same time obtaining cultural appropriate language and interactions.

Dialogue/Communication

The professor should gain valuable information about cultural pedagogy by actively including concepts and activities on the syllabus and in class activities. The professor should include culturally appropriate language on the syllabus that does not promote group exclusion. The professor should encourage students to attend service learning or experiential learning activities that promote culturally sound learning. For instance, there should be an effort to provide students with learning experiences external to the classroom.

Continual Review of the Course

A professor's course should be reviewed annually to ensure the professor is maintaining a course that is culturally sensitive. For example, is there statement about students with disabilities on the syllabus? Is that statement consistent throughout all programs? Is information given regarding who to contact if the student needs certain services (e.g., Office of

Students With Disabilities, student support services, library resources, financial aid)? Is the professor using activities and objectives that follow the Quality Matters curriculum?

Conclusion

This chapter has reviewed researched-based culturally responsive teaching strategies for addressing the learning profiles and needs of a diverse population of students (Delpit, 1992; Gay, 2013, 2018; Ladson-Billings, 1999, 2001). As the review shows, the majority of students who reside in and attend schools in urban areas are highly culturally, ethnically, and socio-economically diverse populations, whereas more than 80% of the teachers who will enter these urban classrooms will be primarily inexperienced teachers who are middle-class White European Americans (Ladson-Billings, 1995). The result is a cultural mismatch between the inadequately prepared homogenous White teachers and the culturally and ethnically diverse students in today's classrooms.

What are the greatest obstacles facing teacher education programs in preparing culturally responsive preservice teachers to teach culturally, linguistically and often students with disabilities? As Wlodkowski and Ginsberg (1995) stated, "Any educational or training system that ignores the history or perspective of learners or does not attempt to adjust its teaching practices to benefit all its learners is contributing to inequality of opportunity" (p. 26). Against the backdrop of a systemic educational reform crisis, there are significant implications for teacher education programs, legislative policy changes, institutional practices, and shifts in power to create opportunity for equity and access for all students (Skepple, 2015). Given the current national trends of decreased student enrollment in teacher education preparation programs, it has become imperative that universities and colleges realign their efforts toward recruitment, retention, and preparation of culturally responsive preservice teachers who can and will teach ethnically diverse student populations beyond their first year.

Questions/Considerations

1. What is culture?
2. Define disability.
3. Is disability a culture? Yes or no? Why or why not?
4. What is culturally responsive teaching?
5. Why is it important to be a culturally responsive teacher?
6. How can an instructor work with a student with a disability?

References

Aaronson, C., Carter, J., & Howell, M. (1995). Preparing monocultural teachers for a multicultural world: Attitudes toward inner-city schools. *Equity and Excellence in Education, 28*(1), 5–9.

Au, K., & Jordan, C. (1981). Teaching reading to Hawaiian children: Finding a culturally appropriate solution. In H. T. True, G. P. Guthrie, & K. H. Au (Eds.), *Culture and the bilingual classroom: Studies in classroom ethnography* (pp. 139–152). Newbury House.

Au, K. H. (2015). Isn't culturally responsive instruction just good teaching? In W. C. Parker (Ed.), *Social studies today: Research and practice* (pp. 105–114). Routledge.

Au, K. H., & Kawakami, A. J. (1994). Cultural congruence in instruction. In J. K. E.R. Hollins, *Teaching diverse populations* (pp. 5–24). State University of New York Press.

Avery, P., & Walker, C. (1993). Prospective teachers' perceptions of ethnic and gender differences in academic achievement. *Journal of Teacher Education, 4*(1), 27–37.

Banks, J. A. (2003). History, goals, status and issues. In J. A. Banks, & C. A. Banks (Eds.), *Handbook of research on multicultural education* (pp. 656–681). Jossey-Bass.

Banks, J. A. (2006). *Race, culture and education: The selected works of James A. Banks.* Routledge.

Barry, N. H., & Lechner, J. V. (1995). Pre-service teachers' attitudes about and awareness of multicultural teaching and learning. *Teaching and Teacher Education, 11*(2), 149–161.

Bennet, C. (2019). *Comprehensive multicultural education: Theory and practice* (9th ed.). Pearson Education.

Brown, R. (2003). *It's your fault: An insider's guide to learning and teaching in city schools.* Teachers College Press.

Cabello, B., & Burstein, N. (1995). Examining teachers' beliefs about teaching in culturally diverse classrooms. *Journal of Teacher Education, 46*(4), 285–294.

Chion-Kenney, L. (1994). Weaving real-life images and experiences into native education. Comment. *R&D Preview, 9*(1), 4–5.

Coballes-Vega, C. (1992). *Considerations in teaching culturally diverse children.* ERIC.

Cochran-Smith, M. (1991). Learning to teach against the grain. *Harvard Educational Review, 51*(3), 279–310.

Council for the Accreditation of Educator Preparation. (2016, July 1). *Demonstrating academic achievement: CAEP board clarifies, refines CAEP standard 3.* Council for the Accreditation of Educator Preparation. http://www.ncate.org/about/news-room/caep-board-clarifies-refines-caep-standa

Curran, M. (2003). Linguistic diversity and classroom management. *Theory Into Practice, 42*(4), 334–340.

Darling-Hammond, L. (2005). Teaching as a profession: Lessons in teacher preparation and professional development. *Phi Delta Kappan, 87*(3), 237–240.

Delpit, L. D. (1992). Education in a multicultural society: Our future's greatest challenge. *Journal of Negro Education, 61*(3), 237–249.

Dickerson, S. (1993). The blind man (and woman) and the elephant: A case for a comprehensive multicultural education program at the Cambridge Rindge and Latin School. In T. A. Perry, & J. W. Fraser (Eds.), *Freedom's plow: Teaching in the multicultural classroom* (pp. 65–89). Routledge.

Erickson, F. (1987). Transformation and school success: The politics and culture of educational achievement. *Anthropology and Education Quarterly, 18*(4), 335–383.

Evertson, C. M. (1990). Bridging knowledge and action through clinical experiences. In D. Dill & Associates (Eds.), *What teachers need to know* (pp. 94–109). Jossey-Bass.

Ewing. (2001). Teacher education: Ethics, power, and privilege. *Teacher Education and Special Education, 24*(1), 13–24.

Florio-Ruane, S. (1994). The future teachers' autobiography club: Preparing educators to support learning in culturally diverse classrooms. *English Education, 26*(1), 52–56.

Foster, M. (2003). African American teachers and culturally relevant pedagogy. In J. A. Banks, & C. A. Banks (Eds.), *Handbook of research on multicultural education* (pp. 570–581). Jossey-Bass.

Gay, G. (2002). Preparing for culturally responsive teaching. *Journal of Teacher Education, 53*(2), 106–116.

Gay, G. (2013). Teaching to and through cultural diversity. *Curriculum Inquiry, 43*(1), 48–70.

Gay, G. (2018). *Culturally responsive teaching: Theory, Research and Practice* (3rd ed.). Teachers College Press.

Gollnick, D. (1992). Multicultural education: Policies and practices in teacher education. In H. Baptise, M. Baptise, & D. Gollnick (Eds.), *Preparing teacher educators to provide educational equity* (Vol. 1). American Association of Colleges for Teacher Education.

Goodwin, A. L. (1997). *Assessment for equity and inclusion: Embracing all our children.* Routledge.

Grant, C., & Secada, W. (1990). Preparing teachers for diversity. In W. R. Houston (Ed.), *Handbook of research on teacher education* (pp. 403–422). MacMillan.

Grant, C., & Sleeter, C. (1989). *Turning on learning: Five approaches for multicultural teaching plans for race, class, gender and disability.* Merrill.

Guillaume, A., Zuniga-Hill, C., & Yee, I. (1995). Prospective teachers' use of diversity issues in a case study analysis. *Journal of Research and Development in Education, 28*(2), 69–78.

Haberman, M., & Rickards, W. H. (1990). Urban teachers who quit: Why they leave and what they do. *Urban Education, 25*(3), 297–303.

Hilliard, A. G. (1998). *SBA: The reawakening of the African mind.* Makare.

Hinchman, K., & Lalik, R. (2000). Power-knowledge formations in literacy teacher education: Exploring the perspectives of two teacher educators. *Journal of Educational Research, 93*(3), 182–192.

Hodgkinson, H. (1996). *Bringing tomorrow into focus: Demographics insights into the future.* Center for Demographic Policy.

Irvine, J. (1991). *Black students and school failure: Policies, practices, and prescriptions.* Praeger.

Irvine, J. J., & Armento, B. J. (2001). *Culturally responsive teaching: Lesson planning for elementary and middle grades*. McGraw-Hill.

Jordan, C. (1985). Translating culture: From ethnographic information to educational program. *Anthropology and Education Quarterly, 16*(2), 105–123.

King, J. (1994). The purpose of schooling for African American children: Including cultural knowledge. In E. R. Hollins, J. E. King, & W. C. Hayman (Eds.), *Teaching diverse populations: Formulating a knowledge base* (pp. 25–56). State University of New York Press.

Kohn, A. (2006). *Beyond discipline: From compliance to community*. Association for Supervision and Curriculum Development.

Kunjufu, J. (2002). *Black students. Middle-class teachers*. African American Images.

Ladson-Billings, G. (1995). Toward a theory of culturally relevant pedagogy. *American Educational Research Association, 32*(3), 465–491.

Ladson-Billings, G. (1999). Preparing teachers for diverse student populations: Critical race theory. *Review of Research in Education, 24*, 211–247.

Ladson-Billings, G. (2001). *Crossing over to Canaan: The journey of new teachers in diverse classrooms*. Jossey-Bass.

Ladson-Billings. (2009). *The dreamkeepers: Successful teacher for African-American children*. Jossey-Bass.

Leavell, A. G., Cowart, M., & Wilhelm, R. W. (1999). Strategies for preparing culturally responsive teachers. *Equity and Excellence in Education, 32*(1), 64–71.

McIntyre, E., Rosebery, A., & Gonzalez, N. (2001). *Classroom diversity: Connecting curriculum to students' lives*. Heinemann.

Melnick, S. L., & Zeichner, K. M. (1997). Enhancing the capacity of teacher education institutions to address diversity issues. In J. E. King, E. R. Hollins, & W. C. Hayman (Eds.), *Preparing teachers for cultural diversity* (pp. 23–29). Teachers College Press.

Mohatt, G., & Erickson, F. (1981). Cultural differences in teaching styles in an Odawa school: A sociolinguistic approach. In H. T. Trueba, G. P. Guthrie, & K. H. Au (Eds.), *Culture and the bilingual classroom* (pp. 105–138). Newbury House.

Oakes, J., Lipton, M., Anderson, L., & Stillman, J. (2018). *Teaching to change the world* (5th ed.). Routledge.

Pang, V., & Sablan, V. (1998). Teacher efficacy: How do teachers feel about their abilities to teach African-American students? In M. Dilworth (Ed.), *Being responsive to cultural difference: How teachers learn* (pp. 39–60). Corwin.

Patton, M. (2015). *Qualitative research and evaluation methods* (4th ed.). SAGE.

Phuntsog, N. (1999). The magic of culturally responsive pedagogy: In search of the genie's lamp in multicultural education. *Teacher Education Quarterly, 26*(3), 97–111.

Phuntsog, N. (2001). Culturally responsive teaching: What do selected United States elementary school teacher think? *Intercultural Education, 12*(1), 51–64.

Ponterotto, J. G., Baluch, S., Greig, T., & Rivera, L. (1998). Development and initial score validation of the teacher multicultural attitude survey. *Educational and Psychological Measurement, 58*(6), 1002–1016.

Scherer, M. (1992). On savage inequalities: A conversation with Jonathan Kozol. *Educational Leadership, 50*(4), 4–9.

Shade, B. (1994). Understanding the African American learner. In E. Hollins, J. King, & W. Hayman (Eds.), *Teaching diverse populations* (pp. 175–189). State University of New York Press.

Shade, B., Kelly, C., & Oberg, M. (1997). *Creating culturally responsive classrooms.* American Psychological Association.

Siwatu, K. O. (2007). Preservice teachers' culturally responsive teaching self-efficacy and outcome expectancy beliefs. *Teaching and Teacher Education, 23*(7), 1086–1101.

Skepple, R. (2015). Preparing culturally responsive pre-service teachers for culturally diverse classrooms. *Kentucky Journal of Excellence in College Teaching and Learning, 12*(6), 57–68.

Sleeter, C. E. (2001). Preparing teachers for culturally diverse schools: Research and the overwhelming presence of Whiteness. *Journal of Teacher Education, 52*(94), 94–106.

Spears, J. D., Oliver, J. P., & Maes, S. C. (1990). *Accommodating change and diversity: Multicultural practices in rural schools.* Rural Clearinghouse for Education and Development.

Swartz, E. (2003). Teaching White preservice teachers: Pedagogy for change. *Urban Education, 38*(3), 244–278.

Tatto, M. T., & Coupland, D. B. (2003). Teacher education and teachers' beliefs: Theoretical and measurement concerns. In J. Rath, & A. C. McAninch (Eds.), *Advances in teacher education series* (6th ed.) (pp. 123–181). Information Age.

Villegas, A. M. (1991). *Culturally responsive pedagogy for the 1990's and beyond.* ERIC.

Villegas, A. M., & Lucas, T. (2002). *Educating culturally responsive teachers: A coherent approach.* State University of New York Press.

Vogt, L. A., Jordan, C., & Tharp, R. G. (1987). Explaining school failure, producing school success: Two cases. *Anthropology & Education Quarterly, 18*(4), 276–286.

Weinstein, C., Curran, M., & Tomlinson-Clarke, S. (2003). Culturally responsive classroom management: Awareness into action. *Theory into Practice, 42*(4), 269–276.

Wink, J. (2010). *Critical pedagogy: Notes from the real world.* Pearson.

Wlodkowski, R., & Ginsberg, M. (1995). *Diversity and motivation: Culturally responsive teaching.* Jossey-Bass.

Zimpher, N. L., & Asuhurn, E. A. (1989). The RATE project: A profile of teacher education students. *Journal of Teacher Education, 40*(6), 27–31.

Chapter 3

Disability Acts and ADA Standards
The Impact on Inclusion

Mable Scott and Bernace Murray

Introduction

Many years prior to 1975, children with certain types of a disabilities, specifically physical and mental disabilities, were kept home. These children did not attend public school, and neither were they home schooled by a parent or school district personnel. Schools had limited accommodations, if any at all (Wright, 2010). For the most part, children with a disability were kept home by parents, mostly hidden from the public, depending on the severity of the disability. If a child had a disability that did not interrupt learning or if the child was deemed capable of learning, parents transported the child to school because school buses were not equipped to transport certain disabilities.

Wright (2010) acknowledges that hundreds of thousands of children were learning trade skills such as, wood works/carpentry, metal work, sewing, cooking, mechanical drawing, and auto mechanics. School personnel were not well trained to teach a wide age range of children with disabilities, and buildings were not architecturally designed to accommodate children with a debilitating disability. Before 1975, most school districts around the country were not held responsible to educate children with a disability. For the next 20 years, school districts struggled to address educating all children, especially those children with a disability.

In 1954, Thurgood Marshal represented African American schools in five states in the civil rights Supreme Court case Brown v. Board of Education, 347 U.S. 483 (1954) that alleged African American children were not given equal educational opportunities as White children. The Supreme Court held that segregating children by race in public schools violated the Equal Protection Clause of the 14th Amendment (The Right of Education, 2019). This decision led many parents of children with a disability to believe that the right to a public education, regardless of race, gender, or disability, applied to all children. This U.S. Supreme Court did not discriminate with the issued landmark civil rights decision that African American children had the right to equal educational opportunities and that segregated schools did not have a place in the field of public education. This decision started the reformation of federally funded school districts to get it right (Wright, 2010).

In 1990, the Americans with Disabilities Act (ADA) was enacted to ensure that all people with a disability were given the same civil rights and privileges as any other American citizen. The ADA is a civil rights law that prohibits discrimination against individuals with disabilities in all areas of public life, including jobs, schools, transportation, and all public and private places that are open to the general public (Wright, 2010). Another important law, No Child Left Behind (NCLB) of 2001 is the expansion of the original Elementary and Secondary Education Act (ESEA) and designed to fix the shortcomings of ESEA. NCLB requires states to have educational content standards, to test students on those standards, and to hold schools and districts accountable for their students' test scores. Test-based accountability for Title I schools included diverse interventions (Wright, 2010).

The Individuals with Disabilities Education Act (IDEA) of 2004, formerly called IDEA, ensured that children with disabilities went to school and were given every consideration to be treated as any other child. Specifically, IDEA required public schools to make available to all eligible children with disabilities a free appropriate public education in the least restrictive environment (LRE) appropriate to their individual needs. For example, IDEA required public school systems to develop an appropriate individual education plan (IEP) for each child, with parent input (Wright, 2010).

Because of these two acts, schools were to practice educating children with disabilities in the classroom alongside children without disabilities. Special education expert Sue Watson (2020) shared that "the inclusive classroom means that all students have the right to feel safe, supported and included at school and in the regular classroom as much as possible" Children with disabilities being included in the regular classroom meant that they had an IEP that stipulated where they were being educated, either in a self-contained classroom or in the least restrictive environment. Parents, teachers, and administrators decided in an IEP meeting where certain subjects were to be taught (Wright, 2010).

The purpose of this chapter is to give the reader a time frame of how long people with disabilities have not been under the jurisdiction of the local and federal government. The Americans with Disabilities Act was the beginning of a means for persons with a disability to be treated with mutual respect, just as other persons. The information in this chapter informs the reader about the struggles that people with disabilities have endured over the years and what the local and federal government have done to change policy with a new legislature. Over the years, working with students with disabilities is still evolving, from students not going to school and others not getting jobs to having trained educators in the schools, recreation centers, and other facilities that focus on accommodating those persons who happen to have a disability.

Who Gets a 504 Plan?

Some students with challenges learning or who have attention deficient issues may not need to be placed in a special education class for individualized instruction or any special education on a one-on basis, but students may need continued support from school accommodations for a student with a 504 plan. These accommodations might include more time to take a test, frequent breaks from the classroom, tutoring assistance, audio or visual enhancements, use of technology for academic assistance, different grading guidelines, less or more homework, and so much more; the school will help remove barriers to learning for a student to be successful in school.

From start to finish, a 504 plan is so much less complicated than an IEP. Students who need academic assistance or assistance due to medical reasons can be recommended in writing by their teacher, a parent, or a school administrator. There are no long periods of behavior observation or trials of intervention or extensive testing. Schools might assess a medical diagnosis, classroom work, standardized test scores, or maybe even grades as a reason to recommend a student for a 504 plan. The 504 plan also involves accommodations in the classroom. Students may get extra time to complete assignments or a quiet place to take tests. But the plan may also include the use of assistive technology, such as computer-aided instruction, or access to therapy. There are no legal requirements about what a 504 plan should include, and the school isn't required to involve parents in developing it (although many schools encourage parents to participate). The most wonderful part of the 504 plan is that the school does not have to wait on the parent to be involved to initiate and implement the plan. The law requires parents to be notified that the child is being assessed for a 504 plan (Wright, 2010).

The school can bring together all personnel involved with the student's academic achievement for a meeting to determine if the student qualifies for a 504 plan and what types of support are needed. The focus of the 504 plan is to ensure that a student is not intentionally or unintentionally discriminated against based on a temporary or permanent disability.

Road to an Individual Education Plan

The Education for All Handicapped Children's Act of 1975 stipulated that "all disabled students must undergo an evaluation leading to an Individualized Education Program (IEP) designed to create a personalized plan to best fit the educational needs of each student" (Moody, 2012). An individual education plan (IEP) is usually initiated by the student's teacher who realizes that something is going on within a student that impedes learning as compared to other students of the same age and gender. The teacher is then given a packet to complete that requires gathering a host of information about the student to determine the type of learning disability, if any, the student may have. The district psychologist or psychiatrist then evaluates the packet information, visits the school to assess the student, and makes recommendations. Parents must be contacted and must be invited to the school to be part of the planning where information is shared about the student. Parents have the right to agree or disagree with the findings about their child.

A group of individuals from multiple backgrounds who meet for a common goal make up the multidisciplinary team. The purpose is to evaluate a student for placement in special education or to create an individualized education program (IEP) for a student. The multi-disciplinary team (MDT) consists of experts with various medical backgrounds such as a psychiatrist, clinical nurse specialist/community mental health nurse, psychologist, social worker, occupational therapist, medical secretary, and sometimes a counselors, drama therapist, art therapist, advocacy worker, or care worker. The MDT also consists of an administrator or designee (guidance counselor or assistant principal), district coordinator, school nurse, teachers who serve the child (adaptive physical education teacher, special education teacher, regular education teacher), psychologist or psychiatrist, physician, parent, and the child.

If parents do not agree with the findings and wishes not to attend the MDT meeting, the school cannot proceed with the MDT meeting and must reschedule and invite the parent again. At this point, the social worker and other support personnel can intervene to reason with the parent. If parents agree to attend the meeting and give the school permission to proceed with accommodations, the student is evaluated by their MDT and placement occurs. The MDT, "sometimes referred to as the Committee on Special Education" (Wikipedia, 2019a), then meets once a year after the initial placement to assess the student's progress.

Most importantly, the parent and student are an essential part of the MDT. Parents and the student know firsthand what is being planned for the student, and they can have input as well. The student gets to hear the input from the parent before a final decision is made and signatures are engraved on the student's educational destination to be on the same level of academic achievement as other students. Parents can speak candidly to their child and make reassurances that the educational plan is in their best interest. Additionally, "the act (IDEA) required that students be integrated into regular classrooms to the greatest degree possible and that they be placed in the least restrictive environment while at the same time being granted access to the extra help and services that they would need" (Moody, 2012).

This special team gathers when the student commits a violent act at school. The team's primary goal is to determine if the violent act was a direct result of the student's disability. If the committed act was a direct result of the disability, then the student is given a short-term suspension not to exceed 10 days. It the act committed was not a direct result of the disability, the student could be suspended for the maximum days allowed or expelled for the remainder of the school year. Keep in mind that that the student cannot have a change of placement without the written consent of the MDT.

Accommodations in the regular education classroom are to be followed as outlined in the IEP. These special accommodations might include allowing extended time on class assignments, reading to students, using assistive technology, permitting tape recording, providing testing arrangements, inclusion, and much more according to the needs of the student. These accommodations are needed to increase the chances for the student to be successful. If special accommodations are not implemented, the school has violated the student's special education civil rights according to the Americans With Disabilities Act (ADA).

Best Practices of Inclusion

In 2004, IDEA was amended to require children with disabilities, when and where possible, to be educated in the least restrictive environment that meets each child's unique needs. Thus, inclusion means a right to be included in all aspects of education without interruption. There are several other definitions that identify *inclusion*. One definition of *inclusion* arose in the context of special education with an individualized education program or 504 plan and is built on the notion that it is more effective for students with special needs to have said mixed experiences for them to more successful in social interactions leading to further success in life. Another definition identified *inclusion* as a powerful cry for those who have been locked out to come in and for those whose abilities have been ignored to be recognized (Asante, 1995).

Functions in the Regular Classroom

In order for children to be identified with a disability and function in the regular classroom, several things need to be taken under consideration: (a) the subject matter, (b) the inclusion classroom, (c) preparing all students for the inclusion classroom, (d) preparing the regular classroom for the student with a disability, (d) making accommodations in the regular classroom, and (e) parents' input and evaluation from the multidisciplinary team. Pairing the child with the disability with the right teacher takes special planning and takes the teacher accepting the child who happens to have a disability with love and respect. At the core of the curriculum is love and at the heart of the teacher should be more love.

Inclusion starts with the subject matter being taught, which should be taken under careful consideration, because when new concepts are taught, some subjects require students to scaffold information in order to be successful. Those subjects also require a lot of connections from new content to old facts and some thinking outside of the box. The reason why some children are in special education is because of their inability to connect facts. Some subjects require students to do a lot of listening and use application skills. With short attention spans, students are unable to listen, so they fall short of applying skills. Some subjects require students to be physical or creative or to use other talents they may not have discovered. Regardless of the subject, students are either interested or they are not interested in what is being taught, which makes a huge difference in how much they comprehend.

McManis explained in his 2017 paper that inclusive education is important in working with youth with disabilities. Therefore, all students can be full participants in their classrooms and in the local community (Alqurani & Gut, 2012). It is the responsibility of the teacher to select the appropriate strategies to use with each of the learning styles that will allow students with special needs and general education students to be successful. Teachers must consider seating arrangements, all distractions, supplies, the presentation of content, assessment, grading, testing, time management, and much more. The classroom should be bright and free of junk and everything in it should be accessible to students for whom the classroom is designed in the first place. Students want to be in a classroom where they are just as important as the next person and expected to learn just as much as the next person. It is part of the teacher's job to make that happen.

Students should be prepared to be singled out of the regular education classroom and then eased back in like other students did not realize that they left in the first place. The team for the student with the learning disability should request a slow and gradual plan to get the student back in the regular education classroom. These students need help making the adjustment back to the regular education class, as some have been out of the class for several months to several years. The special needs teachers and the regular education teachers should work together to ensure the special needs class is ready to meet the needs any child who is on the road to inclusion.

When children fill a classroom, they bring a certain personality to the room, which could range from calm and happy to loud and rugged. All students should be taught that everyone learns differently, and special education should be looked at as being positive, because students with a learning disability get their own tutor at school without a charge to parents. General education students are encouraged that students with disabilities help make up a learning environment that is designed for all students.

A child's IEP must include all modifications or accommodations that the child needs so that they can be successful. An accommodation is a change that helps a student overcome or work around the disability. Teachers are to implement accommodations according to the IEP of that student with special needs. The general education teacher is usually part of the IEP team and is fully aware of the accommodations to implement (Morin, 2019).

Pairing with the Right Teacher

Students view the spirit and energy of the teacher as impressive. The amount of energy a teacher puts into helping motivate students to achieve does not go unnoticed. In order to keep students motivated, the teacher should make the inclusion classroom inviting, interesting, and innovative. It must be a place where students want to come to grow academically. A caring and loving teacher will make the classroom a place where students feel safe, free from ridicule, and in the center of that curriculum, love. All students in the class should be made aware of who is joining the class, why they are joining the class, and when they are joining the class. The teacher should have great expectations for everyone's behavior, and children should always be held accountable for their actions.

Pairing the child with the disability with the right teacher is sometimes a problem, especially in schools where there are few to no choices. Teachers who have no compassion or no conflict resolution skills can sometimes let a small incident grow into a huge outbreak. Power struggles with children can easily be diffused if the teacher realizes that they are about to be caught up in the middle of one. At any rate, the teacher makes the difference in any classroom. Children care and reach goals when they know the teacher cares.

Barriers of Inclusion

The attitudes of teachers can have a great impact on the success of the inclusion of a student in class. "Attitudes held by some teachers also need to be changed before schools become genuinely inclusive for disabled children. A lack of understanding about disability and insufficient training in inclusive education techniques mean that schools are not inclusive" (Baux, 2012). Barriers to inclusion deny students with a disability the resources needed to be successful and to blossom with the confidence to excel. It is most important that there is the working together of the regular education and special education teachers. Both teachers should have training on working with children with special needs.

Another barrier is the teacher providing the one-on-one instruction that may be needed for students with disabilities to get the support that is needed. For sure, parents want a special needs child to get the same attention as a regular education child. Parents want inclusion, but they also want the necessary attention from the teacher, even if it's not equal.

A very important barrier is the essential variable of using peer support in the inclusive classroom. Getting other students to accept and help a student with a disability gives a sense of acceptance and belonging. The child gets an opportunity to know their supporters and place among friends in the classroom community. Supports interfere with the teasing and ridicule that takes place among children, especially when there is not an adult around.

The ADA Standards

From 1975 to 1990 when the Americans With Disabilities Act (ADA) was brought into law, there were many inconsistencies in the schools: from the selection process to the actual placement, to the teaching and learning accommodations for students with a disability. There were some requirement changes; such as, those pertaining to the Individual Education Program (IEP), disability placement qualification criteria, and even multidisciplinary committee meetings. ADA standards for accessible design was regulated under Title III in 1991. This act was designed for people of all races, genders, and ethnicities, and these standards were issued "by the Department of Justice and the Department of Transportation to ensure access to the built environment for people with disabilities" (U.S. Access Board, 2010).

A Closer Look

As noted by a blind certified Braille instructor

In this section of the chapter, students will get a closer look at a disability by hearing a narrative from a person who is blind. Blindness is one disability that most sighted persons do not know how to assist. This disability becomes customized to the person's personality and the degree of acceptance. One can never know the joy or pain of a person who happens to be blind until you have a close friend who loses sight. Being born blind, a student learns by using other senses and does not have to overcome social, emotional, and mental disparities after being able to see and then losing sight. The way of life, love, and laughter changes.

Getting to Know the Student Who Happens to Be Blind

This section will focus on the student who happens to be blind and will explore the many factors that affect the educational process of the visually impaired student. Society has made many assumptions and formed opinions that have determined how a student who happens to be blind is educated. These personal and professional analyses have resulted in good and bad educational plans. Understanding the student who happens to be blind can change some learning processes that lead to better outcomes for the student that prepare them to reach their full potential in life.

With an attempt to dispel any stereotypical views of the blind student and the overall blind community, the student who happens to be blind should first be recognized as a person who did not choose to live with this unfortunate disability. Many of these individuals go through daily activities and situations no different than individuals with no blindness. Others may experience difficulties that limit independence in their day-to-day living. One's independence to successfully complete an education plan and receive a high school diploma or college degree has been such a concern. Many students who happen to be blind travel through the education structure with no realistic goals. The failure of this education process results in the visually impaired student not receiving a high school diploma, but a certificate of completion. There are circumstances that lead to this.

Causes of Blindness

The student population who happen to be blind is affected in many ways. Some students experience blindness through inherited eye diseases, optic nerve disorders, retinal disorders, health issues, traumatic incidences, accidents, and unknown conclusions.

These students' rights to a successful education have to be addressed and taken seriously by those educators who encounter them. All students who are blind are in no way the same mentally, spiritually, or emotionally. So, the education process should be carefully orchestrated to harbor the best results for the student.

Blind, Legally Blind, and Visually Impaired

The terms *blind*, *legally blind*, and *visually impaired* when referring to a person who has experienced vision loss is misunderstood in many cases. Part of the population who use some form of a corrective lens device can be considered legally blind, blind, or visually impaired when not using that device. When using the device, the person can see again. On the other hand, a person is considered blind, legally blind, or visually impaired when their useful sight falls in a certain useful sight range or the sight range does not exist (blind). This range of sight measurement is called visual acuity. Visual acuity simply measures the clarity of vision. In order to be considered legally blind, a person must have vision measurement of 20/200 in their best eye with corrections and/or have a visual field that is limited to 20 degrees or less in contrast with a 180-degree visual field enjoyed by persons with healthy eyes. The visual field is the entire area that a person or animal is able to see when their eyes are fixed on one position.

In the blind community, organizations use interchangeable words in their title to identify a person who happens to be blind. Some national organizations are American Foundation for the Blind, National Federation of the Blind, and American Council of the Blind. There is a comprehensive rehabilitation center for the blind in Atlanta, Georgia, the Center for the Visually Impaired. This rehabilitation facility serves all persons with vision loss, from the lowest vision loss to total blindness. There is also the comprehensive rehabilitation center in Columbia, South Carolina, the South Carolina Commission for the Blind. The rehabilitation mission for the blind is the same in both locations, but one uses "visually impaired" and the other uses the "blind."

The proper and politically correct term currently used today to designate a person who is blind is *visually impaired*. The student who is blind will be referred to as the "visually impaired student." This term will include the totally blind student. The student with no useful vision may have lost their vision later in life or the student may have been born with no useful vision. In this situation, the learning process can be more of a challenge but not an impossible one.

To spotlight, the visually impaired student will be able to see with some remaining useful sight. These students in many cases show no problems that would interfere with the learning process. The student who is totally blind uses their other human senses to see. These human sensory functions are one's hearing, smell, taste, and touch. Students who are visually impaired can see well enough to live a normal life. Others may find it difficult to perform certain life activities. In assisting a visually impaired person to be independent in life activities, there is assistive and adaptive equipment. Let's start with the least adaptive solution. Adjusting the lighting in a room can remove the glare, which prevents a visually impaired person from seeing clearly. Some visually impaired individuals wear tinted eyewear (shades) that serves this same purpose. Depending on the low degree of vision loss to the most severe loss (total blindness), large print and Braille will allow the visually impaired student to read independently. Large print is simply magnifying regular print to the size that will allow the student to be able see it. Braille is a reading method that allows the severe loss of sight to total blindness to independently read using their fingers. This method consists of tactually navigating raised dots to read the entire English language. Other visually impaired individuals use their ability to hear. Devices equipped with audio applications have contributed substantially to the visually impaired population's independence. Computers, tablets, tape recorders, telephones, and other applications associated with these devices have advanced with current times. These tools will give the student much independence to learn.

Characteristics of the Visually Impaired Student

The visually impaired student should not be viewed any different than a sighted student. What does this mean? The visually impaired student sees themselves first as a person who happens to not see things clearly or not at all. This condition does not disqualify the visually impaired student from learning or participating in the education process. Get to know the visually impaired student based on their individual presentation of themselves. The student should acquaint themselves with the teacher in the same manner as anyone else. Remember that no two students are the same in personality, character, emotions, and other human attributions. The education process needs to be planned and implemented according to the visually impaired student's ability to learn. Eliminate any probabilities when engaged in this process. Fewer doubts in this education plan should promote an atmosphere that gives a good chance for success.

The student should inform the teacher of any barriers that can obstruct their ability to learn. An open and well-planned first meeting is necessary in order to promote a positive learning environment and learning experience. Teacher's human skills, professional skills, and common sense should be used to recognize any significant differences in their students. When the need to correct learning and behavior issues arises, those teacher skills must be equitably applied in all cases. The visually impaired student and sighted student should be approached in the same fair manner as the situation warrants.

When everything is said and done, there will be exceptions about the visually impaired student and their learning process. The teacher should address these exceptions according to their professional skills, educational guidelines, policies, and other protocol.

A well-planned and thoughtful educational and learning process for anyone is critical. The quality of one's being will be greatly affected by this process. The education institution in the United States has produced many accomplished and successful visually impaired individuals. Doctors, lawyers, executives, businessmen, massage therapists, and many other careers have been successfully achieved.

The education of the visually impaired population and other disabled groups cannot be expressed enough in this chapter. Each visually impaired student is there to be educated in order to acquire the necessary knowledge and skill sets for gainful employment and to pursue opportunities ahead.

The next section sheds light on the personal life of one of the authors. This experience lends a personal touch on the importance of empowering persons with disabilities. The author's testimony notes the agencies and resources that were helpful in his journey.

Name: Bernace Murray
Born a fraternal twin
Place of birth: Lincolnton, Georgia, moved to Columbia, South Carolina, at the age of 1 year old.
Secondary education: Perrin Thomas Elementary, Florence C. Benson Junior High, Booker T. Washington High
Higher education: Benedict College (4 years athletic basketball scholarship)
Military: U.S. Navy (4 years of service with honorable discharge)
Employment: Southern Bell Telephone (BellSouth Corporation, American Telephone & Telegraph Corporation)
Disability retirement from American Telephone and Telegraph Corporation (AT&T) after 20 years of employment
Entrepreneurship: Braille School (501c3), A Touch of Braille, Inc. (founder, CEO, and primary Braille instructor)
Certifications: Braille Instructor & Peer Support Counselor for the Visually Impaired
What is in a name? The name Bernace Murray represents a real human being. As you read the name Bernace Murray, you may be trying to figure out my gender. If so, this is who I am. Bernace Murray is a real human being of the male gender. My name is associated with Mr. and (Success, Independence, Respect) SIR for the following reasons. Mr. Bernace Murray, SIR, receives correspondence and calls asking for Miss Bernace Murray. Mr. Bernace Murray, SIR, lives by the following life principles daily: Success—strive to be successful in everything you pursue; Independence—use success to forward independence; Respect—my success and independence keep me grounded in respect for others first to receive respect.

A Short Prelude to My Life Story

I, Mr. Bernace Murray, SIR, was not born with total blindness nor with a known visual impairment. My vision problems began later, during adulthood. At that time in my life, I was 38 years of age, in excellent health, and gainfully employed. This unforeseen event was the beginning of a very long downward spiral in my life.

This nightmare started when I awoke one morning to prepare to go to work, and I noticed some blurriness in my left eye. The blurriness did not cause me any concern at that moment. I just thought it might be time to see if I needed glasses since my work required me to stare at a computer screen for a long time daily. This meant that I needed to schedule an appointment to get checked out by an optometrist. My visit with the optometrist discovered that the pressure in both eyes was abnormally high. There was no corrective lens available that would clear up my blurred vision. A scheduled appointment was initiated so that I could be examined by an ophthalmologist, an eye specialist whose final diagnosis showed that I was experiencing the eye disease known as glaucoma. This eye disease is referred to as the "slow robber of sight."

A series of testing, medications, and surgical procedures occurred for 8 years. After experiencing extensive progression of sight loss, I was declared blind in July 1996. Truth be told, I will never forget that life-changing experience, for life can bring adversity at any given time with no advanced warning. I found myself at a crossroads in my life. Of all directions I could move in, I chose to move on with my life as best as I could, which I knew was by no means going to be easy. I knew my family depended on me: my wife of 16 years; a daughter, age 15; and a son, age 5. I clearly understood that their well-being and welfare depended on me. I believe that there is power in everyone to make good or bad decisions. I chose to live a productive life with my disability.

My Story: Life With Vision to Without Vision

I was probably no different from most of you: a normal individual aspiring to get the best that life could offer. This meant doing the necessary things required to get there. I thought I was doing just that. I strived to be successful early in life. As I reflect on how I seriously approached all levels of my secondary education, my academic results placed me in the top 10% of my senior class. I excelled in the sport of basketball at Booker T. Washington High School in Columbia, South Carolina. This achievement rewarded me with a 4-years basketball scholarship to attend a higher education institution, Benedict College. After 2 years at Benedict College, I made a hasty decision to leave. At that time, I genuinely knew it was not a well-thought-out decision, but later, as God would have it, my decision had a very positive outcome. I realized then that I did not completely control the events of my existence. I understand now that my hasty decision has affected my life scheme.

After giving up a 4-year college scholarship, I enlisted in the U.S. Navy for 4 years. I entered the military ahead of other enlistees due to 2 years of college, which qualified me to enter the Military Junior College program. The military provided me with some disciplines and training that were later important in my blindness rehabilitation program. A person's mental and physical condition is critical during adverse circumstances. I can honestly say that my military experience provided me a positive attitude, patience, organization, and stamina, along with skills to move forward in my life after my blindness.

After I fulfilled my obligations in the U.S. Navy, it was time to take my secondary education, 2 years of college, and Navy experiences to the world. I landed a civilian entry-level clerical job with Southern Bell Telephone Company. A significant skill that contributed to me being hired with Southern Bell was the ability to type 60 words a minute. I acquired typing skills while in the U.S. Navy, and my typing skills became very instrumental during my blindness rehabilitation program. Also, my principles of life, SIR, success, independence, and respect, motivated me to work very hard. Southern Bell management promoted me into a first-level management supervisor position. This occurred within the first 9 months of my initial hire. I held this supervisor position for 4 years. With a continued SIR attitude and work ethics, I was again rewarded for my results. Southern Bell management promoted me to a position at the second-level staff management and I was transferred to Atlanta, Georgia. The Southern Bell Telephone Company name changed to BellSouth Corporation due to a federal government action that divested us from American Telephone & Telegraph Corporation (AT&T). I was excited and encouraged about my life success this early in my career. I never gave up on those principles, success, independence, respect (SIR) as I started a higher job level and adjusted into a new geographical environment. The next 7 years with BellSouth were very successful. Unexpectedly, this career success was met by the beginning of my vision problems. Blurred vision in my left eye appeared at that time. It was later diagnosed that I had glaucoma. Glaucoma proved to be very progressive in a life-changing way. As you follow my story, do not lose sight of where I was in my path of life. Mr. Bernace Murray, SIR, was at the young age 38 and married with a family, with a successful career and a sky-is-the-limit attitude.

I continued my employment at BellSouth, but things were not looking too good. My greatest concern was how my vision problem would affect my income needed to support my family. Although I was visiting my doctor regularly and receiving the prescribed course of medical treatment, the disease continued to affect the vision in my left eye. The doctors advised me that their main concern was saving the vision in the right eye. Unfortunately, over the next 8 years, the eye disease eventually robbed me of all vision. My mental-emotional roller coaster ride of almost took me out. The bright sunshine of my life turned to the gloom of darkness, both physically and mentally. I questioned myself. "Can you, Bernace Murray, adapt to total blindness for the remainder of your life?" I, Mr. Bernace Murray, SIR, did a tremendous amount of praying and soul searching for the right answer. My life had to move on with a changed outlook. It is a beautiful thing when one has their life experiences to draw from to help them move forward. I feel very fortunate that I took seriously my secondary education, 2 years of college, the U.S. Navy, and my employment with BellSouth. As you read further, you will see how I had to draw on these institutions that would help me understand and adapt to my world of blindness.

As I struggled with my blindness, I was still employed at BellSouth. The ability to fulfill my job responsibilities became very difficult. Fear, uncertainty, stress, and confusion weakened my soul, but I knew I had to find a way out before I got kicked out. My way out had to be beneficial to my family's welfare. There were no job positions at BellSouth that could be performed with total blindness. What do I do now? I requested a retirement from the company based on my disability. BellSouth Human Resource Department did grant me a retirement disability. Now, what do I do with myself blind and shut in at my home?

Please let me be the first to tell you that I almost lost it being at home alone. All I could do was sleep or listen to television or radio. I was going down for the count each passing day. My fears led to anxiety and panic attacks. This state of mind brought on a condition of deep depression. I screamed out for help. My initial help came from both my Atlanta family and my Columbia family. I was encouraged to leave Atlanta and spend time with a sister and her husband in Columbia, which was no coincidence because my sister's husband was visually impaired since his early childhood. One benefit of spending time with my sister's husband was to help me understand, adjust, and adapt to my new world of blindness. My brother-in-law helped me move forward, adapting in my journey of blindness.

After returning home from this needed and encouraging personal therapy, I was in a better mental state to seek and accept other help and resources that may be available to me. With the concerned support from my spouse and some dear friends, I was assisted in contacting the Georgia Department of Vocational Rehabilitation Services. This governmental agency has since been moved under the Georgia Department of Labor. Notwithstanding the process I went through to receive the services necessary for addressing my disability, this governmental agency granted a rehabilitation program for me. The rehabilitation program was with a private institution known as the Center for the Visually Impaired (CVI).

The Center for the Visually Impaired (CVI) was a new beginning on life. This opportunity presented many tangible and intangible skills necessary to live a productive, independent life. I invite you behind the walls of CVI, a private agency that provides comprehensive rehabilitation services for the visually impaired. This agency's primary goal was to provide the necessary skills for gainful employment. The tangible services offered there included Braille, orientation/mobility, remedial education, technology skills (computers/ Braille writers/recorders/cell phones), daily living skills (domestic/cooking/cleaning/hygiene), and employment (interviewing/job application/job searching). Other services of an intangible nature included support group meetings, social time, and mental fortitude building. I participated in all services offered. I can unequivocally say that these services continue to make a difference each day of my life.

The opportunity to learn Braille was most exciting for me. You may ask why. The ability to read and write independently was lost because of my becoming blind. I thought that if I were asked to clarify how I read and write, my answer would not be to my liking.

My introduction to a process that would allow me to independently read and write again instilled a very positive spirit in me. During those 8 months attending classes at CVI, I gave my best effort, especially in the Braille classes. Upon actual graduation at CVI, I continued studying and practicing the Braille lessons while home alone. I was determined to master the skills necessary to read and write Braille. My literary skills were held hostage at that time. My ability to read small raised dots was accomplished by the year 2000. I took the following progressions in using my newly acquired Braille skills: I volunteered my free time assisting in the Braille classroom at CVI; I successfully completed through the Library of Congress's Library for the Blind and Physically Handicapped, Library of Congress Braille certification course; I received a Braille teaching job that came with a salary; and I provided Braille training for the visually impaired through my own nonprofit 501c3 school at no cost to the student. These accomplishments in Braille gave me a second chance in life. As the widely used phrase emphasizes, "When one door closes, another one opens."

The nonprofit Braille school allowed me to interact with many visually impaired individuals. This is where I had the opportunity to make a difference in someone else's life. These visually impaired students also needed the same independence to read and write. My various life experiences before I lost my sight contributed to my capability and ability to teach the Braille course. I concluded that I was destined to teach Braille. Life gave me a second chance. That second chance allowed me to motivate, encourage, inspire, and teach others daily. I cherished giving back to society in that way.

In conclusion, Mr. Bernace Murray, SIR, participates in life no differently than anyone else. Yes, I am totally blind, but I do not use my blindness as an excused hindrance in my life. The adjustments and adaptations I made allow me those freedoms that I desire. When you meet a person with a disability, see that person as a productive human being in society and not as a disabled individual. Recognize Mr. Bernace Murray, SIR, as a man who happens to be blind, not a blind man. The life of retirement is no different for me as for anyone else. How I lived before I lost my vision and what I achieved along the way has been very beneficial to me as a person who happened to become blind. Mr. Bernace Murray is still a man who happens to be visually impaired, but I give it my best shot to maintain my life independently.

I very much thank my very good friend, Dr. Mable Scott, for this platform to share my story and a book chapter on some best practices when dealing with persons who happen to have a disability. I also thank the persons reading my story and hope my words can be served to you as an encouragement to keep your head to the sky no matter how life challenges you. I thank the publishers putting this book together for accepting my story and putting it out there for readers all over the county or even world.

Conclusion

Disabilities come in a lot of forms, including those whose disability is apparent and those whose disability is somewhat concealed. This chapter disclosed several legislative acts that came into law after the civil rights case of *Brown v. the Board of Education* (1954) for people with a disability. These acts were created to ensure that all students with disabilities had equal educational experiences as those general education students. The multidisciplinary team, which includes the parents and the child, has the responsibility to develop an individual educational program for each child with a disability. Inclusion or inclusive education was identified as a major way to have students with disabilities educated with their peers in the same classroom, with necessary accommodations. The ADA standards affect all people with disabilities and ensure they have rights that were created and supported by the federal government.

Questions/Considerations

1. What is an IEP and how is it written?
2. Which act was put into law that was a direct result of the *Brown v. Board of Education* decision?
3. Describe what takes place in a manifest determination for a student with disability.
4. Who are the professional people on a multidisciplinary team and what is their purpose for being part of the committee?
5. Who is covered under the Elementary and Secondary Education Act of 1965 (ESEA)? Why was a reauthorization act necessary? Name the act and who the act serves.
6. Trace the movement for organized handicapped acts for people with a disability.
7. Describe inclusion and inclusive education.
8. What are two categorical ways to accommodate students with disabilities? Describe two means of accommodations for each.
9. The No Child Left Behind Act is a reauthorization of which act?
10. Who is ultimately responsible to ensure a smooth transition for a child with special needs being accepted into the general education class?
11. How does blindness affect one's everyday activities?
12. Describe the difference between being born blind and losing one's sight.

References

Alquraini, T., & Gut, D. (2012). Critical components of successful inclusion of students with severe disabilities: Literature review. *International Journal of Special Education, 27*(1), 42–59.

Asante, S. (1995). What is Inclusion? Inclusion Network. https://inclusion.com/site/wp-content/uploads/2019/04/What-is-InclusionShafik-Asante.pdf.

Baux, S. (2012). Interview with Stephanie Baux. Mali 2012.

Brown v. Board of Education. (2019). disabilityjustice.org/Right-to-education.

Center for Parent Information and Resources. (2017). Supporters, Modifications and Accommodations for Students. NICHCY.

Elementary and Secondary Education Act of 1965, [As Amended Through P.L. 114–95, Enacted December 10, 2015]. https://www2.ed.gov/documents/essa-act-of-1965.pdf.

Gamson, D. A., McDermott, K. A., & Reed, D. S. (2015). The elementary and secondary act at fifty: Aspirations, effects and limitations. *RSF: The Russell Sage Foundations Journal of Social Sciences*, 1(3), 1–29.

Keirnan, W. (1992-2019). What We Mean When We Talk About Inclusion. Institute of Community Inclusion.

McManis, L. D. (2017). Inclusive Education: What It Means, Proven Strategies, and a Case Study. Course Hero. Concordia University-Portland. Retrieved from /blog/classroom-resources/inclusive-education.

Moody, A. (2012). The Education for All Handicapped Children Act: A Faltering Step Towards Integration. Wordpress.org.

Morin, A. (2014-2019). Common Accommodations and Modifications in School. Understood for All Inc.

OSERS. (2019). United States Department of Education. Ed.gov.

Search Laws. 2019. Elementary and Secondary Education Act. LAWS.com.

The Right to Education. (2019). disabilityjustice.org/right-to-education.

United States Access Board: Advancing Full Access and Inclusion for All (2010). Using the ADA Standards.

U. S. Department of Justice. (2015). *Overview of Title IX of the Education Amendments of 1972, 20 U.S.C. A§ 1681 Et. Seq*. https://www.justice.gov/crt/fcs/TitleIX-SexDiscrimination.

Watson, S. (2020). Special Education and Inclusion. thoughtco.com/special-education-and-inclusion-3111343.

Wikipedia. (2019a). *Special education in the United States https://en.wikipedia.org/wiki/Special_education_in_the_United_States*.

Wikipedia. (2019b). *Inclusion (education)*. https://en.wikipedia.org/wiki/Inclusion_(education).

Wright, P. (2010). *The history of special education law* (2nd ed.). Wrightslaw.

Chapter 4

Cultural Considerations in School Disability Counseling

Freddie Boan, Stephen Patterson, and John Bates

Introduction

Disability counseling, either as a school counselor or through another agency, is a rewarding vocation, yet can be quite challenging. One of the greatest potential challenges can be in developing a strong cross-cultural perspective when counseling. When the counselor and the consumer have different cultural backgrounds, misunderstandings caused by the differences may strongly impact the counseling experience. The insightful counselor will focus on the whole consumer, including not only the disability but also the consumer's cultural norms. The counselor must cultivate an awareness of their own potential cultural biases.

An individual's identity is closely tied to their cultural background. One's perceptions are always formed as part of an inherent cultural identity. This is a fundamental social grouping. Culture provides a normative lens through which individuals see their place in the world, their social relationships, their health and lifestyle choices, their community and political engagement, and their general sense of well-being and wholeness. Each culture shares commonalities with other cultures, and each has variances from other cultures. An individual may be a part of more than one culture and may relate to multiple cultures. Effective counselors must understand both the common and the variant components of the relevant cultures of their consumers, working to become multiculturally competent. Growth as a counselor demands growth in multicultural understanding.

Counselors interact with a variety of people from a variety of backgrounds. While counselors may expect consumers to share many common characteristics, the counselor must also remember that consumers may have views, values, and perspectives that differ from the counselor's own views, based on differing cultural backgrounds. Counselors must take care not to let these differences in culture and worldview impact any part of the counseling relationship. Counselors must work to create a comfortable environment for all consumers and form a relationship built on trust. The successful counselor must remember that the needs of each consumer will differ. Counselors able to understand and accept, without prejudice, the unique cultural perspective of the consumer can build an effective counseling relationship with greater buy-in and less miscommunication. Cultural competence is a core competency required of counselors in most state licensure regulations. The American Counseling Association (ACA) set forth specific guidelines for providing counseling services to ethnically and culturally diverse populations in their ACA (2014) code of ethics.

Preparation for Counselors

Counselors must be aware of how their own cultural background may differ from the consumer's. In multicultural counseling and social justice training, counselors are primarily exposed to information that will help culturally different and oppressed clients, even as these counselors focus on awareness of their own prejudicial experiences and culture (McCloud, 2014). A multiculturally aware counselor must recognize that the norms of their own culture may be culture-specific and not universal, which requires a thorough exploration of the counselor's culture from an objective perspective. Understanding that many normative valuations are based on the shifting perspective of culture enables the prepared counselor to be more effective with the consumer. At the same time, counselors must develop a reasonable familiarity with common cultural norms of the populations they may work with.

What Is Prejudice?

Prejudice refers to any negative beliefs, feelings, judgments, or opinions we hold about people based on their group membership or societal recognition (Sue, 2003). While racial prejudice is often the most commonly discussed, prejudice can take many forms. Counselors can show prejudice based on multiple group categories including religious affiliation, political affiliation, status in a social group, academic or athletic achievement (nerds and jocks), gender, sexual orientation, or socioeconomic status. Prejudicial stereotyping, on any level, often leads to discrimination, judgmental error, inequity, and exclusion. Persistent stereotyping can have a serious negative impact on a consumer's self-esteem, create an environment of persecution and oppression, stunt the actualization potential of the consumer, and limit the counselor's ability to recognize and encourage growth in the consumer (Couillard, 2013). Allport (1954) provided a scale known as Allport's scale that can be used to measure prejudice. Allport's scale is used to measure the amount of prejudice in a society.

Allport's Scale of Prejudice

1. Antilocution: Antilocution occurs when the majority or dominant group freely support negative images of a minority culture or group. Hate speech and other speech that is demeaning to a minority culture are included. This stage may or may not always be harmful; a common theme to look for in this phase would be ethnic jokes.

2. Avoidance: The large or dominant group begins to avoid or neglect contact with smaller minority groups. This creates an atmosphere of isolation and sometimes inferiority for smaller, non-dominant cultures.

3. Discrimination: Discrimination against minority groups can be seen through the denial of opportunities and services. Behaviors of this type are set in place to give an advantage to one group over the other. This also creates a more difficult platform for minority cultures to achieve academic goals. Examples of societal discrimination include Jim Crow laws in the United States and regulations that were in place due to apartheid in South Africa.

4. Physical attack: The larger group feels empowered to vandalize, harm, or destroy property or individuals in the less dominant culture. Many times, this can be labeled as simple bullying but may be symptomatic of a much larger concern.

5. Extermination: The larger culture attempts to remove the less dominant culture through violence or force. Although this is not as common, groups with extermination as an objective target younger students.

What Is a Stereotype?

A stereotype is "a fixed, over-generalized belief about a particular group or class of people" (Caldwell, 1996, p. 5). Stereotyping exists because, in certain limited situations, it is a useful tool. Like other forms of generalization, stereotyping allows one to use the experience to form a framework for dealing with an unfamiliar circumstance or environment. However, like any preconception, stereotyping taken as a rule rather than a guide is often inaccurate and dangerous. Particularly when applied to individuals, who are unique, stereotyping may lead to harmful, untrue assumptions. When a counselor stereotypes, they infer that a person has characteristics, beliefs, and abilities that are the same as all members of a similar group. Stereotypes may lead to social categorization, which is one of the main attributing factors for prejudiced attitudes (i.e., "them" and "us" mentality), leading to biases against groups (Katz & Braly, 1933). Even stereotypes that may appear positive can be harmful to the individual and their personal identity. Stereotyping may lead to the development of counseling "blind spots." Blind spots are factors a counselor has that are unseen and unconscious and prevent that counselor from disseminating relevant data, recognizing different points of view, finding alternative solutions, and understanding foreseeable consequences crucial to effective ethical decision making (Lipschultz, 2018).

Effects of Stereotypical Beliefs in Working With Different Cultures

The book *Public Opinion*, published in 1922 by journalist Walter Lippman (Lippmann, 1922), introduced the term stereotype. He used the term to help paint a mental picture of individuals for various cultural groups. Unfortunately, the impressions many people have of cultural group identity are based on limited interactions and knowledge. Stereotypes become perpetuated by individuals who choose not to look beyond the surface. In a counseling session, the counselor may have consumers from various backgrounds and communities, potentially presenting multiple disabilities.

The presence of stereotypical beliefs can negatively affect how individuals perform or utilize services. Consumers are always more likely to use a service when it feels comfortable. Stereotyping is not just an internal thought process, but many times these beliefs and thoughts are projected onto our consumers. When an individual feels they are stereotyped, they will perform poorly and resist the services. Unconscious thinking leads to an increased risk of failure and of discrimination, creating an unfavorable environment for a productive counseling session.

The Formation of Stereotypes

One of the dangers of stereotyping is that no two people have the exact same cultural background and identity, so making broad generalizations will almost never be accurate. The formation of self-identity necessarily includes discrimination between what is inherently "self" and what is inherently "other." Many facets of these definitions are given to us by our parents, grandparents, and the communities we live in. Our personal identity is shaped and formed by things we experience or observe in the home, in the school, or the church. Personal identity of self and others is further impacted by available media, often shaping how one sees oneself and others as depicted in the media. While every individual is limited in their experiences when developing a self-identity, a culturally aware counselor must continue to expand their self-identity throughout a lifetime. The counselor must avoid falling into the trap of overutilizing stereotypical beliefs and other such false assumptions. Though it is challenging to rise above the stereotype assumptions and ideas, a counselor must strive to do so.

Addressing Cultural Stereotyping

If counselors accept stereotypical labels of students, then the counselor is counseling an imperfect image of a person rather than a whole person. Further organizations and counselors must be aware that such things as prejudicial language and inappropriate jokes subtlety and unconsciously form cultural biases and negative stereotypes. Counselors set the standard for interactions with consumers, and their actions determine how the session progresses or fails. A consumer will not be successful in an environment where they are stereotyped or thought of as different from the nor, just based on cultural background or personal differences in how they see the world.

Mapping Stories: Taking Detours to Challenge Whiteness, by Cary Terwilliger (Terwilliger, 2010, April 1), looks at how race, in a White-dominated society, is used as a category to define people while simultaneously tending to exclude White people. The tendency is for White individuals involved in education to resist the claim that the education system is exclusionary and deny that a problem exists in the imbalance of education.

> It has been suggested that teachers unconsciously favor those students perceived to be most like themselves in race, class, and values; culturally relevant teaching means consciously working to develop commonalities with all the students.
>
> Gloria Ladson-Billings, 1995, p. 466

This leads to a tendency to look at diversity as something that hinders education. Consumers may present challenges related to their diverse backgrounds and family dynamics. When counselors/educators fail to recognize the diversity of students/consumers, the effectiveness of the educational offering or counseling will be negatively impacted. This may be witnessed in academic achievements, a basic understanding of disabilities, racial dynamics, and sexual orientation. Educators, like all people, tend to teach based on their own experiences and understanding of the world. In a White-centered society, the experience is one of Whiteness and middle-classness. The educator's role has an unfortunate history of stagnating (consciously and unconsciously) social and academic change for minorities. Without training and education, educators may enter the field of education and never change their preconceived notions on race and prejudice. This may negatively impact group testing as well as the utilization of resources as defined by the counselor or teacher. Consequently, many times diversity initiatives in education fail because they contradict the original purpose of labeling by race, undermining their intended goal of developing culturally and racially inclusive dispositions and instead reinforcing racial stereotypes (Terwilliger, 2010).

Benefits of Cultural Awareness

Addressing cultural differences for disability counseling will facilitate greater success with the student/consumer. If a counselor can see beyond their own cultural views of disability, the consumer can better feel valued and respected as an individual. While all consumers need validation, this need to feel valued and respected becomes multiplied when the consumer is dealing with a disability. A consumer with a disability may feel out of place in the school and in counseling sessions, affecting how they seek and receive counseling. In many instances, the student with the disability has already been subjected to different treatment throughout their school career. Consumers seeking counseling may have more positive feelings about the encounter if the environment is welcoming. Students should have confidence in the counselor in the offering of assistance and direction.

The interactions between counselor and student will naturally be affected by cultural differences. Factors such as religious beliefs, one's sexual orientation, gender, age, level of maturity, socioeconomic class, family history, and even geographic location all play a role in one's culture. As culture impacts how we interact with others, it is also a factor in self-identification. If cultural differences exist between counselor and student, then the counselor needs the training to address such gaps and understand how one's culture can affect one's acceptance of services and direction. Being aware of cultural differences can help counselors create an environment for a successful session.

Students may not be prepared to deal with cultural differences if the counselor has not addressed them. These differences could create unnecessary tension and distrust between the counselor and the student. Developing an empathetic thought process and a quest for knowledge for other cultures helps a counselor better relate to the perspective of the consumer. One of the easiest ways to understand cultural differences is to ask questions. A willingness to listen and learn how a consumer's culture has impacted their life will allow a counselor to build rapport with consumers while applying appropriate counseling techniques. When a counselor is unsure of cultural nuances, the counselor can ask clarifying questions.

Cultural awareness can also prevent assumptions from being made, assumptions that may harm or derail the counseling session. Assumptions can lead to unfounded feelings and actions. Counselors must always understand why an individual has come into counseling or is seeking services. Then the counselor needs an awareness of how the consumers feel regarding services and the service provider. Counselors need to be mindful of what role the student's culture plays in how they feel regarding counseling. Do their cultural beliefs affect how they interact with the caregiver? If a cultural divide is present, the counselor needs to seek an understanding of how it impacts the student as well as the session. Recognize that the direct approach may not be the most effective approach for some cultures. Showing the client respect for their culture and seeking a common ground of understanding is crucial.

Bogging down on cultural differences can prevent the meeting from moving in a positive direction. Awareness of possible cultural differences facilitates a counselor-consumer relationship that becomes more trustworthy and comfortable for all.

In the offering of services, it is crucial the counselor recognize their view of the world and their personal beliefs. Acknowledging that one's perspective or understanding may not be universally accepted is essential for the counselor to gain awareness of differences that may impede successful interaction and growth between counselor and consumer. Counselors should be open-minded with the need to continually educate themselves on cultural differences that may exist. As a care provider, the need to understand and recognize our own prejudices, feelings, and stereotypical ideas is crucial for establishing a trustworthy and productive counselor-client relationship.

Self-disclosure has been discussed as an intervention that may build trust and credibility in cross-cultural contexts (Constantine & Kwan, 2003). In studies of real therapy, clients have consistently found that self-disclosure had positive impacts on the therapeutic relationship and outcomes when the disclosures were commensurate with the client's cultural values (Kim et al., 2003). When using self-disclosure, the therapist needs to be genuine and not appear to be scripted or going through a process.

One of the strongest mechanisms for building cultural awareness and providing positive outcomes from individuals of all backgrounds is through community involvement. Today's schools have an ever-changing population that is culturally diverse, and to be successful the school should ensure that school-community partnerships operate from both a diverse and responsive point of view. Incorporating resources and involvement from multicultural communities is a powerful component to create diversity in the school-community partnership. This concept is not widely used in practice or in learning environments, so it has not been fully integrated into educational and teacher learning and preparation programs (Bridgie, 2004).

Disabilities and Cultures

Educators must realize that they play a significant role in how an individual will see the culture of disability in the future. The behaviors and attitudes that are modeled by the administration and direct support staff will provide a lens for students to view individuals with disabilities. The primary sources that non-disabled individuals have early in their lives about disability are family, schools, government, and disability peer organizations, and these groups mold and transform individuals' concepts about disability. Educators need to explore their own personal identity, interpersonal and community relationships, and political commitments and how these align with consumers with disabilities. Honest evaluation and reflection on how a school addresses and treats individuals who may have mobility disabilities, blindness, deafness, pain, autism, psychological disabilities, and other issues will impact how students at that institute develop a worldview of these individuals. Reframing the conversation and showing the importance of changing traditional narratives of sorrow and medicalization benefits everyone involved (Bhatia, 2017).

Individuals with disabilities impact all cultures. The World Health Organization (2011) estimates that over one billion people are living with some type of disability worldwide. This number constitutes nearly 15% of the world's population. In the United States, the Census Report for 2010 (*United States Census*, 2010) identified 56.7 million people with a disability; this means 1 in every 5 of those currently living in the United States has had a recognized disability. In the coming years, the number of individuals with disabilities will only increase because of an aging population with a higher health risk related to cardiovascular disease, diabetes, mental disorders, and other health-related issues that face the elderly.

Individuals with disabilities have more significant health concerns and lower educational achievements and live in higher rates of poverty no matter their culture or ethnicity (Cornell University, 2018). Such disadvantages only add to academic and personal stressors that confront students with disabilities. These conditions create additional barriers to accessing services and negatively impact daily living skills and activities. These barriers can create challenges that limit the obtaining of healthcare services, transportation, educational opportunities, and other services that many individuals with no disability may take for granted. Barriers can be actual or perceived, but any barrier may prevent the individual with a disability from being recognized as a contributing citizen to society. The challenges and hurdles the disabled face can be exacerbated by cultural biases that may be present in the individual's family or community.

Only in relatively recent years has society and education systems realized that individuals with disabilities have a voice and know what is best for them and their communities. There is currently a change in conversation from labeling disability as a sickness, abnormal, or less capable. The change requires that educators see individuals with disabilities as normal and wanting the same results from education as students without disabilities (Charlton, 2000). Oppression of students with disabilities impacts not only the student with the disability but also the entire student body. The inclusion of the student, the family, activists, and organizations that support individuals with disabilities should be the practice of every school system and educator. Allowing advocacy groups access to curriculum and educational goals will help to strengthen the school, the educator, and the consumer.

It is widely accepted that those who have a disability face many challenges. In addition to the functional limitations inherent to the disability, many of the difficulties are the results of cultural biases. As already presented, cultural bias not only affects how one deals with disabilities but can impact other areas of society as well. Cultural biases can lead to attitudinal barriers. Attitudinal barriers lead to misunderstandings or false assumptions and beliefs. These attitudinal barriers can create an environment for complacency and distrust, both of which complicate an individual's path to success. Every disability presents a unique challenge, but the problem will be less significant when the counselor takes time to learn about each disability and understands that the functional limitations created by the disability are only a small part of the total person.

In recent years there has been an increase in literature and research regarding children of color with disabilities. However, most of the research is interested in the social and not educational context. Most of the research previously done for individuals with disabilities treats the group as homogenous and having no other cultural differences. This research is primarily based on White, middle-class insured individuals with disabilities (Mitchell, 2013). Understanding the different cultural groups and perspectives that exist for a consumer with a disability is just one part of providing proper services. Identification and developing a familiarity with family and educational contexts that are based on the experiences of children and their lives with disabilities is perhaps the most important part of delivering services. Understanding and learning the differences that disabilities present for different students in different cultures are the best practice for individuals in an educational setting.

A counselor's view on disability will have significant effects on the delivery of services. For the consumer or student, both the disability and culture may impact their ability to participate in services. In many cases, cultural beliefs can result in individuals with disabilities becoming stigmatized. Stigmatization of disabilities contributes to the individual being undesirable or having little value to their culture or community, adding to the discrimination of the individual. Not only will being stigmatized potentially exclude these individuals from being included in some group activities, it can also add to the challenges of socialization or employment (McLaughlin et al., 2004). This applies to loved ones and family members as well. Families can feel social discrimination due to a child or family member having a disability seen as different or unique. In some cultures, the family will choose to avoid counseling, keeping the child or individual with the disability secluded from others a result of fear of the negative view of the family. It is essential for those who are counseling persons with disabilities to understand the ramification of a disability and how it can affect not only the individual but their family and the community where they live as well.

Disability discrimination may not be a conscious action. Conscious or not, the results can be devastating and defeating for the disabled individual. A person who is stigmatized by their disability may face exclusions from activities and have a sense of less personal value, creating an environment of self-doubt and isolation (Buljevac et al., 2012). Stigmatizing an individual is to label them, generally with a set of negative beliefs that may be associated with a specific group of people. This can and will affect clinical consumer relationships and trust. When this occurs, the individual with the disability will become dehumanized by their culture and the society in which they live, adding to the challenges faced by the person with the disability. Gaining acceptance from the community and being seen as a valuable member of the community is crucial for anyone seeking success. If societal stigmas and biases against the person exist because of their disability, the challenge will be enhanced.

Cultural differences can lead to fears and uncertainties on the part of the consumer that are only magnified by the disability. As a counselor, it is essential to recognize the roots of the consumer's fears. Is the concern a result of cultural differences or is it an offshoot of one's disability? Studies indicate that 67% of respondents report being "uncomfortable" interacting with people who have a visible disability (Aiden & McCarthy, 2014). This uneasy feeling contributes to the many challenges faced by individuals with disabilities, especially over employment opportunities. The disabled individual makes up the largest minority group of people who are unemployed or underemployed.

Individuals with disabilities and the counselors that work with them may have a shared fear of approaching cultural differences. Unconscious barriers faced by the individual with a disability could result from fear or a misunderstanding of the public for one's disability. The lack of understanding of disability can contribute to the discrimination and exclusion of disabled individuals brought on by the fear of the unknown. The fear of the unknown can be exacerbated by poor information systems that then contribute to a lack of understanding and awareness of the abilities of individuals with disabilities. Often people fear being trapped by the disability of others. (How will my interaction with the disabled affect my interactions with others?) It is these thoughts that lead to attitudinal barriers for both individuals with and without disabilities. The counselor will be more effective when they do not let their own personal biases influence the working alliance.

Educators, counselors, and administrators all need to become aware of their unconscious prejudices. Everyone should review and give thought to how they talk with or interact with someone with a disability. The severity of the impairment may be a factor in how we react or associate with someone with a disability. It is essential that those in the counseling profession be aware of their unconscious or conscious feeling regarding the disabled.

Counseling and Providing Services for Students With Disabilities

Recognizing and understanding the need for services for students with disabilities is something that was not always practiced and well received. It was not until the early 1960s that the United States made an aggressive effort to begin addressing the needs of students with disabilities. Before this time in history, if a family had a child with a disability public education was not guaranteed. Indeed, for most students with disabilities, education was not available. Families were forced to educate children with special needs in their homes or consider placing the child in a group home or paying for private education. It was not until 1975 that the United States voted to ensure all children would have the right to a public education regardless of their disabilities or differences. The law known as the Education for All Handicapped Children Act (*The Individuals with Disabilities Education Act*, 1974) came into being. This law helped fund the establishment of special education programs in public schools and helped address critical components in education for children with disabilities. The areas of needs identified were as follows:

1. Improve the identification of children with disabilities
2. Evaluate program effectiveness
3. Provide protection and due process for families of and the child with a disability

The law is widely considered one of the first attempts to educate not only the child with a disability but also the community on what a disability is and the addressing of limitations. It was designed to help ensure that individuals with disabilities have an opportunity to enjoy a meaningful life.

Since its inception in 1975, the law has been modified and rewritten in various forms, but it was this original law that laid the groundwork for the Americans With Disabilities Act (*Americans with Disabilities Act*, 1990) that was signed into law by President George H. Bush on July 26th, 1990. This law became known as the ADA Act, and it protects individuals with disabilities from discrimination in all aspects of life, including employment, in accessing public services such as transportation and state and local government programs and services, as well as accessing the goods and services provided by businesses such as restaurants, stores, hotels, and other types of companies such as law offices and medical facilities.

Though the U.S. government has been enacting laws and regulations to aid the disabled, the culture of care for the disabled is still in its infancy. Cultural awareness of disabilities is ever-evolving, and it is important to be responsive to the need for and development of programs designed to help disabled students in addition to educating fellow students and teachers who may not have a disability. It becomes increasingly important for the individual working with individuals with disabilities to have an understanding of how one's culture may influence their response to having a child with a disability or addressing their disability.

Historically the United States has been thought of as a melting pot of cultures, with many cultures assimilating with the American mainstream culture. But over the last 50 years, the term melting pot has been replaced with a salad bowl. Today, a trend of multiculturalism or acculturation exists rather than assimilation. The change in modern thought is that the best practice is for everyone to maintain whatever parts of their culture that they wish and not be forced to blend their cultural beliefs with the majority White culture in the United States (Schwartz et al., 2013).

There has been a rise in subcultures that exist in mainstream American culture. These subcultural groups may share a commonality based on geographical regions or religious beliefs or ethnicity bonds. Each subgroup contributes to the overall American culture. The number of subgroups in American culture supports the need for education and a better understanding of how each group views and relates to individuals with disabilities. There is no one-size-fits-all approach when it comes to society's response to the individual with a disability.

Finally, understanding that counseling services for an individual with a disability may have a profound impact on their education, both positive and negative, is important. Just being labeled an individual with a disability in need of services will have a profound impact on how a student is treated by classmates. Students with disabilities are disproportionately recognized as receiving or being the victim of bullying in schools (Rose et al., 2015). Despite this information, there have been few studies that have investigated the relationship between disability identification and special education services However, the results from studies that have been produced suggest that students with disabilities experience higher rates of victimization and are involved in more physical altercations than will students attending the same school without disabilities (Rose et al., 2015). Students with learning disabilities and autism spectrum disorders are more visibly at risk for victimization in inclusive environments because of the ability of other students to see the impact of the disability. However, students with intellectual disabilities and emotional- and behavioral-based disabilities may have a higher rate of victimization by both staff and other students because the disability may be "hidden" and only viewed as bad conduct, behavior, or upbringing. Students who are subjected to this type of treatment tend to, over time, either develop aggressive behaviors or create coping mechanisms that can be unhealthy and hinder their learning experience.

Conclusion

Counseling with cross-cultural competence is a skill that counselors have to master. Counselors cannot use the logic or thought process that once they have mastered the skill of cultural competence, the skill will be retained forever. Remaining culturally competent requires constant work, research, study, self-reflection, and development throughout a counselor's career. Some counselors fall into the incorrect belief that reading a chapter or taking a class allows them to declare themselves culturally competent. There are other counselors who believe that they are competent because they have been exposed to many cultures or the counselor has a family history of diversity. This is a false narrative.

As an educator or counselor, look at cultural competence in the same manner that you look at your professional license or certifications. With licensure, an individual is constantly learning and attending seminars, professional lectures, and classes to maintain the skills necessary to keep the license current. Cultural competence is a target that constantly changes and demands constant training. It cannot be underestimated how important it will be to constantly strive for cultural competence. Without this competence, a counselor will never achieve the highest level of effectiveness.

The dynamics and populations of nations are constantly changing, and the world is becoming a place that is more diverse. Understanding the need to expand our "worldview" and accepting that we see the world through our own personal perspective may impact the delivery of services. By gaining cultural competence a counselor will have the ability to work with a consumer from the consumer's cultural perspective, and that allows issues to be resolved in a more advantageous manner for the consumer.

A counselor's work is never done when it comes to multicultural competence; the profession must continue to reach a higher level of understanding. The counseling profession has come a long way in disseminating research about multiculturalism in counseling, but there is still a lot of work to be done. Research shows that counselors in training and practitioners still resist the topic of diversity and multicultural counseling. Counselors need to continue to evaluate their personal resistance to multicultural counseling. Individuals are more likely to embrace something they know, so counselors need to constantly seek new information and research on how to be more culturally competent. Since this will always be a moving target, the goal needs to be a lifetime of learning.

The most important thing for an educator to understand is that inclusive culturally-based education is beneficial to everyone involved in the system. There are many groups impacted by this type of education. Families have a vision that their children will be able to accomplish all their educational goals. Parents have a desire for their children to be liked, even loved, by their peers and educators. Parents want their children to be accepted as "normal and regular" by their peers. This takes work and investment by an educator to ensure that all students will be included. This paradigm is based on accepting individuals as they are and not labeling or limiting based on their culture, race, ethnicity, disability, religion, or sexual orientation.

Students and faculty begin to develop a positive understanding of both themselves and others that may appear to be different than them. When children attend schools where the administration highlights both the similarities and differences of people in a positive sense, everyone involved begins to understand how diversity contributes to society. In fact, students will begin to acknowledge and strive to learn more about diversity and other individuals. Respect for cultural differences grows for both students and educators when they are submerged in a positive learning environment that involves a multicultural setting.

Relationships that were not possible before inclusion begins to emerge and continue. Educational settings are where many children will learn societal views and develop their most lasting and impactful relationships. Students of all types learn to form bonds with students of different cultures through inclusiveness. Individuals begin to look past stereotypes, disabilities, and perceived societal norms. Even educators will learn different teaching styles and communication styles through interaction with diverse individuals. Our personal development is crafted through our perceived worldview and personal experiences By increasing that interaction, the educator will also be expanding the worldview and understanding of their students and the consumer.

Students learn academically from one another. In inclusive classrooms, students are expected to meet the same academic requirements. This allows students with and without disabilities to strive to reach a higher academic level. By including diversity in the classroom, the educator will have to include instruction or counseling for diverse learning styles and capabilities. The more styles that are incorporated the more likely an individual will be to find a learning style that works for them and utilize this skill. Also, students learn as much from each other as they do from professionals; taking time to explain, work with, and learn from each other only increases the amount of knowledge gained. It is the expectation that all staff will provide a diverse learning environment so that it will be beneficial to all students.

Students not only learn academically by being together, but they also learn skills that are beneficial for society. In a culture with ever-increasing diversity, the skill of learning inclusion and acceptance becomes more important every day. Educational settings are more than just what is in a book or a smartboard; they are the formation of many individuals' beliefs about interactions with others that are different than them. Educational settings can provide the springboard for corporations, governments, and societies to gain a larger and more welcoming worldview. Also, understanding that more than one possibility may be in existence for the desired outcome is the crux of critical thinking. Inclusiveness and cultural awareness require a great deal of critical thinking, which is the foundation for life-long academic learning.

Finally, inclusion is the right thing to do in all settings. To bridge the gap and disparity that exist in both educational and noneducational settings, inclusion is necessary. Cultural understanding and inclusion on a larger scale will help formulate ideas about diverse topics that would have otherwise gone unnoticed. Concepts such as equality, social justice, and advocation begin with a culturally diverse and accepting environment. Providing this in a school setting will help to cure many of the problems that currently exist in culture. The conversation will always change and shift, and the dynamics may differ, but the goal should always be to provide a cross-cultural learning and counseling environment for everyone involved.

Questions/Considerations

1. Why is cultural understanding important to the counseling process with consumers?
2. How do a counselor's personal beliefs impact their attitude when counseling the culturally diverse?
3. How can you ensure that each student has an effective counseling session?
4. How do you identify the impact of family and culture on behavior and learning?
5. What ongoing learning are you using to practice culturally sensitive advising?
6. How do you recognize the gifts and strengths provided by cultural diversity?
7. What are your personal blind spots and biases?
8. How do you prevent your biases from impacting your counseling?
9. How do you distinguish between consumers?
10. How does your cultural background affect your perception of normal?

References

2014 ACA code of ethics [PDF]. (2014). American Counseling Association. https://www.counseling.org/resources/aca-code-of-ethics.pdf

Aiden, H., & McCarthy, A. (2014). *Current attitudes toward disabled people* [PDF]. http://www.scope.org.uk/Scope/media/Images/Publication Directory/Current-attitudes-towards-disabled-people.pdf.

Alport, G. (1954). *The Nature of Prejudice*. Perseus Books Group.

Americans with disabilities act. (1990). United States Congress.

Bhatia, A. (2017). *Barriers and Belonging: Personal Narratives of Disability*. Temple University Press.

Buljevac, M., Majdak, M., & Leutar, Z. (2012). The stigma of disability: Croatian experiences. *Disability and Rehabilitation*, 34(9), 725–732. https://doi.org/10.3109/09638288.2011.616570

Caldwell, M. (1996). *The dictionary of psychology*. Fitzroy Dearborn.

Charlton, J. I. (2000). *Nothing about us without us: Disability, oppression, and empowerment* (1st ed.). University of California Press.

Constantine, M. G., & Kwan, K.-L. (2003). Cross-cultural considerations of therapist self-disclosure. *Journal of Clinical Psychology*, 59(5), 581–588. https://doi.org/10.1002/jclp.10160

Couillard, L. (2013). *The impact of prejudice on society*. The Daily Collegian. https://www.collegian.psu.edu/news/crime_courts/article_a86ea0dc-270a-11e3-ad90-0019bb30f31a.html

Disability statistics. (2018). Cornell University. http://www.disabilitystatistics.org/reports/cps.cfm?statistic=poverty

Ford, B. A. (2004). Preparing special educators for culturally responsive school-community partnerships. *Teacher Education and Special Education: The Journal of the Teacher Education Division of the Council for Exceptional Children*, 27(3), 224–230. https://doi.org/10.1177/088840640402700302

Katz, D., & Braly, K. (1933). Racial stereotypes of one hundred college students. *Journal of Abnormal Psychology, 28*(3), 280–290. https://doi.org/10.1037/h0074049

Kim, B. K., Hill, C. E., Gelso, C. J., Goates, M. K., Asay, P. A., & Harbin, J. M. (2003). Counselor self-disclosure, east asian american client adherence to asian cultural values, and counseling process. *Journal of Counseling Psychology, 50*(3), 324–332. https://doi.org/10.1037/0022-0167.50.3.324

Ladson-Billings, G. (1995). Toward a theory of culturally relevant pedagogy. *American Educational Research Journal, 32*(3), 465–491. https://doi.org/10.3102/00028312032003465

Lippmann, W. (1922). *Public Opinion.* Harcourt, Brace and Company.

MacLeod, B. P. (2014, January 27). *Addressing clients' prejudices in counseling.* Counseling Today. https://ct.counseling.org/2014/01/addressing-clients-prejudices-in-counseling/

McLaughlin, M. E., Bell, M. P., & Stringer, D. Y. (2004). Stigma and acceptance of persons with disabilities: Understudied aspects of workforce diversity. *Group & Organization Management, 29*(3), 302–333. https://doi.org/10.1177/1059601103257410

Mitchell, D. D. (2013). *Crises of identifying: Negotiating and mediating race, gender, and disability within family and schools.* Information Age Publishing.

Rose, C. A., Stormont, M., Wang, Z., Simpson, C. G., Preast, J. L., & Green, A. L. (2015, December). Bullying and students with disabilities: Examination of disability, status, and educational placement. *School Psychology Review, 44*(4), 425–444.

Schwartz, S. J., Unger, J. B., Zamboanga, B. L., & Szapocznik, J. (2013). Rethinking the concept of acculturation: Implications for theory and research. *Journal of American Psychology, 65*(4), 237–251. https://doi.org/10.1037/a0019330

Sue, D. (2003). *Overcoming our racism: The journey of liberation.* Jossey-Bass.

Terwilliger, C. (2010, April 1). Mapping stories: Taking detours to challenge whiteness. *Making Connections, 11*(2), 14–25.

The individuals with disabilities education act. (1974). United State Congress.

United States Census. (2010). United States Census Office.

Vignoles, V. L., Owe, E., Becker, M., Smith, P. B., Easterbrook, M. J., Brown, R., Gonzalez, R., Didier, N., Carrasco, D., Cadena, M. P., Lay, S., Schwartz, S. J., Des Rosiers, S. E., Villamar, J. A., Gavreliuc, A., Zinkeng, M., Kreuzbauer, R., Baguma, P., Martin, M., & Bond, M. H. (2016). Beyond the 'east–west' dichotomy: Global variation in cultural models of selfhood. *Journal of Experimental Psychology: General, 148*(8), 966–1000. https://doi.org/10.1037/xge0000175

World report on disability. (2011). World Health Organization. http://www.who.int/disabilities/world_report/2011/report/en/

Chapter 5

Boots on the Ground
Meeting the Needs of Veteran Students With Disabilities in Higher Education

Quiteya Walker and Tammara P. Thomas

Introduction

Those who have served in the Armed Forces made immeasurable sacrifices to ensure that we continue to enjoy our freedom here in the United States of America. It is through the sacrifices of these men and women we have the liberty to pursue our dreams. Notably the traditional American dream may include establishing a career that is both professionally and personally meaningful. Work provides meaning in the lives of many, while also ensuring that quality of life is financially sustainable. However, becoming a skilled and effective professional for many veterans requires education and training after separation from the Armed Forces. The passage of the New Post-9/11 GI Bill has provided millions of veterans with the opportunity to obtain higher education, but there are continued concerns that veteran students with disabilities (VSDs) are not receiving the support needed to successfully complete their academic goals. According to the Department of Veterans Affairs Education program beneficiaries fiscal year (FY) 2000 to 2016 statistics, as of 2016 the total number of veterans utilizing educational benefits in 2016 was 1,000,089. These statistics suggest a steady increase since FY 2000. Although there has been increased growth in veterans taking advantage of educational benefits, the success rate of completion remains lower as compared to nonveteran students. VSDs have needs that are uniquely different, and these needs can pose barriers to successfully completing postsecondary programs.

Over the last 10 years there has been increased research that is aimed at addressing veterans' issues, specifically as they relate to transition, academic progress, retention and success once they enter college and university settings (DiRamio et al., 2008; Semer & Harmening, 2015). A review of the literature has provided notable findings in regard to the experiences of nontraditional students such as veterans when compared to traditional students. Typically nontraditional students are older than traditional students. They often times have responsibilities that may include taking care of families and participating in employment that help to support them. These responsibilities may contribute to less activities that would expose them to student-centered activities and engagement and as a result could contribute to feelings of isolation and disconnectedness in postsecondary settings (Dill & Henley, 2010; Forbes et al., 2011; Kim & Cole, 2013). Further, the Million Records Project (Cate, 2014) in the largest study on student service members/veterans' (SSM/Vs) performance and retention in higher education indicated that over the span of 10 years SSM/Vs earn postsecondary degrees at rates (51.7% completion rate) similar to other students but it takes them longer to do so. These findings strongly support that when compared to traditional students, despite challenges, VSDs are overcoming these factors and are successfully meeting their educational goals. A review of the literature does indicate that there is a bit of confusion when analyzing VSDs' postsecondary outcomes. Collection, analysis, interpretation of data on a national level has made it difficult to provide clarity on overall outcomes (U.S. Department of Veterans Affairs, 2018). Based on research results from the VSDs of America Research Brief Profile of the Contemporary VSDs (U.S. Department of Veterans Affairs, 2018) more than 340,000 veterans have completed a postsecondary degree or certificate under the GI Bill (72% success rate since 2009). Other reports suggest that there are factors that may contribute to VSDs' noncompletion rates such as the greater propensity for VSDs to take breaks and then reenroll, which makes it difficult to ascertain if the VSD will later complete those degrees (Ochinko & Payea, 2018). Ochinko and Payea (2018) posit that nontraditional and first-generational students are predisposed to atypical risk factors such as being the first in the family to attend college, having a disability, being single or married with dependents, not having a traditional high school diploma, not being in a classroom setting for quite some time, and working full time. It is clear that efforts aimed to address concerns about VSDs' drop-out rates and transitioning issues that impact veterans who leave the military and enter higher education are needed. Further, there has been considerable agreement regarding the impediments veterans who depart active duty military service, specifically problematic transitional processes that veterans undergo as they transition into post-secondary institutions, face (Jenner, 2017).

Veterans are currently enrolling in postsecondary education at a higher rate than in previous years. According to the U.S. Department of Veterans Affairs (2018), over 200,000 veterans since 2015 are pursuing postsecondary education for the first time. The Department of Veteran Affairs (VA) provides educational benefits such as tuition payment/reimbursement, books, and housing to encourage and support veterans in the pursuit of higher education. As of 2013, 877,000 VSDs have utilized the Post-9/11GI Bill to enroll in college course at over 6,000 institutions (Bosari et al., 2017; Sander, 2013); therefore, it is important that the development of effective processes to support this population is made a priority within institutions of higher education. Veterans have received the benefit of access to higher education since World War II, yet historically institutions of higher education have underserved students from specific demographic groups in which veterans belong, such as first-generation and "nontraditional," low-income students and students of color (Canaday, 2003; Jenner, 2017). According to the National Center for PTSD (2014), 62% of VSDs with disabilities are first-generation students. Despite the longstanding precedence of existing barriers that seem to be systemically threaded through the fabric of institutions of higher education, it is critical that efforts to facilitate the effective transition and integration of veterans into postsecondary settings be as intentional as the legislative strides made to ensure access. There have been concerted efforts made legislatively to ensure that service men and women receive the well-deserved benefit of higher education.

Legislative Acts That Supported Veterans on College Campuses

Following World War II, there was an increase in the number of returning veterans seeking vocational and educational goals (Madaus et al., 2009). The precursor to the increase in veteran attendance in postsecondary schools was the creation of different legislation. **The Commission on National Aid to Vocational Education** (1914) provided vocational education to individuals returning from World War I. The **Vocational Rehabilitation Act of 1918** provided the beginning of educational assistance for veterans (Madaus, 2000). The **Servicemen's Readjustment Act of 1944 (GI Bill of Rights)** allowed veterans to attend "approved institutions and to take courses of 1 to 4 years' duration, depending on length of service, for which the government would pay expenses up to $500 per school year" (Strom, 1950, p. 23). **Vietnam Era Veteran's Readjustment Assistance Act** increased educational benefits provided to veterans. The **Post-9/11 Veterans Educational Assistance Act of 2008** (the **New GI Bill**) expands educational benefits for veterans serving since 9/11 through the provision of financial benefits to veterans pursuing an associate's degree or higher (Veterans Administration, 2008). More specifically this bill provides support for tuition, books, and housing (Sander, 2012). **The Americans With Disabilities Act Amendments Act of 2008** (ADAAA) expands the definition of disability and eligibility for services and accommodations.

According to the National Survey of Student Engagement (NSSE, 2010), VSDs attending 4-year colleges and universities perceive lower levels of campus support and interact less with faculty than nonveterans. Further, the results of the survey found that VSDs spent twice as many hours per week working and six times as many hours taking care of dependents. Last, compared to nonveteran students, about one in five combat veterans in college reported having a disability, which is twice that of nonveterans. Additionally, some studies have identified an 88% dropout rate and a 3% graduation rate for VSDs (Ginder-Vogel, 2012).

However, it is difficult to ascertain if these numbers are due to variables such as deployment, military transfer, financial issues, and other relevant issues. Regardless of the varied circumstances that may impede a VSD from being successful in an institution of higher learning, it is without question that challenges VSDs face are uniquely different from their colleagues. It is critical that every VSD is equipped with the knowledge, skills, and support needed to negotiate an environment that is vastly different from the one mastered during active duty. Failure to address and meet the needs of VSDs creates barriers that negatively impact VSDs' success, transition, and acculturation within college and university settings.

Challenges

VSDs are among an increasing population on college campuses today. Considering the increasing number of veterans who are in an effort to adequately serve this unique population it is critical for institutions providing postsecondary education to establish more effective pathways that will support successful transition. VSDs who seek continued education aim to improve their professional civilian career growth. Despite aspirations for reintegration from soldier to civilian, VSDs continue to face myriad challenges in higher education (Lim et al., 2018; Rumann & Hamrick, 2010). VSDs are faced with various impediments that impact their ability to reintegrate and adjust to civilian life. These challenges often relate to personal, social, academic, and vocational concerns (DiRamio & Jarvis, 2011). It is important that the higher education community is aware of these challenges and make reasonable efforts to provide the support needed to assist VSDs in their academic journey. In order to better support VSDs into transition into higher education settings it is important to attend to the following: (a) cultural differences; (b) faculty and staff perspectives, expectations and training needs; (c) social connectedness; and (d) establishment and maintenance of collaborative relationships with stakeholders (e.g., Veterans Administration).

Social Connectedness

The military has been a way of life among veterans, and entering an institution of higher learning could pose significant challenges. The military is a more structured environment as compared to campus settings. Veterans spend active duty being fully immersed and indoctrinated to the culture that exists on military bases and in the Armed Forces. While in the Armed Forces active duty soldiers worked as a unit toward a common goal, which is to protect us from threats both foreign and domestic. They understand what is required of them, and they excel at executing the mission. Shared military missions, goals, and values help create comradery and a sense of belonging among soldiers who serve. According to an examination of Maslow's "Theory of Human Motivation," human motivation requires five need levels to be met: physiological, safety, affiliation, achievement, and self-actualization (Hall & Nougaim, 1968). The need for *affiliation* refers to "belonging" and is noted as the third most important level of need, which means close affective relationships are necessary for people to have life satisfaction. Affiliation speaks to concern over establishing and maintaining a positive affective relationship with another person or group in the work situation (Hall et al., 1968). VSDs often report difficulty connecting socially to their traditional civilian student counterparts because their experiences are so different from others (Bosari et al., 2017; Parks et al., 2015). This disconnect may be related to VSDs' perception that civilians lack an understanding and appreciation for the military experience and that traditional students hold misperceptions about war conflict and U.S. policy (Dunwoody et al., 2014). This lack of perceived understanding may lend themselves to inappropriate questions, behaviors, and comments, and as a result VSDs may feel uncomfortable or find integrating with traditional students unattractive. An inability to develop a sense of belonging can pose a great challenge for VSDs who are entering the academic setting for the first time or after an extended period of time. Integration into campus environments are not only beneficial for the development of support systems, but necessary when establishing a sense of belonging, thus minimizing the feeling of isolation. Further, when VSDs encounter these uncomfortable interactions with traditional students the challenge of forming a positive identity may occur. In other words, VSDs could see themselves as different from other students and may prefer to only engage with other veterans (DiRamio et al., 2008; Ellison et al., 2012).

Faculty and Staff Perceptions

Due to the diversity that exists on campuses across the United States it stands to reason that each individual may have differences in their abilities. Faculty and staff within postsecondary settings must have an understanding of these differences, in particular as it relates to providing support to the VSD population. VSDs present unique cultural challenges that may pose an issue for DSS staff who are not culturally competent as it relates to the military culture. The VSD with the disability has become accustomed to the military culture of structure and cohesion, so when they transition into the university setting they now must adapt to the new culture, which may leave them disgusted with the behaviors of postsecondary student, whereby they lack this structure (Elliot & Naphan, 2015). Emphasis should be placed on how faculty perceive this group, specifically as it may relate to disabilities that may require understanding and accommodation. Faculty and staff awareness should begin with the importance that all students should be positioned for success in postsecondary environments. Foreman et al. (2001) indicated that in order for adult learners to be successful, their needs must be uniquely addressed, especially since there is such variance in disability, and they must also be respected as competent learners with strengths needed to learn. Instead of viewing VSDs from a *deficit,* a shift is warranted whereas a strengths-based approach to helping is considered more desirable.

Further, it is important to address the cultural implications of a disability diagnosis. African Americans, U.S. Latinos, and American Indians have a higher rate of PTSD diagnosis (Beals et al., 2002; Hinton & Lewis-Fernández, 2011). According to Kessler et al. (2005) females have a higher prevalence of PTSD, which can be attributed to the fact that they are more likely to experience a traumatic event such as rape or domestic violence. Butcher et al. (2013) note that biological factors such as gender and sociocultural factors such as belonging to a minority group can affect how an individual responds to a traumatic event.

It is important for DSS staff to recognize culturally based behaviors that are not intended to be disruptive. If DSS staff are not sensitive to these cultural differences, they may respond inappropriately to minority group members. VSDs will learn best when DSS staff, professors, and other administrators take cultural factors into consideration.

Cultural Challenges

The military has a longstanding history of established traditions and values. Scholars are in agreement that there is a distinctive culture that upholds agreed-on social standards (Collins, 1998; Lim et al., 2018; Reger et al., 2008). The Armed Forces are a unique cultural group that has its own language, manners, behavioral norms, belief system, and values, while each university and college setting also has espoused traditions, norms, values, and belief systems that are distinctive to campus life. In essence, each organization has an organizational culture that is threaded through the fabric of these entities, which govern the interactions that take place in these environments. It may be particularly challenging for VSDs to transition to an environment in which the cultural norms are so different from the expectations of their previous military environment; therefore, it is important that cultural exposure to campus life is a positive experience. VSDs represent a nontraditional cultural group, so it is critical to take into account the need for postsecondary faculty and staff to be aware of their unique needs and work diligently to improve cultural competence in providing academic services.

Cultural competence is a term that was coined in a seminal article (Sue, 1998) that argued that clinicians lack the competency to provide mental health services to ethnically diverse people (e.g., African Americans, American Indians, Asians, Latinos). Although this concept has been traditionally used to describe clinical relationships, it stands to reason that the idea of cultural competency would also be relevant when exploring the needs of VSDs. The concept that there is a disconnect in the articulation of cultural norms and language aptly describes the issues that impede the transition of veterans into institutions of higher learning. Sue (2001) proposed the multidimensional model of cultural competence (MDCC) that reflects three primary components a provider should possess: (a) cultural competence defined in terms of provider awareness, knowledge, and skills; (b) provider self-awareness of their own attitudes about diverse cultural groups and being knowledgeable about these diverse groups; and (c) engagement in practices that advocate and promote the well-being of people from diverse groups. Atuel and Castro (2018) illuminated the importance of non-serving civilians to ensure that they give attention to establishing a therapeutic alliance with veterans. Atuel and Castro admonish that the failure to gain the respect and trust of veterans will erode the relationship, hence the importance of developing "military cultural competence." Military cultural competence pertains to *"a provider's attitudinal competence, cognitive competence, and behavioral competence in working with service members and veterans"* (Atuel & Castro, 2018, p. 77). Although it is not practical to understand the facts surrounding every nuance of military life, it is possible to be aware of your beliefs about the specific cultural group, which can help safeguard against biases that may serve to sabotage the helping relationship. Also, cognitive competence speaks to a provider's knowledge regarding military culture, which also includes cultural norms, organizational structure, and social identities that are relevant to the veteran (Atuel, & Castro, 2018). Last, behavioral competence refers to the helper's skill in assessing and treating veterans. This is particularly relevant because although VSDs will not ideally receive treatment and assessment from postsecondary settings, it is important to be aware of common disabilities VSDs experience. Working knowledge of these disabilities may provide much needed insight as to what additional services and referrals may be warranted while also avoiding any unintentional behaviors and interactions that may trigger negative responses. Developing competencies aimed at providing better service to VSDs in postsecondary education may require faculty and staff to engage in training opportunities and also realign current curricula strategies that support successful outcomes.

Training Needs

Staff, administration, and faculty play an essential rolling in assisting an estimated one million U.S. VSDs pursue postsecondary educational and training that will yield the promise of college degrees. By providing the necessary assistance that will ease their transition, it will enable VSDs to be more prepared to navigate the unique challenges they may encounter while on the academic journey. Also, the provision of timely and relevant support VSDs can maximize educational benefits, thereby avoiding extended time spent in academic programs and also increasing the number of successful completions of beneficiaries. Third, by receiving more education and training VSDs are better positioned to pursue financial stability and experience the benefit of feeling a sense of purpose and life meaning that is the byproduct when one is engaged in a thriving career. Individuals who are employed in postsecondary settings and participate in student engagement activities (e.g. faculty, administration, student life, advisors, staff) can be highly beneficial to the transition of VSDs if they are keenly aware and sensitive to the differences and unique challenges that veterans experience as compared to students who are nonveterans. They typical "cookie-cutter" approach to working with traditional students is even less effective when dealing with VSDs who have broader life experiences than their counterparts. A better understanding of how these differences can possibly impact a veteran who is just now entering an institution of higher education could have positive implications as it relates to integration in the classroom. There is a trend in which colleges and universities are housing designated staff and offices for veterans to receive "tailored" attention; it is not enough (Wilson, 2014). Monroe (2008) noted not all colleges have experience accommodating veterans with disabilities. Wilson (2014) noted the need for other services to VSD such as a detailed orientation, student services, and social support services provided by institutions. Additionally, individuals in these various areas need to be trained on the proper way to provide services specifically to VSDs. There are distinct differences between college-aged students with disabilities, nontraditional students with disabilities, and VSD. DSS staff would benefit from specific training on the needs of veterans with disabilities on college campuses. Veterans have various types of disabilities, some of which are traumatic brain injuries and post-traumatic stress disorder, which are hidden. It would be beneficial for the DSS staff, teachers, and staff to be knowledgeable about different disability types and how they can work together to assist veterans.

Faculty play a critical role in ensuring that VSDs are presented with the appropriate learning environment in which they can equally thrive. As a result of military and life experiences, VSDs have a different set of skills, knowledge, and aptitudes that should be seen as strengths and can provide positive learning opportunities for class. However, educators have to remain committed to ensuring they have developed the competence needed to work with VSDs. For example, many VSDs have disabilities that are seen (visible) and those that are not so readily seen (invisible). In other words, VSDs may need support that may require educators to reevaluate learning strategies and curriculum. An example of the this is perhaps the use of *group projects*. Placing students in group projects can be an effective way of teaching specific skills and encouraging teamwork. However, for a VSD who may be experiencing issues with post-traumatic stress disorder or mental health issues such as anxiety, this simple assignment may present an unpleasant and perhaps hostile experience. Educators who lack knowledge and understanding of these types of disabilities could inadvertently contribute the barriers that already exist for VSDs working to transition back into civilian life. Therefore, if educators had the ability to recognize and understand how *invisible and visible* disabilities, such as the impact of painful combat memories, how traumatic brain injury effects cognition, processing, and mood, and how amputation, and disfigurement can evoke bias, stigma, and stereotyping, then they would be in a better position to support VSDs in the classroom (DeCoster, 2018).

Collaboration

Veterans with disabilities require various services from several areas throughout the college campus. For example, the financial aid counselor must be knowledgeable about the similarities and differences between GI educational benefits and financial aid (Madaus et al., 2009). Therefore, it would be important for the financial aid counselor and DSS to work together to assist the veteran with navigating through the financial process. Collaboration between VA staff and DSS staff is also beneficial because veterans also receive services from the Veteran's Administration office (Fredman et al., 2018). The VA counselor is knowledgeable about the needs of the veterans they serve and can be a link between the student and the DSS office.

Standardize How the Term *Disability* Is Defined

The Americans With Disabilities Act (ADA) (1990) defines *disability* as a physical or mental impairment that substantially limits one or more major life activities, has a record of such impairment, or is regarded as having such an impairment. While the ADA has their definition of disability that DSS offices use, the military and VA use different standards to determine disability (U.S. Department of Education, 2008), which could pose problems for veterans with disabilities on college campuses qualifying for services. DSS staff and VA administration should use consistent language when they define the term *disability* so that this will not be a barrier for VSDs qualifying for services in the postsecondary setting.

Social Support Strategies to Enhance Veteran Student Success in Postsecondary Setting

In addition to academic needs, the VSD also has social support needs, which can also have an impact on their academic success in the postsecondary setting. Social support is an integral part of transition for VSDs. Furthermore, many VSDs are experiencing various life adjustment, such as reintegration into their family (Knox et al., 2010). VSDs often have difficult transitions from the military culture to the university culture. Kato (2010) noted VSDs with disabilities have difficulty developing a support system, relating to their university peers, and finding meaning and purpose in the postsecondary setting. Moreover, Jones (2013) notes VSDs have difficulty starting over in the university setting and often have difficulty developing a support system because of their inability to relate to college-aged students. Research shows the age and maturity differences between VSDs and traditional students are potential barriers to developing social relationships. Traditional college students are less structured and childlike, whereas veteran students are more established with vocational, social, and family roles (Bosari et al., 2017; Smith-Osborne, 2012).

The DSS staff must be multifaceted in their approach to working with VSDs and be able to provide academic accommodations in addition to counseling. In circumstances when the DSS staff is not qualified to provide individuals counseling, the student should then be referred to the counseling center. Oftentimes, individual counseling is beneficial because sometimes VSDs need to address social and emotional problems so that they can focus in the academic environment.

VSDs' Physical and Mental Health Issues

According to Vachi (2012) 30% of veterans are diagnosed with physical and mental health disabilities in the postsecondary setting. Wilcox et al. (2013) noted veteran students have higher rates of mental health issues when compared to nonveteran students. Some of those disabilities commonly diagnosed to VSDs are post-traumatic stress disorder, anxiety, depression, traumatic brain injury, and mobility issues.

Post-Traumatic Stress Disorder

The American Psychological Association's (APA, 2013) *Diagnostic and Statistical Manual* (5th edition; DSM-5) defines *post-traumatic stress disorder* as "the development of characteristic symptoms following exposure to one or more traumatic events (p. 274). Post-traumatic stress disorder is one of the most common mental health issues experienced by veteran service members (APA, 2013; Tanielian & Jaycox, 2008). Moreover, PTSD is the most common mental health issue among VSDs (Bryan et al., 2014; Campbell & Riggs, 2015).

There are several diagnostic features of the PTSD diagnosis that may impact VSDs in the postsecondary setting. According to the DSM-5, individuals with PTSD may be quick tempered and aggressive and have a heightened sensitivity to external stimuli (APA, 2013). The APA also says individuals with a PTSD diagnosis can engage in aggressive behaviors with no provocation. Additional symptoms that may have an impact in the academic setting include difficulty with concentration, memory, and focusing. As a result of the aforementioned diagnostic features, VSD are more likely to have a lower grade point average, lower academic self-efficacy, and lower academic persistence and effort regulation (Barry et al., 2012; Eakman et al., 2016; Ness et al., 2015).

Anxiety

The features of anxiety disorder are excessive fear and anxiety (APA, 2013). The APA (2013) defines *fear* as "the emotional response to real or perceived imminent threat, whereas anxiety is anticipation of future threat" (p. 189). Performance in the postsecondary setting is one of the areas that can cause stress for individuals with this diagnosis. Identified physical symptoms that can impede VSD performance in the postsecondary setting are "restlessness or feeling keyed up or on edge; being easily fatigued; difficulty concentrating or mind going blank; and irritability" (APA, 2013, p. 190). In the academic setting VSDs may have difficulty focusing in class and retaining information provided from the lectures.

Depression

Research has shown veterans are more likely to experience depressive symptoms, particularly those who have served in combat (Gould et al., 2014). Moreover, depression has a negative impact on academic performance. Symptoms of depression are depressed mood, weight loss, inability to sleep or sleeping too much, fatigue, feelings of worthlessness, and/or loss of interest or pleasure (APA, 2013). In a study conducted by Fortney et al. (2015) veteran students had a higher prevalence of positive depression screens than nonveterans. Individuals who suffer from depression are more likely to miss class and/or not complete assignments.

Traumatic Brain Injury

Traumatic brain injury (TBI) is an invisible wound of war that has affected an estimated 313,816 service members (U.S. Department of Defense, 2019). Traumatic brain injury (TBI) is defined as a blow or jolt to the head or a penetrating head injury that disrupts the functioning of the brain. Symptoms of TBI include behavioral, emotional, and personality changes; cognitive changes; loss of senses; physical changes; and sleeping difficulties. Academic implications of these symptoms include shortened attention span, impulsivity, limited social skills, disorganization, lack of memory, limited comprehension, difficulty catching on to new material, and disorganized thinking.

Mobility Issues

According to Parks and Walker (2014), about 30,000 American soldiers have been wounded in action since the beginning of the war in Iraq in 2003, and many of these soldiers have experienced psychological and physical trauma. Engagement in intense combat has left many soldiers returning from combat with varied forms of disability that may impact not only cognition and behavior, but also their physical mobility. Many types of impairments can impact mobility, such as amputation, paralysis, stroke, spinal cord injury, and arthritis. After acquiring a disability that impacts the ability to negotiate physical environments, veterans face the arduous adjustment to the changes in their bodies but also to how to best access the campus environment. Students who do not have mobility issues may take a walk to their next class for granted without having to give any thought as to whether the entrance of the building is wheelchair accessible. Further, the student without disabilities can also carelessly rush off to their next class with the understanding that they have 10 minutes to get there, and they fully expect to make it to their class on time. However, for the veteran who has a disability that can make negotiation of the campus more difficult, and the veteran would find that these unspoken traditions and expectations may not be easily met. The Americans With Disabilities Act (ADA) and Section 504 of the Rehabilitation Act mandates that students with disabilities receive equal access to programs and services in higher education (Disability Compliance for Higher Education, 2013). These standards apply to places that are considered public, commercial, state, and local facilities. Despite the ADA mandate for access, at times these institutions may marginally meet the requirement, especially if compliance would be an undue hardship for these entities. For example, the college or university may have a building that does have a wheelchair accessible ramp, but it may be located in a location that is not necessarily very convenient.

In order for VSDs to be successful in a college/university setting, institutional-wide commitment to accessibility and inclusion must be adopted. This attitude of inclusion can be demonstrated by intentionally creating campus environments that promote student success. A ways in which this can be accomplished is by implementing universal design in postsecondary settings (Scott et al., 2003). Universal design by definition refers to the creation of products and environments that can be utilized by as many people as possible (which includes people with disabilities) in such a manner that adaptations and accommodations are not needed (Connell et al., 1997). Faculty commitment to inclusion in postsecondary settings would create a culture that would lend itself to modifying curriculum that embodies the spirit of inclusive instruction. Development of inclusive environments and implementation of inclusive curriculum can be beneficial for veteran students with disabilities who may have difficulty negotiating their physical environments and would also meet the diverse needs of a wide range of learning styles.

Strategies for Veteran Success in Post-Secondary Setting

Disability support staff have an increased responsibility when providing services to veterans with disabilities because of their unique experiences with combat and adjustment to civilian life (Madaus et al., 2009). Adequate services for veterans with disabilities on college campuses dates back to the 1950s. Strom's (1950) report identified four procedures campuses should employ to support the success of veterans with disabilities on college campuses: (a) centralization of responsibility to a designated staff member, (b) identification of students in need of assistance, (c) increased faculty and staff awareness of the needs of students, and (d) continuous follow-up to ensure that services were adequate. Nearly 70 years later, those are still strategies that can be implemented on college campuses.

Training for DSS Staff, Other Staff, and Faculty

Wilson (2014) noted having a designated staff and office for VSD is not enough. Additionally, Monroe (2008) noted not all colleges have experience accommodating veterans with disabilities. Wilson noted the need for other services for VSDs such as a detailed orientation, student services, and social support services. Additionally, individuals in these various areas need to be trained on the proper way to provide services specifically to VSD. There are distinct differences between college aged students with disabilities, nontraditional students with disabilities, and VSD. DSS staff would benefit from specific training on the needs of veterans with disabilities on college campuses. It would be beneficial for the DSS staff, teachers and staff to be knowledgeable about different disability types and how they can work together to assist veterans.

Disability Support Services Process

Monroe (2008) noted veterans with disabilities do not know how to seek out services in the postsecondary setting. In the process for receiving services in the postsecondary setting state an individual must disclose their disability in order to receive services. Students who transition from high school would typically be advised by the school counselor on the steps to receiving services when they enter college. However, veterans who acquire an injury in combat later in life may not already know the steps to receiving disability support in the college setting. DSS should reconsider their approach to students with disabilities when that individual is a veteran.

Ethical Considerations

When working with VSDs, it is important to consider potential ethical issues that may arise. The disability support service provider should not only understand ethical issues, but also understand how violations can impact the veteran student. While there is not a specific code of ethics that govern disability support service providers, the American Counseling Association's (2014) code of ethics could serve as a guide to ensure ethical practice. Ethical principles and practice that should be adhered to when working with veterans are autonomy, informed consent, confidentiality, and competence.

The DSS administration should provide adequate information about the process the veteran student with the disability has to take to receive services. This will allow the VSD to make informed decisions throughout the process. The counselor should also work to ensure confidentiality of the information disclosed by the veteran. Herlihy and Corey (2015) defined *confidentiality* as "the counselor's obligation to respect the client's privacy and to our promise to clients that the information they reveal during counseling will be protected from disclosure without their consent" (p. 108). The ACA (2014) code of ethics states, "Counselors practice only within the boundaries of their competence, based on their education, training, supervised experience, state and national professional credentials, and appropriate professional experience" (C.2.a). DSS staff should ensure they are knowledgeable about veterans and their needs in order to provide adequate services.

Conclusion

VSDs are attending postsecondary institutions at a much higher rate. As more veterans receive support from the government to attend postsecondary institutions the numbers will continue to increase. Postsecondary institutions must be prepared to provide quality academic, social, and emotional support to veterans as they matriculate.

Questions/Considerations

1. Discuss one social and cultural challenge that a veteran student with a disability may encounter.
2. Identify and discuss three barriers to VSDs' success in the postsecondary setting.
3. Discuss one major legislative act and the impact it has on veteran students with disabilities' success in the postsecondary setting.
4. Discuss two strategies you would implement to promote the success of VSDs in the postsecondary setting.

The Case of X: A College Student With PTSD

X is a Hispanic male majoring in a science at a 4-year postsecondary institution. His academic goal is to receive a science degree in order gain entrance into medical school. X served many years in the military, and during that time he was deployed for three tours. During these tours X served on the front lines of all wars and saw a great deal of fighting and bombings. In a conversation with the college counselor, X stated that he has vivid memories of what he saw, has night sweats, and is afraid of sitting in the back room. Although he met with a counselor, he was never referred to anyone for academic accommodations.

X's professor describes him as very helpful in the laboratory setting and very knowledgeable about the course content. The professor states X always comes to class on time and prepared. He is also very respectful toward the professor and often engaged in conversations about his academic and career goals. The professor is concerned because X does not relate well to his peers and often performs poorly on group assignments. One day X made a mistake in the lab and dropped something; he immediately began to uncontrollably yell out obscenities and went into a fit of rage, scaring the other students and professor. The professor became concerned about X's fixation with danger and fits of rage. After at least two occasions of at-risk behaviors, the professor asked to the student to leave.

One day while taking a break in the conference room, the professor overheard two other faculty discussing X and his PTSD diagnosis. The professor was unaware that X had this diagnosis but now understood why he was having so much difficulty in the classroom. The professor later spoke with the student and referred him to the Disability Support Services Office.

Case Study Discussion Questions

1. What could have been done to ensure X received veteran support services at the university?
2. What individuals need to collaborate to ensure the success of X moving forward at this institution?
3. Identify one academic, social, and cultural barrier to X's success in the classroom.
4. What is a potential ethical issue in this case?

References

American Council on Education (ACE). (2010). *Accommodating student veterans with traumatic brain injury and post-traumatic stress disorder: Tips for campus faculty and staff.* https://www.acenet. edu/Documents/Accommodating-Student-Veterans-with-Traumatic-Brain-Injury-and-Post-Traumatic-Stress-Disorder.pdf

American Counseling Association (ACA). (2014). *2014 ACA code of ethics.* http://www.counseling.org/docs/ethics/2014-aca-code-of-ethics.pdf?sfvrsn=4

American Psychiatric Association. (2013). *Diagnostic and statistical manual of mental disorders* (5th ed.). Author.

Americans With Disabilities Act of 1990, Pub. L. No. 101-336, 104 Stat. 328 (1990)

Atuel, H. R., & Castro, C. A. (2018). Military cultural competence. *Clinical Social Work Journal, 46,* 74–82. https://doi.org/10.1007/s10615-018-0651-z

Barry, A. E., Whiteman, S. D., & MacDermid Wadsworth, S. M. (2012). Implications of posttraumatic stress among military-affiliated and civilian students. *Journal of American College Health, 60,* 562–573.

Beals, J., Manson, S. M., Shore, J. H., Friedman, M., Ashcraft, M., Fairbank, J. A., & Schlenger, W. E. (2002). The prevalence of posttraumatic stress disorder among American Indian Vietnam veterans: disparities and context. *Journal of Traumatic Stress: Official Publication of the International Society for Traumatic Stress Studies, 15*(2), 89–97.

Borsari, B., Yurasek, A., Miller, M. B., Murphy, J. G., McDevitt-Murphy, M. E., Martens, M. P., ... & Carey, K. B. (2017). Student service members/veterans on campus: Challenges for reintegration. *American Journal of Orthopsychiatry, 87*(2), 166.

Bryan, C. J., Bryan, A. O., Hinkson, K., Jr., Bichrest, M., & Ahern, D. A. (2014). Depression, posttraumatic stress disorder, and grade point average among student service members and veterans. *Journal of Rehabilitation Research and Development, 51*(7), 1035–1046.

Butcher, J. N., Hooley, J. M., & Mineka, S. (2013). *Abnormal psychology* (16th ed.). Pearson.

Campbell, R., & Riggs, S. A. (2015). The role of psychological symptomatology and social support in the academic adjustment of previously deployed student veterans. *Journal of American College Health, 63*(7), 473–481. https://doi.org/10.1080/07448481.2015.1040408

Canaday, M. (2003). Building a straight state: Sexuality and social citizenship under the 1944 G.I. Bill. *The Journal of American History, 90*(3), 935–957.

Cate, C. A. (2014). *Million Records Project: Research from VSD's of America.* https://projects.ncsu.edu/www/ncsu/design/sod5/cud/about_ud/udprinciplestext.htm

Collins, J. (1998). The complex context of American military culture: A practitioner's view. *Washington Quarterly, 21*(4), 213–228. https://doi.org/10.1080/01636600809550359

Connell, B. R., Jones, M., Mace, R., Mueller, J., Mullick, A., & Ostroff, E. (1997). *The principles of universal design.* https://projects.ncsu.edu/www/ncsu/design/sod5/cud/about_ud/udprinciplestext.htm

DeCoster, V. A. (2018). The needs of military veterans returning to college after service. *International Journal of Arts & Sciences, 11*(1), 11–20.

Dill, P. L., & Henley, T. B. (1998). Stressors of college: A comparison of traditional and nontraditional students. *The Journal of Psychology: Interdisciplinary and Applied, 132*(1), 25–32. https://doi.org/10.1080/00223989809599261

DiRamio, D., Ackerman, R., Garza Mitchell, R. L. (2008). From combat to campus: Voices of student-veterans. *NASPA Journal, 45*(1), 73–102. https://doi.org/10.2202/1949-6605.1908

DiRamio, D., & Jarvis, K. (2011). Veterans in higher education: When Johnny and Jane came marching to campus. *ASHE Higher Education Report, 37*(3), 1–144. https://eric.ed.gov/?id=EJ940516

Disability Compliance for Higher Education (2013). *Medical school students with disabilities. Disability Compliance For Higher Education, 18*(10), 16.

Dunwoody, P. T., Plane, D. L., Trescher, S. A., & Rice, D. (2014). Authoritarianism, social dominance, and misperceptions of war. *Peace and Conflict: Journal of Peace Psychology, 20*(3), 256-266.

Eakman, A. M., Schelly, C., & Henry, K. L. (2016). Protective and vulnerability factors contributing to resilience in Post-9/11 veterans with service-related injuries in postsecondary education. *American Journal of Occupational Therapy, 70*(1), 1–10.

Elliott, M., & Naphan, D. E. (2015). Role exit from the military: Student veterans' perceptions of transitioning from the U.S. military to higher education. *The Qualitative Report, 20*(2), 36–48.

Ellison, M. L., Mueller, L., Smelson, D., Corrigan, P. W., Torres Stone, R. A., Bokhour, B. G., Najavits, L. M., Vessella, J. M., & Drebing, C. (2012). Supporting the education goals of post-911 veterans with self-reported PTSD symptoms: A needs assessment. *Psychiatric Rehabilitation Journal, 35*(3), 209–217.

Forbus, P., Newbold, J. J., Mehta, S. S. (2011). A study of non-traditional and traditional students in terms of their time management behaviors, stress factors, and coping strategies. *Academy of Educational Leadership Journal, 15*, 109–125.

Foreman, P., Dempsey, I., Robinson, G., & Manning, E. (2001). Characteristics, academic and post-university outcomes of students with a disability at the University of Newcastle. *Higher Education Research & Development, 20*(3), 313–325.

Fortney, J. C., Curran, G. M., Hunt, J. B., Cheney, A. M., Lu, L., Valenstein, M., & Eisenberg, D. (2015). Prevalence of probable mental disorders and help-seeking behaviors among veteran and non-veteran community college students. *General Hospital Psychiatry, 38*, 99–104.

Fredman, S. J., Marshall, A. D., Le, Y., Aronson, K. R., Perkins, D. F., & Hayes, J. A. (2018). Interpersonal relationship quality mediates the association between military-related posttraumatic stress and academic dysfunction among student veterans. *Psychological Trauma: Theory, Research, Practice, and Policy, 11*(4), 415–423.

Ginder-Vogel, K. (2012). *Supporting the soldier-to-student transition: Ensuring the success of active duty military students and student veterans.* The Evolllution. https://evolllution.com/opinions/supporting-the-soldier-to-student-transition

Gould, C. E., Rideaux, T., Spira, A. P., & Beaudreau, S. A. (2014). Depression and anxiety symptoms in male veterans and non-veterans: The Health and Retirement Study. *International Journal of Geriatric Psychiatry, 30*(6), 623–630.

Green, L., & Hayden, S. (2013). Supporting student veterans: Current landscape and future directions. *Journal of Military and Government Counseling, 1*(2), 89-100.

Griffin, K. A., & Gilbert, C. K. (2015). Better transition for troops: An application of Schlossberg's transition framework to analyses of barriers and institutional support structures for student veterans. *The Journal of Higher Education, 86*(1), 71–97.

Hall, D. T., & Nougaim, K. E. (1968). An examination of Maslow's need hierarchy in an organizational setting. *Organizational behavior and human performance, 3*(1), 12–35.

Hall, L. (2011). The importance of understanding military culture. *Social Work in Health Care, 50*(1), 4–18.

Herlihy, B., & Corey, G. (2015). *ACA ethical standards casebook* (7th ed.). American Counseling Association.

Hinton, D. E., & Lewis-Fernández, R. (2011). The cross-cultural validity of posttraumatic stress disorder: Implications for DSM-5. *Depression and Anxiety, 28*(9), 783–801.

Jenner, B. M. (2017). Student veterans and the transition to higher education: Integrating existing literatures. *Journal of Veteran Studies*, 2(2), 26–44.

Jones, K. C. (2013). Understanding student veterans in transition. *The Qualitative Report*, 18(37), 1.

Kato, L. (2010). The psychological adjustment of veterans returning from Afghanistan and Iraq. *Order*, (3426110).

Kessler, R. C., Chiu, W. T., Demler, O., & Walters, E. E. (2005). Prevalence, severity, and comorbidity of 12-month DSM-IV disorders in the National Comorbidity Survey Replication. *Archives of General Psychiatry*, 62(6), 617–627.

Kim, Y. M., & Cole, J. S. (2013). Student veterans/service members' engagement in college and university life and education. Retrieved from https://vtechworks.lib.vt.edu/bitstream/handle/10919/97817/StudentVeteransEngagement.pdf?sequence=1

Knox, K. L., Pflanz, S., Talcott, G. W., Campise, R. L., Lavigne, J. E., Bajorska, A., ... & Caine, E. D. (2010). The US Air Force suicide prevention program: implications for public health policy. *American Journal of Public Health*, 100(12), 2457-2463.

Lim, J. H., Interiano, C. G., Nowell, C. E., Tkacik, P. T., & Dahlber, J. L. (2018). Invisible cultural barriers: Contrasting perspectives on student veterans' transition. *Journal of College Student Development*, 59(3), 291–308.

Madaus, J. W. (2000). Services for college and university students with disabilities: A historical perspective. *Journal of Postsecondary Education and Disability*, 14(1), 4–21.

Madaus, J. W., & Miller, W. K. & Vance, M. L. (2009). Veterans with disabilities in postsecondary education. *Journal of Postsecondary Education and Disability*, 22(1), 10–17.

Monroe, S. J. (2008). *Dear colleague letter*. U.S. Department of Education, Office for Civil Rights. https://www2.ed.gov/print/about/offices/list/ocr/letters/colleague-201104.html

National Center for PTSD. (2014). *VA campus toolkit*. https://www.mentalhealth.va.gov/studentveteran/docs/ed_todaysStudentVets.html

National Survey of Student Engagement. (2010). *Veterans in college perceive lower levels of campus support and interact less with faculty than nonveterans, survey finds*. https://newsinfo.iu.edu/news/page/print/16325.html

National Veteran Education Success Tracker (NVEST). (2017). *A report on the academic success of student veterans Using the post-9/11 GI Bill*. *https://www.luminafoundation.org/files/resources/veteran-success-tracker.pdf*

Ness, B. M., Middleton, M. J., & Hildebrandt, M. J. (2015). Examining the effects of self-reported post-traumatic stress disorder symptoms and positive relations with others on self-regulated learning for student service members/veterans. *Journal of American College Health*, 63(7), 448–458.

O'Herrin, E. (2011). Enhancing veteran success in higher education. *Peer Review*, 13(1), 15.

Ochinko, W., & Payea, K. (2018). *Postsecondary non-completion among veterans: Contributing factors and implications.* https://vetsedsuccess.org/postsecondary-non-completion-among-veterans-contributing-factors-and-implications/

Parks, R., & Walker, E. (2014). Understanding student veteran disabilities. *College and University, 90*(1), 53–74.

Parks, R., Walker, E., & Smith, C. (2015). Exploring the challenges of academic advising for VSD's. *College and University, 90*(4), 37–52.

Reger, M. A., Etherage, J. R., Reger, G. M., & Gahm, G. A. (2008). Civilian psychologists in an Army culture: The ethical challenge of cultural competence. *Military Psychology, 20*(1), 21–35.

Rumann, C., & Hamrick, F. (2010). Student veterans in transition: Re-enrolling after war zone deployments. *Journal of Higher Education, 81*(4), 431–458.

Sander, L. (2012, March 11). Out of uniform: At half a million and counting, veterans cash in on post-9/11 GI Bill. *The Chronicle of Higher Education.* Washington D.C.

Sander L. (2013, January 5). Veterans' graduation rates are focus of new partnership. *The Chronicle of Higher Education.* 2013. Washington D.C.

Scott, S. T., McGuire, J. M., & Shaw, S. F. (2003). Universal design of instruction: A new paradigm for adult instruction in postsecondary education. *Remedial and Special Education, 24*(6), 369–379.

Semer, C., & Harmening, D. S. (2015). *Exploring significant factors that impact the academic success of VSD's in higher education.* http://www.m.www.na-businesspress.com/JHETP/SemerC_Web15_7_.pdf

Smith-Osborne, A. (2008). Mental health risk factors and protective mechanisms for post-secondary educational attainment among young adult veterans.. Retrieved from https://kb.osu.edu/bitstream/handle/1811/32069/2/20_4smith-osborne_paper.pdf

Strom, R. J. (1950). *The disabled college veteran of World War II.* American Council on Education.

Sue, D. W. (2001). Multidimensional facets of cultural competence. *The Counseling Psychologist, 29*(6), 790–821.

Sue, S. (1998). In search of cultural competence in psychotherapy and counseling. *American Psychologist, 53*(4), 440–448.

Tanielian, T. L., & Jaycox, L. (2008). *Invisible wounds of war: Psychological and cognitive injuries, their consequences, and services to assist recovery* (Vol. 1). Rand Corporation.

U.S. Department of Defense. (2019). *Traumatic brain injury: Department of Defense special report.* https://dod.defense.gov/News/Special-Reports/0315_tbi/

U.S. Department of Education. (2008). *So you want to go back to school.* https://www2.ed.gov/about/offices/list/ocr/letters/colleague-20071226.pdf

U.S. Department of Veteran Affairs. (2015). *Profile of veterans: 2012: Data from the American Community Survey.* https://www.va.gov/vetdata/docs/SpecialReports/Profile_of_Veterans_2012.pdf

U.S. Department of Veterans Affairs. (2018). *National Center for Veterans Analysis and Statistics* https://www.va.gov/vetdata/

Vachi, D. T. (2012). Considering student veterans on the twenty-first-century college campus. *About Campus*, 17(2), 15–21.

Veterans Administration. (2008). *VA benefits and health care utilization.* https://catalog.data.gov/dataset/va-benefits-health-care-utilization

Wilcox, S. L., Finney, K., & Cedarbaum, J. A. (2013). Prevalence of mental health problems among military populations. In B. A. Moore & J. E. Barnett (Eds.), *Military psychologists' desk reference* (pp. 187–196). Oxford University Press.

Wilson, C., Sour, A. J., Miller, L. A., Saygbay-Hallie, M., Miller, C., & Daniels, R. A. (2016). A standardized tool for measuring military friendliness of colleges and universities. SAGE Open, 6(2). https://doi.org/10.1177/2158244016644009

Wilson, K. B. (2014). Thank you for your service: Military initiatives on college campuses. *New Horizons in Adult Education & Human Resource Development*, 26(3), 54–60.

Chapter 6

Undiagnosed Post-Traumatic Stress Disorder

Implications for Counselor Education Programs at Historically Black Colleges and Universities

Sheila Witherspoon

Introduction

The stigma of mental illness is very prevalent in the so-called African American community. Though many have been exposed to trauma related to physical, sexual, and/or psychological ordeals, African Americans seeking help from counselors, psychologists and/or psychiatrists are typically discouraged by family, friends, and themselves. Identifying any type of mental disorder and/or illness as a remnant of being exposed to a traumatic event(s) is often viewed as a weakness. Moreover, this "weakness" must be shrouded in silence as to not bring attention to the dysfunction, recognized or not, that is or has been present in their lives, especially in their families. Additionally, cultural mistrust of counselors, psychologists and/or psychiatrists may contribute to African Americans' denial of symptoms related to mental illness, and subsequently seeking help.

Help-seeking behaviors of African Americans may be more connected to talking with clergy, which tends to be more socially acceptable and less stigmatizing. Moreover, engaging in high levels of codependency (i.e., helping others to the detriment of care for self) is also seen as acceptable, and in some cases a badge of honor (i.e., the "strong Black woman") even to the detriment of one's physical, medical, mental, and/or financial health. Coping mechanisms such as self-medicating (e.g., substance abuse, emotional eating, gambling, etc.) though not socially acceptable, could be viewed as "better" than going to a counselor, psychologist and/or psychiatrist. Yet many African Americans who have experienced symptoms of mental illness, specifically those relative to post-traumatic stress disorder gravitate toward helping professions that serve others who they affiliate and associate with but not necessarily for their own healing (Wallace & Constantine, 2005). Basically, some African Americans pursue careers in helping professions such as counseling because of their desire to help others so they don't have to go through what they went through, yet are reluctant to participate in counseling themselves.

Essentially, the probability of African American preservice counseling students who will counsel counselees, clients, and/or consumers who have experienced trauma yet avoid help-seeking behaviors that lead to participation counseling or counseling-related services can be higher due to their own beliefs about counseling as it relates to themselves. Especially concerning is the possibility that undiagnosed post-traumatic stress disorder (PTSD) could be a major part of graduate students' lives. For those who attend historically Black colleges and universities (HBCUs), a traditional culture of some African Americans relative to staunch religious (church) beliefs can also be fostered and reinforced among students, staff, and faculty who may not see counseling services as important or necessary. Coupled with family and community beliefs, counseling may not be a viable option when dealing with exposure to traumatic events.

Thus, what happens when African Americans enrolled in graduate counseling programs who not only maintain these attitudes about persons with mental disorders but are reluctant to face their own diagnosis? Moreover, what happens if these students are living with undiagnosed PTSD?

This chapter will explore implications for students undiagnosed with PTSD, especially those enrolled in master's-level counseling programs who attend HBCUs. Aware that racial ethnic groups other than African Americans attend HBCU counseling graduate programs, a pervasive stigma related to mental health and mental illness persists among African Americans; as such, that the focus will be on this group.

Moreover, this chapter delineates how undiagnosed PTSD affects graduate students' counseling disposition inclusive of the propensity to engage in transference and/or countertransference, boundary crossings, and/or boundary violations with consumers. A case study and critical analysis questions to stimulate thought on how to address issues of undiagnosed PTSD, and the ability to encourage help-seeking behaviors in preservice counseling students at HBCUs will be examined.

Post-Traumatic Stress Disorder

The American Psychiatric Association's (2013) *Diagnostic and Statistical Manual of Mental Disorders* (DSM-5) defines PTSD Criteria A as "exposure to actual or threatened death, serious injury, or sexual violence in one (or more) of the following ways:

1. Directly experiencing the traumatic event(s).
2. Witnessing, in person, the event(s) as it occurred to others.

3. Learning that the traumatic event(s) occurred to a close family member or close friend. In cases of actual or threatened death of a family member or friend, the event(s) must have been violent or accidental.

4. Experiencing repeated or extreme exposure to aversive details of the traumatic event(s) (e.g., first responders collecting human remains; police officers repeatedly exposed to details of child abuse)" (p. 271).

Symptoms associated with PTSD are inclusive of but not limited to the. following:

- Flashback and nightmares that replay traumatic events

- Consciously avoiding people, places, and things that bring back memories of the traumatic events that have the capacity to paralyze emotions and movement

- Enhanced hypersensitivity, irritability, and agitation (Pai et al., 2017)

PTSD is diagnosed after a person experiences symptoms for at least 1 month following a traumatic event (Pai et al., 2017). However, symptoms may not appear until several months or even years later. Victims may suppress these symptoms through avoidance of rehashing the exposure to the traumatic event as well as trauma experienced directly. Persons who are undiagnosed may engage in this suppression as a form of denial, as well as maintain their ability to continue living their lives without interruption. Essentially, the capacity to interrupt work and home life management is seen as detrimental, more so than the symptoms they may recognize yet are unable to tend to.

Moreover, if parents and/or caretakers are aware of symptomology, it may be characterized by family and friends as something that if one stops thinking about it will reduce and/or eliminate their reactions to those events. Being unable to do anything about it (e.g., live in the home where the trauma took place, the perpetrator is family or supports the family financially, etc.) as well as simply not knowing what to do about it (as many adults have experienced trauma to the point where it becomes normalized) may be one reason why these events and the remnants thereof are ignored as problematic. Basically, if the trauma experienced isn't considered "extreme" it may not be taken seriously by family or friends. Too, if helping professionals such as social workers or law enforcement are not involved as to lead to an adverse consequence such as removal of children from the home or an arrest that results in incarceration, the ability to hide or deny is becomes easier.

Thus, the number of African American graduate students who attend HBCUs and have witnessed and/or experienced trauma in their lives has the propensity to largely be tucked away in silence. The mantra of many families, especially some African American families, is "What happens in this house stays in this house." In other words, any conversations, incidents, and/or events that occur, whether positive or negative, are not to be disclosed with anyone. Much of the rationale surrounding this mindset is the perceived and/or real adverse effects that comes from others outside the family unit's (teachers, counselors, law enforcement, etc.) ability to jeopardize their way of life.

This mindset can nullify the traumatic experience, further stifling disclosure as well as seeking help for post-traumatic stress disorder. This is relative to physical violence (domestic violence, homicide) suicide, sexual violence (rape, incest, spousal/couple, childhood), and/or emotional, verbal, and substance (alcohol, narcotics) abuse. In many cases, law enforcement may not be called, and if called the victims may not be taken seriously, especially when there is a lack of funds for quality legal representation or the perception that lower-income African Americans are only experiencing what is believed to be "normed" within the culture.

Additionally, while educated, upper-income African Americans may have the financial wherewithal and resources to seek help from a counselor, psychologist, and/or psychiatrist, a veiled silence about mental health and mental illness may have similar connotations relative to the stigma associated by the so-called African American community. As well, African American professionals must protect their careers and financial status, especially in the face of White colleagues and counterparts. Essentially, any type of perceived weakness around or in front of Whites in the workplace where African American professionals maintain high-powered careers (lawyer, doctor, corporate America, etc.) can literally end a high financial status. Thus, even with African American professionals livelihoods being extremely different from lower- income and working-class African Americans, the perceived outcome and stigma associated with mental illness can be the same.

When resources are minimal or even plentiful, and cultural mistrust is evident, Black families may be reluctant to rehash events that the victim may be asked to keep quiet. Thus, undiagnosed PTSD may result in psychological issues such as extreme anger, lack of emotional intelligence, or extreme codependency. This can also affect people at home, work, and the community, especially if unresolved.

As a result, undiagnosed PTSD has the propensity to manifest in a graduate student's counseling disposition. Some of the ways this can be compromised is in future counselors' ethical conduct in the form of boundary crossings, boundary violations, transference, and/or countertransference. The thought is, how does undiagnosed PTSD affect counseling dispositions? Can unresolved issues relative to witnessing violence against others and/or themselves affect counseling disposition? How does this impact transference and/or countertransference? What happens if PTSD is undiagnosed for too long? How does this affect the future counseling practice of preservice counselors? This will be discussed via the stigma of mental illness among African Americans, as well as cultural mistrust of helping professionals, which possibly contributes to preservice counseling students' attending HBCUs reluctance to seek help from counselors, psychologists, and/or psychiatrists.

The Stigma of Mental Illness Among African Americans

"In the 16th century, the beginning of African enslavement in the Americas until the ratification of the Thirteenth Amendment and emancipation in 1865, Africans were hunted like animals, captured, sold, tortured, and raped. They experienced the worst kind of physical, emotional, psychological, and spiritual abuse. Given such history, isn't it likely that many of the enslaved were severely traumatized? And did the trauma and the effects of such horrific abuse end with the abolition of slavery?" (DeGruy, 1994, p. 20)

Cultural Mistrust of Helping Professionals

African Americans have been largely suspicious of helping professionals throughout history. With the enslavement of Africans since 1619 during the Transatlantic Slave Trade, subsequent oppressive disenfranchisement via Jim Crow Laws (enforced from the early 19th century until 1965) and Black Codes (1865) that governed and relegated African Americans to segregation and other discriminatory practices, specific events relative to health and medicine were extremely impactful. Historical events such as the Tuskegee Syphilis Experiment (1932–1972) where scores of African American men were infected with syphilis with the expectation of being inoculated with a cure but were left infected and subsequently went blind, suffered mental illness, were sterilized, passed the infection on to their wives and children, and/or died created a foundation of cultural mistrust among helping professions.

A similar egregious human subject medical practice via the Eugenics Board in North Carolina was the sterilization of largely poor African American girls and women from 1933 until 1972. As generations of African Americans began seeing so-called "helping" initiatives as a means of population control, and/or a means by which to further disenfranchise the race, surrendering any type of data or information about themselves and/or their families had the potential to disrupt the family system's economy relative to work or housing, or open up the possibility to be incarcerated as a result. Thus, many African Americans shied away from participating in medical studies. In addition, other data-gathering activities such as the U.S. Census was also riddled with the belief that any information collected about their family and household could and would be used against them in any way.

The Census, which is a means of data collection of households for providing resources for particular communities, has also been a sources of mistrust by the so-called African American community. A belief in African American households is that any information can be used against the household, which can adversely affect the economic structure of the family. In other words, knowing where people are can be deemed helpful to police and/or helping professionals and thus take a breadwinner out of the home. Also, housing can be interrupted if Census information is available. Essentially, the diminishing information available to helping professionals, law enforcement, and/or medical professionals provides a safety net for African American families who may feel more vulnerable to adverse effects to their family and economic structure. Essentially, the ability to avoid any disclosure about people and their behavior within the family seeks to protect the unit, even if verbal, emotional, or mental behavior is detrimental to the person's home, work, and community. Thus, seeking help can be construed as a means of placing African Americans at a disadvantage to be victimized by systems that can radically change their lives. This may be especially evident with overdiagnoses of African Americans.

An example relative to mental illness and help-seeking behaviors is attention deficit hyperactivity disorder (ADHD), which is disproportionately assigned to African American boys during their K–12 academic years. A diagnosis of ADHD is noted as the gateway to African American men disproportionately diagnosed with schizophrenia. This diagnosis has the capacity to institutionalize and/or incarcerate scores of African American men, as the school-to-prison pipeline heavily documents research that targets children as young as 8 years old to build and thrive off a billion-dollar industry by predicting how many African American boys will be primed for prison (Mallett, 2017).

Basically, whether lacking adequate health insurance or using the emergency room during crisis, many African Americans seeking help from a preventative and/or proactive measure may be affected by historical events. Helping professionals were also caught in the fray of being listed as those who would not be helpful to African Americans by disclosing information that may warrant intervention on behalf of social workers, counselors, psychologists and/or psychologists, which could result in loss of employment, housing, and/or children. How then does the understanding of African Americans' help-seeking behaviors encourage and/or discourage graduate students at HBCUs who are training to become counselors to get counseling for themselves? Could graduate students' at HBCUs interest in helping professions be a type of resistance to how information gathered after a traumatic event affected their lives and the lives of their families? What notions and experiences with helping professionals inform preservice counseling student's help-seeking behaviors as well as helping mechanisms for others?

Living in Denial: Effect on Help-Seeking Behaviors

"Ain't nothing wrong with them!"

Pastors of Christian churches are most often identified as the most viable resource for many African Americans who may be experiencing symptoms or have been diagnosed with PTSD. As the civil rights movement touted the so-called Black church as the bastion of help for almost all types of situations and concerns, clergy were often consulted before approaching lawyers, law enforcement, or organizations such as the NAACP. In many cases, a pastor's word carried so much weight that even if they maintained minimal power to do something, it was deemed more socially acceptable to talk to pastors than psychologists, psychiatrists, and/or counselors. In other words, the ability of pastors to engage in denial and "convince" an individual who was exposed to trauma and/or experienced trauma that those events did not happen or that their perception of what happened was skewed has the capacity to contribute to consumers ability to not disclose actual events.

Also, a pastor who does not understand mental illness or believe in mental health, particularly PTSD, may attempt to pray it away. The use of scriptures and prayer can continue to encourage denial—even if the symptomatic behavior such as a physical or verbal outburst of a disturbing nature are evident and visualized during church worship service or in the confidentiality of the pastor's office. Essentially, until there is an extreme reaction or response regarding behavior as problematic, the urgency to be concerned can be lost.

There are notions among some African Americans that unless a family member or friend's behavior is extreme (e.g., client "went off" verbally, suffered broken bones, required a hospital stay, was arrested by law enforcement, etc.) outward, socially acceptable behavior of expressing oneself verbally or kinesthetically is not a crisis. In other words, the pressures and vestiges of racism existent in everyday life, particularly at work or the community, should be considered normal though irritating. Essentially, it is to be expected that racism affects the mental and physical well-being of African Americans. Thus, that type of stress manifesting into mental illness may not be considered based on the criteria of PTSD. Yet, the stress management of that symptomology may develop a level of codependence that is unhealthy to families and friends associated with the person who is experiencing PTSD.

Codependence, Denial, and Self Medication

"They're just going through something"

Codependence is characteristic of a family member or friend of a person experiencing symptoms and/or who has been diagnosed with PTSD and who enables that person to engage in behaviors that can ultimately be destructive relative to their personal and professional life. Basically, if a person who is living with undiagnosed PTSD is displaying symptomology and engaging in self-medication (e.g., food, alcohol, narcotics, gambling, etc.) that is adversely affecting their personal and professional life, persons who are codependent may enable these behaviors as a form of denial. Thus, they will give in by giving money to persons who are engaging in self-medication, particularly those who are addicted, as to maintain a role in their lives, even though they know their codependency is enabling them (Cook & Barber, 1997).

Essentially, to maintain a role in that person's life, as they cannot control their family member, significant other, spouse and/or friend's addiction or symptoms of undiagnosed PTSD, they will enable their behavior instead of abandoning their denial. They will give them money with the inner knowledge that they will spend it on drugs or gamble it away. Other ways of being codependent are purchasing unhealthy foods in gross amounts, as well as cooking food in an unhealthy manner for an individual who is morbidly obese or is an emotional eater—with the knowledge that either will actively contribute to their eventual demise though distressed by their actions to the point of almost secondhand PTSD. Outside of making financial contributions, other ways people engage in codependence are lying about the extent of how that person's behavior is recurring, as well as the extreme and frequency to which it is happening.

For example, family members may complain and/or discuss how a person who may be experiencing undiagnosed PTSD behavior is impacting their life, and someone who is codependent will completely deny it, even though they were there. Comments such as "Oh, they are just going through something" or "It's just a phase" can be irritating. Additionally, truth telling about family members, especially within the so-called African American community, can result in passive aggressive "shutting down," meaning raising voices, pointing out flaws of the person who is not in denial, as well as accusations of "forgetting where one comes from" and/or "being bougie [bourgeoisie]." Moreover, pointing out the obvious may also get that person accused of thinking like a "White person." Essentially, the thought that Black people keep secrets no matter what and then suggesting that clinical mental health counseling is needed may be perceived as moving in the mentality of a White person and that these actions break the code of silence relative to protecting and/or maintaining the codependence that is perceived to maintain the family or community image. Many African Americans carry this mentality and code of silence as masters-level preservice counseling students.

Preservice Counselor Education Students at HBCUs

"I don't need no counseling"

Undiagnosed PTSD and Counseling Disposition

Counseling disposition of master's-level students is often evaluated throughout The Council for Accreditation of Counseling and Related Educational Programs approved (CACREP) counseling programs. Defined as "the commitments, characteristics, values, beliefs, interpersonal functioning, and behaviors that influence the counselor's professional growth and interactions with clients and colleagues (CACREP Counseling Dispositions, 2015), these qualities provide counselor educators the ability to provide early alert support to students who may experience challenges based on their personality, worldview, and/or perspective. The ability to provide remediation and professional development for preservice students in the early stages of their graduate studies may prove helpful before becoming professional counselors. While remediation may include self-exploration and observation of self, a referral to counseling services may be met with fierce resistance. Basically, while learning to become counselors may be the goal for preservice counselors, analyzing themselves during their graduate program may be their help-seeking behavior. In other words, if one can avoid seeking counseling altogether, they can help themselves without truly facing the events of their lives that may be indicative of the onset of or living with PTSD.

As a preservice counseling student, the realization of having to engage in self exploration, as well as being encouraged to seek counseling during their counseling program may be unsettling. Moreover, when placed in the context of counseling disposition, similar symptomology for PTSD may manifest itself in the form of triggers when topics discussed in class are relative to their life's story. A lack of understanding of this can manifest in counselor ethical issues, particularly boundary crossings and boundary violations. These ethical dilemmas can become most evident during their practicum and internship experience.

Practicum and Internship

Culminating phases of counselor education programs are practicum and internship courses. Preservice counseling students will practice counseling in schools, agencies, and/or private practice counseling. With a site/clinical supervisor and a university professor, counseling dispositions are closely monitored relative to their performance at the practicum and internship site. Counseling dispositions observed are within the counselor-consumer counseling relationship, as well as the counseling supervisor (site and university) and counseling intern relationship. This is inclusive of individual and group counseling, as well as psychoeducational sessions.

While engaging consumers and/or clients in counseling, preservice counseling interns may experience transference or countertransference, as the probability to hear events associated with PTSD can be heightened. For students who have unresolved, undiagnosed PTSD, triggers associated with consumer and/or client stories can manifest. As practicum and internships have required direct and indirect hours, the ability to complete internship may be compromised by unresolved issues that interns have not sought help for—further exacerbated by transference and/or countertransference.

Transference and Countertransference

"I just don't want them to experience what I did!"

The definition of these two terms are very important to the counseling profession. While both deal with boundary crossings that can graduate to boundary violations, Corey (2017) defines both terms as the process whereby clients project onto their therapists past feelings or attitudes they had toward significant people in their lives. With this, Corey (2017) suggests that counselors be aware of how they react to a consumer's transference; even though he states that all reactions are not a sign of transference, counselors must be cognizant of how it can become an ethical dilemma, as transference can place counselors in a very vulnerable position. Regarding preservice counseling students, recognizing transference is an important skill set that must be practiced via self-exploration. Whether during class experiences and exercises that allow self-exploration and evaluation, pre-service counselors may in a stage of realizing that what he or she witnessed or experienced in the form of traumatic events may manifest in the form of undiagnosed PTSD. Unchecked, countertransference can impede and impair preservice counseling students' skills and abilities to proceed as counselors.

Counselors experiencing countertransference (which is defined as a therapist or counselor's response to a consumer's disclosure) evokes an emotional response and they enmesh themselves at a heightened level in a client's feelings, losing objectivity, and their own unresolved issues can destroy the counseling relationship. The consumer can then be adversely affected, as can the counselor's ability to maintain a healthy counseling relationship. Ways in which countertransference can affect the counselor's practice are being overprotective with the consumer, engaging in frequent and consistent communication with the consumer outside the counseling relationship, as well as becoming sexually and/or romantically attracted to the consumer (Corey, 2017).

Countertransference can place counselors in a position to engage in boundary violations with clients/counselees/consumers. Preservice counseling students may not recognize countertransference, especially if undiagnosed PTSD exists. Essentially, counselors have the capacity to respond to the disclosures of their clients/counselees/consumers based on unresolved issues and/or concerns from their lives, be it their past, their families, and/or their personal experiences. While transference can be a type of boundary crossing where counselors ethically help for the growth of the consumer, countertransference can be a type of boundary crossing or boundary violation where the consumer's best interest is not considered based on unresolved issues of the counselor, who may go too far in the counseling relationship.

In other words, the counselor becomes more emotionally entrenched with the consumer based on their disclosure in the counseling relationship. Reminiscent of a scene in the movie

Prince of Tides when the psychologist and client become involved in a sexual relationship, though the therapist was able to help the client relive and accept the trauma experienced, their dual relationship was a form of boundary violation and countertransference on the part of the therapist. This can also reveal itself during practicum or internship.

Boundary Crossing, Boundary Violations, and Cultural Humility

"That's not unethical ... it's how we help!"

For many counselors who have worked with counselees, clients, and/or counselees who have been disenfranchised economically and/or psychosocially, going above and beyond to provide counseling services may not be abnormal. Boundary crossings is defined as ethical conduct of counselors who seek to help counselees, clients, and/or counselees with an immediate need (Corey, 2019). Moreover, ethical conduct of counselors who counsel marginalized counselees, clients, and/or consumers may participate in boundary crossing to help in ways that maintain their dignity while providing much needed help momentarily. An example of this is a school counselor assisting a counselee with college applications that require an admissions fee, or a school counselor talking with parents who are reluctant to allow their son or daughter to attend a college tour where, if accepted, it would require they will live away from home in a dormitory. These are examples of ethical conduct that can be beneficial to a counselee for their postsecondary academic endeavors. Yet, even something as helpful as going above and beyond in the context of a boundary crossing can, if affected by transference or countertransference, become a boundary violation.

Boundary violations may also appear as ethical conduct of counselors; however, the help extends into unethical and/or dual relationships as a contingency to continue receiving help necessary to support the academic, career and social-emotional development of counselees. Referring to the school counselor example, a boundary violation would be offering to continue to assist with college application admissions fees if a school counselor's sexual advances are welcomed and discontinuing help with college admissions fees if those advances are rebuffed. Additionally, relative to the second example of boundary crossings, the school counselor who convinced parents to allow the counselee to attend college fairs may look for other opportunities where travel is involved to isolate a counselee for illicit purposes, particularly if they have the parents' trust.

Thus, when examining undiagnosed PTSD and boundary crossing as symptoms appear a counselor may suggest or refer to a colleague who specializes in PTSD and charges a nominal consulting fee they may cover due to lack of financial resources. A boundary violation then would be to continue urging this client to seek their colleague's services but ask for sexual favors as a means of continued financial help for counseling.

Boundary violations may also affect practice after becoming licensed or certified as a counselor. Some colleges and universities require their preservice counseling students to go to a counseling session so that they can understand what it is like to be a client or consumer, but some institutions do not. Even though counselor educators may suggest that students seek counseling based on impaired counseling dispositions, there are institutions that cannot force students to provide proof of counseling. Thus, there may be preservice counseling students in practicum and internship who may elicit symptomology of undiagnosed PTSD via transference and/or countertransference, as well as boundary crossings and boundary violations.

Considerations for Counselor Educators and Supervisors

Undiagnosed post-traumatic stress disorder affects many people across the world. Preservice graduate counseling students attending HBCUs who are African American can be adversely affected, particularly as it relates to counseling disposition. Essentially, the stigma of mental illness may impede the ability to get help, as well as acknowledge that they experienced or witnessed physically, mentally, emotionally, and/or psychologically violent events in their lifetime. Living in denial or being admonished by family that those events were to be contained within the family and not be discussed, regardless of pain experienced, has the propensity to manifest in the counseling relationship. Thus, points for HBCU counseling programs to consider are as follows: cultural humility when assessing counseling dispositions, evidence-based practices in supervision, collaboration with university counseling services, and connection to alternative spiritual helping approaches.

Cultural Humility

Cultural humility must be central in working with African American graduate students in counseling programs. As kinship ties within families and community are paramount and essential to spiritual connectivity and student support systems, having a deeper understanding of the stigma associated with admitting and acknowledging mental illness in the so-called African American community is critical. Essentially, counselor educators and supervisors will be able to engage students in helping services that may not be relative to traditional counseling yet have the capacity to serve as a safe space to discuss trauma and trauma-related events they have witnessed and/or experienced. Also, counselor educators and supervisors' insight into the worldview of African American students experiencing trauma but whose families are more comfortable "sweeping it under the rug" can shed light on their help seeking behaviors. In other words, approaching African American preservice counseling students who attend HBCUs and have yet to recognize that their help-seeking behaviors and counseling dispositions could manifest into transference and/or countertransference could be value added. Although counselor educators and supervisors may recognize symptoms of PTSD in preservice counseling students, and the need to suggest or refer to counseling services, there must be an empathic response that garners an empathetic worldview as to why preservice counseling students at HBCUs may not seek counseling from counselors, psychologists, and/or psychiatrists though pursuing a career in counseling. Thus, calls for an examination into pre-service counseling readiness to become counseling interns must be examined and explored.

Collaboration With University Counseling Services

While some counselor education programs require preservice counseling to engage in counseling, it is important to explore how African American dispositions are affected by going to counseling before being accepted and enrolled in internships. Essentially, if symptoms and/or remnants of undiagnosed PTSD are evident in their tenure at a counseling program, and the program has the capacity to require attending counseling sessions to move forward in their program, this could be a precautionary step as well as a move toward active help-seeking behaviors. Moreover, if preservice counseling students are formally diagnosed with PTSD and it becomes evident that their counseling dispositions are impacting their internship counseling relationships with consumers, how do graduate school and/or programmatic policies protect counselor educators and supervisors when having to interrupt and/or terminate students' internship experiences?

Connection to Alternative Spiritual Helping Approaches

Moreover, if an internship must be interrupted and/or terminated due to countertransference or boundary violations possibly related to PTSD, what type of remediation is available where helping resources alternative to traditional counseling services are acceptable to the preservice counseling student? As many universities cannot force a student to attend counseling services, behaviors can negatively impact a consumer relative to an intern's counseling disposition. As ecumenical institutions provide counseling based on spiritual beliefs systems (Christianity, Islam, Judaism, Buddhism, etc.) or spiritual-based counseling relative to mindfulness, yoga, or meditation, there will be more of a willingness to engage in help-seeking behaviors prior to graduation, especially if counseling dispositions are hindering progress.

Evidence-Based Practices in Supervision

From a research perspective, would it be advantageous for counseling programs housed at HBCUs to promote mental wellness at the center of their graduate programs via evidence-based practices? How might these practices impact supervision from a remediation perspective, infused with cultural humility when understanding a reluctance to disclose events that are indicative of symptomology related to PTSD? How would the mantra of mental health and wellness counseling services support preservice counseling students from the so-called African American community and provide a safer space to work through undiagnosed PTSD? Would students begin to see asking for help as an advantage versus a means of admitting weakness? Would students understand how unresolved issues of trauma and undiagnosed PTSD could affect their counseling disposition to the point of the inability to complete their internships as well as secure employment as a counselor?

These are questions that counselor educators and supervisors must consider when teaching and researching how undiagnosed PTSD can affect African American preservice counseling students. Understanding and securing empirical data can be insightful, particularly from a standpoint of social justice advocacy for populations who may be distrustful of helping professionals.

Conclusion

The stigma of mental illness in the so-called African American community is strong and seen as damning if a suggestion of seeking help via counseling is discussed. Mental illness and mental health can be regarded as a weakness if admitted to family and friends. For many preservice counseling students at Historically Black Colleges and Universities, those who have experienced traumatic events may not have recognized how it affects their social-emotional lives. Moreover, many may not realize that not seeking counseling may spill over into their counseling dispositions in the form of transference and/or countertransference, which can leave preservice counseling interns susceptible to ethical dilemmas such as boundary crossings and/or boundary violations. Though counselor educators cannot force students to go to counseling, monitoring counseling dispositions with a population that can engage in cultural mistrust of helping professionals may become a gatekeeping strategy, not for punitive measures. This gatekeeping would be from a social justice advocacy perspective where counselor educators and supervisors can serve as a resource to help students. Many times, students at HBCUs build a kinship rapport with professors. As many may believe that African American professors may understand their worldview, and are more likely to be helpful, there is an assumption that they are culturally competent. Also, a level of expectation and cultural humility may be assumed by African American students, even if they are reluctant to seek out helping professionals.

Thus, it is important to encourage self-care and wellness, especially as it relates to undiagnosed PTSD. As in the case of X who did not believe that witnessing his mother stabbing his father to death was affecting his counseling disposition during his internship as he engaged in boundary violations, X also did not consider his self-medicating using pills versus alcohol (he was addicted yet not using). In other words, his decision to self-medicate was viewed as more socially acceptable than going to counseling to resolve and confront childhood trauma. X's witnessing of this event is considered a characteristic of PTSD, which if not addressed could carry into counseling practice. His approach could be indicative of the response to the stigma African Americans associate with mental health and mental health disorders. Though seen as a weakness if acknowledged, having the opportunity to engage in remediation could strengthen African American preservice students who attend HBCUs help seeking behaviors.

Questions/Considerations

1. Define post-traumatic stress disorder.
2. What is cultural mistrust?
3. Define transference and countertransference.
4. Based on the chapter, what are healthy ways to manage stress?

References

American Psychiatric Association (2013). *Diagnostic and statistical manual of mental disorders* (5th ed.) Author.

The Council for Accreditation of Counseling and Related Educational Programs (CACREP) Counseling. (2015). *Dispositions*. https://www.cacrep.org/glossary/professional-dispositions/

Constitutional Rights Foundation. (n.d.). *Southern Black codes*. https://www.crf-usa.org/brown-v-board-50th-anniversary/southern-black-codes.html

Cook, D. L., & Barber, K. R. (1997). Relationship between social support, self-esteem and codependency in the African American female. *Journal of Cultural Diversity*, 4(1), 32–38.

Corey, G. (2017). *Theory and practice of counseling and psychotherapy* (10th ed.) Cengage.

DeGruy, J. (1994). *Post traumatic slave syndrome: America's legacy of enduring injury and healing* (rev. ed. 2017) Portland, Oregon: Joy DeGruy Publications Inc.

Mallett, C.A. (2017). The school-to-prison pipeline: Disproportionate impact on vulnerable children and adolescents. *Education and Urban Society*, 49(6), 563–592. https://doi.org/10.1177/0013124516644053

Pai, A., Suris, A. M., & North, C. S. (2017). Posttraumatic stress disorder in the DSM-5: Controversy, change, and conceptual considerations. *Behavioral Sciences, 7*(1), 7. https://www.ncbi.nlm.nih.gov/pmc/articles/PMC5371751/

Wallace, B. C., & Constantine, M. G. (2005). Africentric cultural values, psychological help-seeking attitudes, and self-concealment in African American college students. *Journal of Black Psychology, 31*(4). 369–385.

Chapter 7

Engaging College Students with Learning Disabilities Through Universal Design

Courtney Ward-Sutton, Antoinette C. Hollis, Crystal M. Giddings, and Bridget Hollis-Staten

Introduction

This chapter will engage readers by discussing modern knowledge, strategies, and principles to improve outcomes for college students with learning disabilities.

Prevalence of Students With Learning Disabilities (LD)

Enrollment trends in the United States indicate an increasing number of students in postsecondary education with a disability, many of the students only being diagnosed after the start of these programs. Students with learning disabilities have received far less empirical attention in the literature, although it has been more than a decade since the 2004 reauthorization of the Individuals With Disabilities Education Act, which placed a greater emphasis on improving the postsecondary outcomes for all students with disabilities (Theobald et al., 2019). Moreover, this is particularly surprising given that learning disability is the most prevalent disability served by special education and the U.S. Department of Education's Office of Special Education Programs has identified postschool outcomes for students with disabilities as a monitoring priority (Showers, & Kinsman, 2017; Theobald et al., 2019). Nearly 60% of young adults with disabilities reported having continued to postsecondary education within 8 years of leaving high school, now enrolling at a closer rate to the general population, 67%. However, the rates of students with learning disabilities completing their degree is 41% compared to 52% of their peers without disabilities (Cortiella & Horowitz, 2014).

Across different data sets and literature it is well documented that students with learning disabilities attend vocational, technical, or business school as well as 2-year or community college at higher rates than their peers without disabilities and are less likely to attend a 4-year college or university (Joshi & Bouck, 2017). In 2015, the disability rate was higher for persons with less education than for those with higher educational attainment. The disability rate was 16% for 25- to 64-year-olds who had not completed high school, compared to 11% for those who had completed high school, 10% for those who had completed some college, 8% for those with an associate's degree, 4% for those with a bachelor's degree, and 3% for those with a master's or higher degree (U.S. Department of Education, National Center for Education Statistics, 2019). In the fall 2017 academic school year, approximately 20 million undergraduate students were enrolled in degree-granting postsecondary institutions. According to the latest data provided by the National Center for Education Statistics (NCES, 2019, 19.4% of undergraduate students self-reported a disability, and 11% reported having a learning disability, meaning more than 200,000 students entering postsecondary education have some type of learning disability.

As students with learning disabilities matriculate into postsecondary education the frequency of requested accommodations is unclear. In 2011, the National Longitudinal Transition Study (NLTS-2) examined a nationally representative sample of students with documented disabilities as they transitioned from secondary to postsecondary institutions. The NLTS-2 the largest study its kind described the secondary and postsecondary experiences of students with disabilities across the country, allowing for a national population estimate to be reported via SPSS Complex Samples instead of focusing only on students who participated (Joshi & Bouck, 2017). It was reported that 32.7% of students with learning disabilities attended any postsecondary education in comparison to 61.8% of peers without disabilities who left school around the same time (Joshi & Bouck, 2017; NCES, 2009). Other reports from the NLTS-2 further highlighted that although 87% of students received accommodations in high school, only 19% sought accommodations in college (Newman et al., 2011). Frequently endorsed student accommodations received from the study consisted of additional time on tests or testing in a different room, tutoring, access to special technology, a reader or interpreter/in-class aide, and a scribe/note taker (Weis et al., 2016). A conclusion from the study suggests that while students with learning disabilities may face extra challenges and hurdles, they will be more likely to complete postsecondary education if early on they obtain accommodations and develop skills and knowledge in secondary education needed to complete rigorous academic courses (Yu et al., 2018).

Transitional experiences from secondary to postsecondary education may vary in preparing students with learning disabilities to be successful. Learning disabilities constitute 34% of all disabilities for students enrolled in K–12 public schools (U.S. Department of Education, 2020). The Individuals With Disabilities Education Improvement Act (IDEIA, 2004) entitles students in primary and secondary schooling to special education, transition planning, and other services to help them achieve their highest potential. A transition plan is required for all students receiving special education services who have an individualized education plan (IEP). An IEP focuses on identifying and developing goals and objectives to facilitate a student's transition from secondary to postsecondary education, employment, or independent living. Additionally, transition planning is individualized and based on a student's needs, strengths, and interests. Therefore, the ultimate goal of transition planning is to prepare students for life after secondary school.

While 94% of secondary students with learning disabilities receive some form of assistance, only 17% of postsecondary students with learning disabilities take advantage of learning assistance resources. Perhaps due to the postsecondary level, it is not mandated to identify students with disabilities, whereas at the primary and secondary level, it is Harris et al., 2016). Furthermore, in postsecondary education, IDEIA is no longer provided. Instead students are protected by the Americans With Disabilities Act Amendment Act (ADAAA, 2008) and Section 504 of the Rehabilitation Act (1973), which prevents others from discriminating against them because of their disability. Contrary to IDEIA that promotes youth success through secondary schooling, ADAAA and Section 504 ensure adults access to higher education but do not guarantee successful outcomes (Lovett et al., 2014; Weis et al., 2016). Contrary to IDEIA that promotes youth success through secondary schooling, ADAAA and Section 504 ensure adults access to higher education but do not guarantee successful outcomes (Lovett et al., 2014; Weis et. al., 2016). Considering postsecondary education institutions are unable to influence students' secondary academic achievement or other influential factors that might attribute to their educational outcomes once enrolled, understanding learning disabilities is vital. Even though a great deal is known about learning disabilities in the classroom, controversy still exists over educators and other professionals' accountability in postsecondary education to serve these students.

LD Defined

The following section provides operational definitions for a learning disability, specific disability, and learning differences in addition to the three types of learning disorders: dyslexia, dysgraphia, and dyscalculia.

Key Terms

The term *learning disability* refers to ongoing problems in one of three areas, reading, writing, and math, which are foundational to one's ability to learn. Learning disabilities is an "umbrella" term describing a number of other more specific learning disabilities, such as dyslexia and dysgraphia. A *specific learning disorder* (SLD) is a medical term for diagnosis and often referred to as a learning disorder. The definition of SLD used in federal education laws refers to disorders that adversely affect learning but are not primarily the result of other disorders such as intellectual disability or hearing impairment (Gartland & Strosnider, 2018). Learning disability is not a synonym for SLD, for the reason that one with a diagnosis of a SLD will likely meet the criteria for a learning disability and have the legal status of a federally recognized disability to qualify for accommodations and services in school. The term *learning disability* is a term used by both the educational and legal systems.

The term *learning disability* denotes "a heterogeneous group of disorders manifested by significant difficulties in the acquisition and use of listening, speaking, reading, writing, reasoning, or mathematical abilities. These disorders are intrinsic to the individual, presumed to be due to the central nervous system dysfunction, and may occur across the life span" (National Joint Committee on Learning Disabilities (NJCLD), 1990, p. 3). Standards for identification of LD at the postsecondary level vary widely (Sparks & Lovett, 2009), but most institutions require standardized test scores that reveal a significant discrepancy between ability and achievement, deficits in academic achievement relative to normative expectations, or underlying cognitive processing problems (Weis et al., 2012).

The definition and identification of LD are contentious; federal law describes the construct and provides eligibility criteria (Maki et al., 2015). The Individuals With Disabilities Education Improvement Act (IDEA, 2004) describes LD using three broad components: achievement deficits, conditions included as LD, and conditions excluded from LD. Another term utilized within the learning disability realm is *learning difference*, as it does not label individuals as disordered (American Psychiatric Association, 2013). Learning disabilities can occur in various forms across one's life span, such as language delays or deficits appearing in early childhood before primary education begins and continuing into adulthood (NJCLD, 2011). Additionally, they can occur across races, cultures, languages, genders, or socioeconomic statuses, but may differ from one culture or language to another. Learning disability may coexist with other disorders and disabilities. The National Alliance on Mental Illness (NAMI) reported in 2016 that one in five students enrolled in United States' colleges and universities has a mental health condition (as cited in Koch et al., 2016). Granted that individuals with learning disabilities may share some characteristics with individuals who have other disabilities, the defining characteristic of a learning disability is that the cognitive process affecting learning underlies the educational difficulties that the individual with learning disabilities experiences (Gartland & Strosnider, 2018). Moreover, according to the DSM-5, a learning disorder can only be diagnosed after formal education starts through a combination of observation, interviews, family history, and school reports. To be diagnosed with a SLD, a person must meet four of the following criteria:

1. Have difficulties in at least one of the following areas for at least 6 months despite targeted help:

a. Difficulty reading (e.g., inaccurate, slow and only with much effort)
b. Difficulty understanding the meaning of what is read
c. Difficulty with spelling
d. Difficulty with written expression (e.g., problems with grammar, punctuation, or organization)
e. Difficulty understanding number concepts, number facts, or calculation
f. Difficulty with mathematical reasoning (e.g., applying math concepts or solving math problems)

2. Have academic skills that are substantially below what is expected for the child's age and cause problems in school, work, or everyday activities.

3. The difficulties start during school age even if in some people don't experience significant problems until adulthood (when academic, work and day-to-day demands are greater).

4. Learning difficulties are not due to other conditions, such as intellectual disability, vision or hearing problems, a neurological condition (e.g., pediatric stroke), adverse conditions such as economic or environmental disadvantage, lack of instruction, or difficulties speaking/understanding the language.

There are several types of learning disorders, but most fall into three categories: dyslexia, dysgraphia, and dyscalculia. Dyslexia refers to the difficulty with reading and problems identifying speech sounds and learning how they relate to letters and words (decoding). Also called reading disability, dyslexia affect areas of the brain that process language. Dyslexia is a common learning disability that causes problems with reading, writing, and spelling. An estimated 80% of people have some degree of dyslexia. Dysgraphia is a term used to describe difficulties with putting one's thoughts on paper and is classified as a neurological disorder that generally appears when children are first learning to write. Associated problems with dysgraphia can include writing difficulties with spelling, grammar, punctuation, and handwriting. Lastly, dyscalculia is a learning disorder used to describe difficulties in learning number-related concepts or using the symbols and functions to perform math calculations.

Disabilities' Effects on Learning

It's possible that each classroom may have a student with LD. Symptoms of LD are short attention span, poor memory, and difficulty in eye-hand coordination, just to name a few. Students with learning disabilities face more psychological problems in thinking and writing at the same time, experience feelings of frustration, anger, sadness or shame, psychological difficulties such as anxiety, depression, or low self-esteem, and have behavioral problems such as substance abuse or juvenile delinquency. The extreme focus on their disability causes low self-concept and emotional immaturity or imbalance in the minds of the child and will lead to feelings of inferiority (Vettiyadan et al., 2018). A learning disorder can vary in severity from mild to severe. Individuals with mild learning disorders experience some difficulties with learning one or two academic areas but may be able to compensate. Moderate learning disorders consists of significant difficulties with learning, requiring some specialized teaching and some accommodations or supportive services. A severe learning disorder affects several academic areas and requires ongoing intensive, specialized teaching. Most students with learning disabilities have an uneven pattern of strengths and weaknesses that affect their learning. Challenges these students experience vary in severity and pervasiveness as they pursue postsecondary education (Weis et al., 2016).

Students with a learning disability report significantly more problems than their peers understanding lectures, completing assignments, and performing well on exams. Higher levels of anxiety and increased study hours to keep up with their coursework were reported as well. They are also more likely to require remedial instruction or special tutoring to help meet the demands of the curriculum designed in their program of study. Additionally, learning disabilities can interfere with higher-level skills such as organization, time planning, abstract reasoning, long- or short-term memory, and attention. Other challenges include interfering with functioning, disruptive medication side effects, failure to use academic accommodations, and inadequate support from disability service offices (Koch et al., 2016). Attending and completing any form of postsecondary education assists an individual in obtaining a meaningful and fulfilling vocation as well as securing monetary independence (Shaw & Dukes, 2013). Individuals who enroll in but do not complete postsecondary education fail to realize the full employment and earnings benefits of being a college graduate (Ma et al., 2016). It is important to realize that learning disabilities can affect an individual's life beyond academics and can impact relationships with family, friends, and coworkers.

Another factor associated with disabilities' effects on learning at the postsecondary education level includes self-disclosure. Many students may wish to not disclose their disability status and seek accommodations because they do not wish to be stigmatized or labeled as incompetent (Banks, 2014; Harris et al., 2016). Cost, in both time and money, may further serve as an obstacle to disclosure. Learning disability assessments at the postsecondary level is usually paid for by students, not the institution, and range from $500-$2,500. Since learning disabilities are hidden, the challenges faced by those students are often unnoticed or misunderstood (McGregor et al., 2016). Interviews of students with learning disabilities in a postsecondary setting revealed poor knowledge of available accommodations, negative self-perceptions, skepticism about the usefulness of accommodations, and the wish to maintain a "typical" identity as additional reasons for not disclosing (Cole & Cawthon, 2015).

Universal Design (UD)

Beginning in the 1950s, an architectural movement known as universal design (UD) began a focus on the removal of physical environmental barriers for individuals with disabilities. Over the past 40 years the concept of UD has shifted to other domains, like education. The principles of UD provide access to learning environments for the broadest range of learners with respect to the spectrum of ability, disability, learning preference, native language, and demographic composition (e.g., age, race, and ethnicity) (Burgstahler, 2015; U.S. Department of Education, 2014). Universal design (UD) in the setting of postsecondary education is a proactive design of instruction that aims to be inclusive of different learners and helps to reduce barriers for students with disabilities (Black et. al., 2015).

The basic concept behind UD is design features that are essential for individuals with disabilities but are also useful for people without, hence highlighting the idea of access for all individuals. Traditional accommodations tended to be unappealing restricted persons with disabilities and were costly. However, today building structures and product features using UD benefit the disabled and nondisabled alike and are often less expensive (Rogers-Shaw et al., 2018). In regard to learning and instruction, UD involves assorted techniques, such as presenting material in multiple formats, for students with different abilities and backgrounds, including students with English as a second language, students from multi-cultural backgrounds, and students with disabilities (Black et al., 2015). Examples of UD include building ramps, electronic door openers, and use of large-print signage.

Researchers Scott et al. in 2001 added two more principles to the seven already established UD principles and also developed a framework for postsecondary education by the name of universal design instruction (UDI): a community of learners and an instructional climate. Apart from UDI, there are two other terms within the UD concept: universal design for learning (UDL) and universal instructional design (UID). The term *universal design for learning* (UDL) entails a unique concentration founded in the concept of accessibility to course content for all learners. Universal design for learning curriculum focuses on the need for flexibility and encourages instructors to consider the framework for designing courses that provide multiple means of choices and alternatives in the material's content, context, and support. UDL is guided by three basic principles (i.e., representation, expression, and engagement) (CAST, 2020; Coolidge et al., 2015; Izzo & Bauer, 2015). UDL and UDI are similar concepts but distinct in their focus. UDI is grounded in Mace's (1985) original UD principles, in addition to focusing on the environment and accessibility, that is primarily applied in postsecondary education. However, UDL focuses on the learner and is founded in neuroscience and neurocognitive fields that were initially implemented in middle schools. UID, another UD term, involves a proactive teaching framework that considers the learner's needs and is a deliberate design of curriculum and pedagogy to support the learner.

Overall, UID outcomes in instructional methods are intended to engage all learners (Rao et al., 2015). Each UD framework (i.e., UDI, UDL, and UID) has its unique focus in providing useful guidelines for instructors to establish settings that address a wide range of learners with and without a disability, grounded in the concept of accessibility to course content for all (Levey, 2018; Rao et al., 2015).

What Is UDI?

Universal design for instruction (UDI) is an approach to teaching that uses proactive design and inclusive instructional strategies to benefit a broad range of learners in postsecondary education (Black et al., 2015). As a comprehensive instructional design approach for creating an inclusive learning environment by which faculty anticipate a variety of teaching and learning needs for a broad range of students with diverse ways of learning, UDI can be used to guide faculty designing and implementing course content and evaluating learning objectives (Levey, 2018; Shaw, 2011). In addition, UDI is centered in social justice principles and the transformation of oppressive social relationships among students, faculty, and the culture of academic institutions. Over the past decade, multiple pedagogies (e.g., technology, materials, resources, evaluations, and physical/social environments) have adopted the UDI principles, which have granted accessible learning in postsecondary education to countless students with disabilities in a global context. (Levey, 2018). The basis for UDI principles include the following: (a) Classrooms include students from diverse populations and the role of faculty is to teach all students effectively, without lowering academic criteria and expectations, and (b) inclusive teaching practices are incorporated into course development and instructional design for all learners as a way to circumvent individual student learning needs or accommodations as they arise (Fenrich et al., 2018; McGuire, 2014; Park et al., 2017; Rodesiler & McGuire, 2015).

The use of UDI principles provides accessibility to learning environments without forcing disclosure from students with disabilities (Shaw, 2011). Thus, by allowing learning environments to be equitable for more than just students with a learning disability, it becomes equitable for all students (e.g., English as a second language (ESL), those temporary disabilities, and those with difficulties with traditional learning formats) (Levey, 2018). Increasingly teachers educate primary and secondary students who are diverse in culture, language, socioeconomic status, and ability (Kieran & Anderson, 2018). According to the National Center for Education Statistics (NCES, 2016) from 2003–2013 enrollment in U.S. public schools shifted from 59% of students who identified as White to 50%, and the number of Hispanic or Latino students increased from 19% to 25% during the same period. African American, Native American, and Asian or Pacific Islander accounted for the remaining 25% of students. At the postsecondary level, the student population is becoming more diverse as well, reflecting an increase in historically underrepresented students, including students with disabilities. For instance, in 2017 enrollment in U.S. postsecondary institutions approximately 41% of students identified as White, 36.5% as African American, 36.2% as Hispanic, 64.2% as Asian, 32.6% as Pacific Islanders, and 20.1% of American Indians/Native Alaskans (Mcfarland et al., 2018). UDI principles in the 21st century embrace the current and ever-growing heterogeneous postsecondary education population. Educators should strive to develop varied ways to design and plan course instruction to embody the UDI principles, inclusive of student learners' needs from diverse backgrounds. Additionally, this will allow the opportunity for students to demonstrate the skills they have acquired while enrolled in college. (Levey, 2018; Rogers-Shaw et al., 2018).

Components of UDI

The nine principles of UDI comprise a professional development tool to inform the instructor's planning and practice (Scott et al., 2001). The principles can be applied to the overall design of instruction as well as to specific instructional materials, facilities, and strategies (e.g., lectures, classroom discussions, group work, Web-based instruction, labs, and fieldwork) (Burgstahler, 2015). Additionally, the principles offer a flexible means for responding to diverse learners that can be practiced through planning, delivering instruction, or evaluating student learning (Rodesiler & McGuire, 2015). The nine principles of UDI include (a) equitable use, (b) flexibility in use, (c) simple and intuitive, (d) perceptible information, (e) tolerance for error, (f) low physical effort, (g) size and space for approach and use, (h) a community of learners, and (i) instructional climate. UDI principles, definitions, and examples are listed in Table 7.1.

TABLE 7.1   Principles of Universal Design for Instruction

Principles	Definition	Example(s)
1. Equitable use	The purpose of instruction is to be useful to and accessible by all individuals with diverse abilities. One should administer the same means of use for all students, being identical when possible or equivalent when not.	Available course notes, instruction, or syllabus available online and accessible in the same manner by all students, regardless of diverse abilities (e.g., vision or hearing abilities, learning or attention disorders). Additionally, students should be able to access and utilize assistive technologies with the provided online content.
2. Flexibility in use	Instruction methods accommodate a broad range of individual abilities. Include a variety of options in methods of use.	Incorporate different instruction methods or practices, such as interactive lecture design with a visual or audio effect, group work, case studies, learning out of the classroom, online discussions, and response posts. Flexibility in usage will provide students with different ways of learning and with enhanced experiences.

(continued)

TABLE 7.1 *(Continued)*

3. Simple and intuitive	The best instruction design consists of simple, short, easy-to-follow, transparent demonstrations or examples. One should remove as much difficulty and irrelevancy as possible. Students should be able to grasp instruction despite their level of comprehension, experience, and knowledge.	Syllabus and grading rubrics clearly state expectations for course material (e.g., exams, papers, and projects). Provide comprehensive, up-to-date information and resources (e.g., reading material, manuals, tutor/writing lab connections) to assist students through challenging assignments.
4. Perceptible information	Instruction design consists of vital information and is communicated effectively to the student(s) regardless of their environmental conditions or sensory skills.	Deliver instructional supports (e.g., textbooks, reading material, notes, and exams) in electronic form or options that students with diverse needs (vision, hearing, cognitive, English language learners) can access and use materials through hard copy or with technological supports (e.g., screen reader, text enlarger, text to speech, amplified hearing device, language translation dictionary).
5. Tolerance for error	With instruction, prepare for fluctuation among student(s)' learning speeds and preliminary skill set transitions.	For long-term projects, offer students the option of submitting individual components separately for constructive feedback and assimilation into the final assignment; considering online instruction, add practice exercises that complement course instruction.
6. Low physical effort	Provide delivery of basic instruction that will minimize students' nonessential physical actions to grant maximum attention and focus on learning. Applying this core fundament is excluded when physical activity is a requisite to a course's essential requirements.	Access and usage to software such as Word processor, Grammarly, SafeAssign, and Turnitin for writing/editing papers or exams will assist in the facilitation of editing and checking for plagiarism without physical exertion of rewriting portions of a text. Plus, this will help with instructor time management and students with fine motor skills, handwriting, or organizational difficulties.
7. Size and space for approach and use	The instructional design application for appropriate size and space considers manipulations and use, aside from a student's body size, posture, mobility, or communication needs.	Classroom space encourages learning. Provide adequate space for assistive technology devices or personal assistance and provide a clear view of sight for important information for students standing or seated.

| 8. A community of learners | The instructional, environmental setting strengthens active interaction and communication in peer-to-peer learning and between students and faculty. | Cultivate communication both inside and outside the classroom by organizing course content (e.g., assignments, discussion groups/posts, e-mail, electronic mailing lists) in a personable and motivational method, for example, the use of motivational/positive language, acknowledgment of students' names, and exceptional achievements. |
| 9. Instructional climate | Embody a welcoming and inclusive method of instruction, one that immerses great confidence in students. | Interactive course assignments are required for students to communicate and experience elements of diversity and social justice that share in the responsibility of the course learning process. Cocreate a learning atmosphere where students feel empowered to think critically or are liberated for development and application for the real world. |

Adapted from Florida State University, "Principles of UD for Instruction (UDI)," https://dsst.fsu.edu/oas/faculty/universal-designaccessibility. Copyright © by Florida State University.

Disability-Specific Legislation That Supports UDI

Over the years, various U.S. public policy legislation has helped to support the foundation of UDI. Below we will highlight legislative priorities and available literature to promote UDI use among working with college students with learning disabilities.

ADA

UDI calls for instructors to go beyond legal compliance to proactively design an accessible course and integrate practice so that other students benefit as well (Burgstahler, 2015). The enthusiasm for greater inclusivity and accessibility in education came in part from policy innovations. Accessibility, in general, refers to the Americans With Disabilities Act (ADA) of 1990, mandating public facilities and services to be fully accessible to people with disabilities. These public facilities and services include access to public spaces, patronizing private businesses, and participating in programs that receive federal funding from the U.S. Department of Education. Moreover, the ADA extends into Sections 504 and 508 of the Rehabilitation Act of 1973 mandating equal opportunity for people with disabilities, including providing auxiliary aids as necessary and meeting accessibility standards for software, hardware, websites, video, and other information technology (Rukel, 2015). IDEA was established on the rights of students ages 3 to 21 years old in K–12 educational settings with disabilities to be included in mainstream classes ((About IDEA). The ADA more broadly affects individuals with disabilities throughout their life span by ensuring them access to lifelong learning programs on an equal basis with other individuals (Ruukel, 2015).

The ADA of 1990 defines someone with a disability as a person with an ailment, either physical or mental, that significantly limits one or more of their life activities. Laws connected with the ADA advocate equal access for all individuals with disabilities and are designed to protect them as equal members of society. Accessible specified by the ADA is providing a person with a disability the opportunity to obtain the same information, have the same interactions, and participate in the same services as a person without a disability. Additionally, the ADA requires that the information is easily obtainable in methods similar to those without a disability. Title II of the ADA ensures that programs of public education such as postsecondary institutions provide qualified individuals with disabilities the right to engage in services provided (McGinty, 2018). In conjunction, these public education programs are required to provide accommodations to individuals with disabilities for them to participate fully. Title III of the ADA additionally requires private entities to also provide physical and academic accommodations to individuals with disabilities. Moreover, the ADA ensures that participation for individuals with disabilities is accomplished through equal and integrative ways in society. Updated in 2017 the ADA laws were amended to clarify the meaning and definition of the term *disability* to assure that it would be broad reaching and applied without the need to consistently revisit and modify the ADA laws (McGinty, 2018).

University Services and Federal Mandates

The ADA of 1990 has protected mandates regarding the participation of students with disabilities. Specifically related are individuals with learning disabilities in postsecondary environments. Another safeguarding federal law for individuals with disabilities is the Rehabilitation Act of 1973, Section 504. The Rehabilitation Act of 1973, Section 504, prevents discrimination against people with disabilities, from which the ADA laws were developed. Furthermore, the Rehabilitation Act of 1973 requires that institutions allow reasonable accommodations to all qualified program participants. Each postsecondary institution has to determine its accessibility policies and plans to meet the requirements of providing reasonable accommodations. Policies must ensure that students with learning disabilities have access to knowledgeable instruction, appropriate related services, and a high-quality education (Gartland & Strosnider, 2018).

In postsecondary education, accommodations extend to student services, curriculum design, and pedagogical practice. Additionally, disability services have served a vital role in making postsecondary education accessible to students through the UDI framework. Use of UDI allows numerous students of all abilities to have a more holistic learning experience, produce greater outcomes, and decrease barriers to graduation (Hartsoe & Barclay, 2015). The principles of UDI push forward a modern pedagogical model by efficiently meeting the needs of students who encompass a diverse array of ability levels (Black et al., 2014, 2015).

Hence, by integrating UDI through university services not only will students with a disability be served but so will generations of postsecondary students to come who learn and process information in a fundamentally different way than their peers and past generations (Black et al., 2014; Hartsoe & Barclay, 2015).

Types of Accommodations

The U.S. Department of Education considers a reasonable accommodation to be any accommodation that will allow equal participation for individuals with disabilities. Educational accommodations refer to making existing facilities readily accessible and usable by individuals with disabilities. Furthermore, they must remove restrictions to students' participation in educational activities without changing students' learning experiences, lowering academic standards, or threatening the validity of exam scores (Lovett, 2014). Accommodations are mandated by law when a student provides documentation of a disability under the American With Disabilities Act Amendments Act of 2008. For postsecondary students to qualify for reasonable accommodations they must prove that their disability limits their participation. To document a disability an individual needs to be evaluated by a licensed psychologist (U.S. Office of Personnel Management, 2017). At the postsecondary level, a qualified person with a disability is a person who meets the admission, academic, and technical standards (nonacademic prerequisites for admission, not essential functions for employment) or participates in program educational activities (U.S. Department of Education, 2015). Educators at postsecondary institutions can help students with a disability who are seeking documentation by informing them of the resources available to them and creating an inviting atmosphere that readily implements accommodations for students with disabilities, such as learning (McGinty, 2018).

Instructional and test accommodations are two general accommodation categories. Instructional accommodations alter how students learn (e.g., note taking during class, having interpreter, and obtaining permission to record lectures). Test accommodations alter how students demonstrate their learning (e.g., additional time for exams or modifications, use of word processor or a calculator during exams (Weis et al., 2016). While accommodations can be used to address some of the needs of students with disabilities, they may include additional steps and barriers created in the accommodation process. Given accommodations are typically developed after the design of the instructional setting, curriculum, and teaching methods. Thus, selecting accommodations for a learning disability can be difficult, and laws do not specify what accommodations a postsecondary institution must provide. Although the UDI framework itself is not a type of accommodation, UDI in postsecondary education aims to alleviate such challenges and barriers by classroom, curriculum, teaching methods, and postsecondary procedures developed with those considerations and accommodations for individuals with disabilities already constructed within (Black et al., 2015).

The decision making in accommodations is made by disability specialists at each post-secondary institution (Banerjee et al., 2015. To assist in making these decisions, disability specialists rely on the evaluation and recommendations of psychologists and other specialists with expertise in the assessment and accommodations of adults with learning disabilities (Lovett et al., 2014). Learning disabilities in adults is not a one-size-fits-all approach. Most effective postsecondary educators should be familiar with foundational information that describes different types of disabilities and understand that there are accommodations they can provide for their students (Grasgreen, 2013; Ingeno, 2013). There are several existing approaches for providing inclusive and accessible learning environments for adults with a learning disability. When considering UDI accommodations, knowing the campus procedures for addressing accommodation requests from students for whom the course design does not automatically provide full access is important (Burgstahler, 2015). Additionally, by planning an accommodations section in the course syllabus, instructors can further ensure the course experience is equivalent for all students. Types of accommodations may include materials in alternate formats, (e.g., iPads with digital versions of textbooks), use of captioned videos, transcriptions for audio videos, rescheduling of classroom locations, the use of apps (e.g., U-Listen, InftyReader, iThoughts, and iStudiezPro), digital pens, and audio recording. Other common classroom accommodations include large print material, consideration of room temperature, distractions from equipment sounds, and seating arrangements that allow for free movement around the classroom (McGinty, 2018).

UDI Strategies for LD

Consistent with available frameworks found in the literature and discussed in this chapter, the next section will equip college educators with UDI strategic tools for LD and implementation.

From Syllabus to Final Exam

The practice of offering information to students regardless of accommodations shows that the instructor is knowledgeable about accessibility and accepting toward individuals with an array of disabilities. As a beginning step, postsecondary instructors can include a statement of accessibility in the course syllabus and organizational materials (McGinty, 2018). The main goal of UDI is to maximize student learning with a wide variety of characteristics by applying UD principles to all aspects of instruction. Burgstahler (2017) says UDI instructors should consider the potential variation in student skills, learning styles and preferences, age, gender, sexual orientation, culture, abilities, and disabilities as they select appropriate content and strategies for the delivery of instruction and then apply UDI to all courses activities and materials. Instructors are recommended to incorporate the following UDI process steps:

1. *Identify the course.* Describe the course, its learning objectives, and its overall content.
2. *Define the universe.* Describe the overall population of students eligible to enroll in the course and then consider their potential diverse characteristics (e.g., with respect to gender; age; ethnicity and race; native language; learning style; and ability to see, hear, manipulate objects, read, and communicate).
3. *Involve students.* Consider student perspectives with diverse characteristics, as identified in step 2, in the development of the course. If they are not available directly from students, gain student perspectives through diversity programs and the campus disability services office.
4. *Adopt instructional strategies.* Adopt overall learning and teaching philosophies and methods (e.g., differentiated instruction, constructivism, the "flipped" classroom). Integrate them with UD to ensure the full inclusion of all students.
5. *Apply instructional strategies.* Apply UD strategies in concert with good instructional practices (identified in step 4) to the overall choice of course teaching methods, curricula, and assessments. Then apply UD to all lectures, classroom discussions, group work, handouts, Web-based content, labs, fieldwork, assessment instruments, and other academic activities and materials to maximize the student learning with the wide variety of characteristics identified in step 2.
6. *Plan for accommodations.* Learn campus procedures for addressing accommodation requests (e.g., arrangement of sign language interpreters) from specific students for whom the course design does not automatically provide full access. Include the information in the syllabus.
7. *Evaluate.* Monitor the effectiveness of instruction through observation and feedback from students with the diverse set of characteristics identified in step 2, assess learning, and modify the course as appropriate (Burgstahler, 2017).

The Motivated Learner

Motivation refers to an internal state or condition that activates behavior and gives direction; a desire or want that energizes and directs goal-oriented behavior; or an influence of needs and desires on the intensity and direction of behavior (Francois, 2014). There is evidence that enhancing self-determination results in more positive school and postschool outcomes for students with disabilities (Shogren et al., 2012, 2015). Self-determination theory (SDT) is a comprehensive theory of human motivation that provides a framework for understanding choice of behavior, quality of motivation and engagement, and overall development and well-being (Ryan & Deci, 2000). Understanding and using these key components of SDT can help promote self-determination among students with disabilities. For instance, researchers have suggested that if students transition into postsecondary education settings with a better understanding of their disability and their needs, they are more likely to succeed (Test et al., 2007; Wehmeyer & Palmer, 2003). Thus, the earlier students can enhance their self-determination and develop appropriate skills, the more positive their outcomes will be when compared to adults who are not fully self-determined. Additional research findings from O'Shea and Meyer (2016) indicate the importance of the subjective experience of a match between students with disabilities' perceived needs and their motivation to utilize support services. Overall, the findings point very strongly to students' experiences of disability support in high school as an important psychological foundation for their motivational processes related to disability disclosure in college.

In the college environment motivations and perceptions may differ in different settings (e.g., different courses and social groups) and among students from different backgrounds with different characteristics, disabilities, experiences, and sense of academic autonomy. Disability offices can promote students' needs of autonomy, competence, and relatedness within the context of various support services (Niemiec & Ryan, 2009). The diversity of interactive activities through a community of learners as a class or small group discussion encourages learning and increases motivation. Moreover, establishing high expectations for all students is important for UDI. Instructors who set different or lower expectations for students with disabilities nevertheless decrease student motivation and violate the UDI principle of instructional climate (CAST, 2020). Providing open communication and a positive instructional climate using UDI principles can help students with learning disabilities become motivated and decrease insecurities they may have about their disabilities (Black et al., 2015).

UD Resources

Understanding UDI in postsecondary education takes an extensive amount of work and does not occur overnight (Lombardi et al., 2013). More research is needed focusing on the concept of UDI if postsecondary institutions are ever to be truly accessible (Black et. al., 2015; Hartsoe & Barclay, 2015). One of the most critical components to implementing UDI is resources. Instructors as a resource for professional development and trainings to promote UDI can help postsecondary institutions intentionally design instruction that is more inclusive and responsive to multiple ways diverse students learn (Rodesiler & McGuire, 2015). In addition to professional development initiatives, mentorship programs to build awareness and increase familiarity for faculty concerning working alongside students with disabilities could serve as a vital resource. By promoting a mentorship collaboration and network between faculty, students, and other academic experts on campus (e.g., disability support services office, counselor offices, and advisors) students could become more aware of their rights, available accommodations, self-advocacy, and self-awareness (Black et al., 2015). When developing learning material resources, the UDI framework embraces UD and UDL principles and applies them to all instruction aspects. The following shortened checklist serves a fundamental resource providing examples of UDI practices and was field tested at more than 20 postsecondary institutions nationwide. Please note the numbers in brackets at the end of items in the checklist refer to UD and UDL principles to which the practice is most relevant (Burgstahler, 2017).

Class Climate

Adopt methods that reflect high values with respect to diversity, equity, and inclusiveness. [UDI 2, 5; UDL 2, 3]

Interaction Encourage

Provide regular and effective interactions between students and with the instructor. For example, utilize different communication methods and establish communication methods that are accessible to all participants. [UD 1-5; UDL 2, 3]

Physical Environments and Products

Ensure that facilities, activities, materials, and equipment are physically accessible to and usable by all students. Additionally, attempt to note all potential student characteristics are addressed in safety considerations. [UD 2-7; UDL 1-3]

Delivery Methods

Use multiple instructional methods that are accessible to all learners. [UD 1-5; UDL 1-3]

Information Resources and Technology

Offer course materials, instruction, notes, and other information resources that are engaging, flexible, and accessible for all students. [UD 2-4; UDL 1, 2]

Feedback and Assessment

Frequently assess students' progress and provide specific feedback on a regular basis using multiple accessible methods and tools. Adjust flexibility in instruction accordingly, if necessary. [UD 2-5; UDL 2, 3]

Accommodation

Plan for accommodations for students whose needs are not fully met by the instructional design. [UD 1-4, 6]

Conclusion

The observations made in this chapter address an ongoing interest of greater accessibility, effectiveness, and happiness in individuals with learning disabilities completing college through the UDI framework. Current techniques for designing and practicing instructional curricula place students with learning disabilities at a disadvantage under the traditional paradigm's content delivery. Instructors should take into consideration the various types of accommodations needed for students with learning disabilities. The major advantages of UDI involve reduced reconstructing of a course when accommodations are requested; eliminating forced disclosure of a disability; anticipating and embracing multiple ways of learning; and improving assessment of authentic learning (Levey, 2018). Furthermore, UDI offers principles, and practices instructors can reflect their instructional practice and pro-actively design and implement more inclusive curricula and pedagogies (Park et al., 2017). Additionally, increasing knowledge and inclusive design content will allow instructors to help decrease the need for accommodations after course materials have been created. Such new strategies can increase student enrollment and retention rates for individuals with learning disabilities, ultimately transforming the postsecondary level to a welcoming learning environment equally benefitting all students.

Questions/Considerations

1. Define universal design for instruction (UDI).
2. Name and define the nine principles of UDI.
3. Define reasonable accommodations.
4. What are different types of reasonable accommodations?
5. Name and define the process steps identified by Burgstahler (2017).

References

About IDEA. https://sites.ed.gov/idea/about-idea/.

American Psychiatric Association. (2013). *Diagnostic and statistical manual of mental disorders* (5th ed.). Author.

Americans With Disabilities Act Amendments Act, Pub. L. No. 110–325 § 3406 (2008)

Americans With Disabilities Act of 1990, Pub. L. No. 101-336, 104 Stat. 328 (1990)

Banerjee, M., Madaus, J. W., & Gelbar, N. (2015). Applying LD documentation guidelines at the post-secondary level: Decision making with sparse or missing data. *Learning Disability Quarterly, 38*(1), 27–39.

Banks, J. (2014). Barriers and supports to postsecondary transition: Case studies of African American students with disabilities. *Remedial and Special Education, 35*(1), 28–39.

Black, R., Weinburg, L., & Brodwin, M. (2015). Universal design for learning and instruction: Perspectives of students with disabilities in higher education. *Exceptionally Education International, 25*(2), 1–16. https://ir.lib.uwo.ca/eei/vol25/iss2/2

Black. R. D., Weinberg, L. A., & Brodwin, M. G. (2014). Universal design for instruction and learning: A pilot study of faculty instructional methods and attitudes related to students with disabilities in higher education. *Exceptionality Education International, 24*(1), 48–64.

Burgstahler, S. (2015). Preface. In S. Burgstahler (Ed.), *Universal design in higher education: Promising practices.* University of Washington. https://www.washington.edu/doit/sites/default/files/atoms/files/Universal%20Design%20in%20Higher%20Education_Promising%20Practices_0.pdf

Burgstahler, S. (2017, January 30). *ADA compliance for online course design.* Educause Review. https://er.educause.edu/articles/2017/1/ada-compliance-for-online-course-design

Burgstahler, S. (2020). Equal access: Universal design of instruction. https://www.washington.edu/doit/equal-access-universal-design-instruction

CAST. (2020). *Research & development.* http://www.cast.org/research/index.html

Cole, E. V., & Cawthon, S. W. (2015). Self-disclosure decisions of university students with learning disabilities. *Journal of Postsecondary Education and Disability, 28*(2), 163–179.

Coolidge, A., Doner, S., & Robertson, T. (2015): *BC Open Campus: Textbook accessibility toolkit* (2nd ed.). http://opentextbc.ca/accessibilitytoolkit/

Cortiella, C., & Horowitz, S. H. (2014). *The state of learning disabilities: Facts, trends and emerging issues.* National Center for Learning Disabilities.

Francois, E. J. (2014). Motivational orientations of non-traditional adult students to enroll in a degree-seeking program. *New Horizons in Adult Education & Human Resource Development, 26*(2), 19–35.

Fenrich, P., Carson, T., & Overgaard, M. (2018). Comparing traditional learning materials with those created with instructional design and universal design for learning attributes: The students' perspective. *Bulgarian Comparative Education Society.* https://eric.ed.gov/?id=ED586138

Gartland, D., & Strosnider, R. (2018). Learning disabilities: Implications for policy regarding research and practice: A report by the National Joint Committee on Learning Disabilities. *Learning Disability Quarterly, 41*(4), 195–199. https://doi.org/10.1177%2F0731948711421756

Grasgreen, A. (2013, July 26). *Audiobooks aren't enough.* Inside Higher Ed. https://www.insidehighered.com/news/2013/07/26/settlements-put-colleges-duty-ensure-blind-students-access-materials-under-new#.VgBe7GcFEBs

Hartsoe, K. J., & Barclay, R. S. (2017). Universal design and disability: Assessing faculty beliefs, knowledge, and confidence in universal design for instruction. *Journal of Postsecondary Education and Disability, 30*(3), 223–236.

Harris, P., Mayes, R., Vega, D., & Hins, E. (2016). Reaching higher: College and career readiness for African American males with learning disabilities. *Journal of African American Males in Education, 7*(1), 52–69.

Individuals With Disabilities Education Act, 20 U.S.C. § 1400 (2004)

Individuals With Disabilities Education Improvement Act of 2004, Pub. L. No. 108–446, 118 Stat. 2647 (2004). https://ies.ed.gov/ncser/pdf/pl108-446.pdf

Ingeno, L. (2013). *Online accessibility: A faculty duty.* Inside Higher Ed. https://www.insidehighered.com/news/2013/06/24/faculty-responsible-making-online-materials-accessible-disabled-students

Izzo, V., & Bauer, W. (2015). Universal design for learning: enhancing achievement and employment of STEM students with disabilities. *Universal Access in the Information Society, 14*(1), 17–27. https://doi.org/10.1007/s10209-013-0332-1

Joshi, G. S., & Bouck, E. C. (2017). Examining postsecondary education predictors and participation for students with learning disabilities. *Journal of Learning Disabilities, 50*(1), 3–13.

Kieran, L., & Anderson, C. (2018). Connecting universal design for learning with culturally responsive teaching. *Education and Urban Society, 51*(9), 1202–1216. https://doi.org/10.1177/0013124518785012

Koch, L., Mamiseishvili, K., & Wilkins, M. (2016). Postsecondary integration and persistence: A comparison of students with psychiatric disabilities to students with learning disabilities/attention deficit disorders. *Rehabilitation Research, Policy, and Education, 30*(3), 259–275.

Levey, J. (2018). Universal design for instruction in nursing education: An integrative review. *Nursing Education Perspectives, 39*(3), 156–161. https://doi.org/10.1097/01.NEP.0000000000000249

Lombardi, A., & Sala-Bars, I. (2013, July). An international examination of postsecondary faculty attitudes and actions toward inclusive instruction: Comparing the United States and Spain [Paper presentation]. Eighth International Conference on Higher Education and Disability, Innsbruck, Austria.

Lovett, B., Nelson, J., & Lindstrom, W. (2014). Documenting hidden disabilities in higher education: Analysis of recent guidance from the Association on Higher Education and Disability (AHEAD). *Journal of Disability Policy Studies, 26*(1), 44–53. https://doi.org/10.1177/1044207314533383

Lovett, B. J. (2014). Testing accommodations under the Amended Americans With Disabilities Act: The voice of empirical research. *Journal of Disability Policy Studies, 25*(2), 81–90.

Ma, J., Pender, M., & Welch, M. (2016). Trends in higher education series: education pays 2016: The benefits of higher education for individuals and society. College Board. https://files.eric.ed.gov/fulltext/ED572548.pdf

Mace, R. L. (1985). Universal design: Barrier free environments for everyone. *Designers West, 33*(1), 147-152

Maki, K. E., Floyd, R. G., & Roberson, T. (2015, January 12). State learning disability eligibility criteria: A comprehensive review. *School Psychology Quarterly, 30*(4), 457–469. http://doi.org/10.1037/spq0000109

McFarland, J., Hussar, B., Wang, X., Zhang, J., Wang, K., Rathbun, A., Barmer, A., Forrest Cataldi, E., & Bullock Mann, F. (2018). The condition of education 2018 (NCES 2018-144). National Center for Education Statistics. https://nces.ed.gov/pubsearch/pubsinfo.asp?pubid=2018144

McGinty, J. (2018). Tips for creating inclusive and accessible instruction for adult learners: An overview of accessibility and universal design methods for adult education practitioners. *PAACE Journal of Lifelong Learning, 27*, 1–20.

McGregor, K., Langenfeld, N., Van Horne, S., Oleson, J., Anson, M., & Jacobson, W. (2016). The university experiences of students with learning disabilities. *Learning Disabilities Research & Practice, 31*(2), 90–102.

McGuire, J. (2014). Universally accessible instruction: Oxymoron or opportunity? *Journal of Postsecondary Education and Disability, 27*(4), 387–398.

National Center for Education Statistics [NCES]. (2019). *The NCES fast facts students with disabilities.* https://nces.ed.gov/fastfacts/display.asp?id=60

National Center for Education Statistics. (2009). *Recent high school completers and their enrollment in college, by sex: 1960 through 2008.* http://nces.ed.gov/programs/digest/d09/tables/dt09_200.asp

National Center for Education Statistics. (2020). *The condition of education.* https://nces.ed.gov/programs/coe/

National Joint Committee on Learning Disabilities. (1990). *Learning disabilities: Issues on definition.* http://www.ldonline.org/pdfs/njcld/NJCLDDefinitionofLD_2016.pdf

National Joint Committee on Learning Disabilities. (2011). *Learning disabilities: Implications for policy regarding research and practice.* file:///C:/Users/court/Downloads/LD%20Validity%20Paper%20FINAL%203.30.11.pdf

Newman, L., Wagner, M., Knokey, A.-M., Marder, C., Nagle, K., Shaver, D., Wei, X., Cameto, R., Contreras, E., Ferguson, K., Green, S., & Schwarting, M. (2011). *The post–high school outcomes of young adults with disabilities up to 8 years after high school. A report from the National Longitudinal Transition Study–2.* Institute of Education Sciences. http://www.nlts2.org/reports/2011_09_02/nlts2_report_2011_09_02_complete.pdf

Niemiec, C. P., & Ryan, R. M. (2009). Autonomy, competence, and relatedness in the classroom: Applying self-determination theory to educational practice. *Theory and Research in Education, 7*(2), 133–144.

O'Shea, A., & Meyer, R. (2016). A qualitative investigation of the motivation of college students with nonvisible disabilities to utilize disability services. *Journal of Postsecondary Education and Disability, 29*(1), 5–23.

Park, H., Roberts, K., Delise, D. (2017). The effects of professional development on universal design for instruction on faculty perception and practice. *Journal of Postsecondary Education and Disability, 30*(2), 123–139.

Rao, K., Edelen-Smith, P., & Wailehua, C. (2015). Universal design for online courses: Applying principles to pedagogy. *Open Learning: The Journal of Open, Distance and E-Learning, 30*(1), 35–52. https://doi.org/10.1080/02680513.2014.991300

Rodesiler, C., & McGuire, J. (2015). Ideas in practice: Professional development to promote universal design for instruction. *Journal of Developmental Education, 38*(2), 24–26.

Rogers-Shaw, C., Carr-Chellman, D., & Choi, J. (2018). Universal design for learning: Guidelines for accessible online instruction. *Adult Learning, 29*(1), 20–31. https://doi.org/10.1177/1045159517735530

Rukel, R. (2015, June). Higher education blogs: Blog U. Inside Higher Ed. https://csd.uconn.edu/wp-content/uploads/sites/607/2014/04/A-Case-for-Accessible-Usable-and-Universal-Design-for-Learning.pdf

Ryan, R., & Deci, E. (2000). Intrinsic and extrinsic motivations: Classic definitions and new directions. *Contemporary Educational Psychology, 25*(1), 54–67.

Sasaki, M., Kozaki, Y., & Ross, S. (2017). The impact of normative environments on learner motivation and l2 reading ability growth. *The Modern Language Journal, 101*(1), 163–178. https://doi.org/10.1111/modl.12381

Scott, S. S., McGuire, J. M.,& Shaw, S. F. (2001). *Principles of universal design for instruction.* Center on Postsecondary Education and Disability.

Shaw, R. A. (2011). Employing universal design for instruction. *New Directions for Student Services, 2011*(134), 21–33.

Shaw, S., Scott, S., McGuire, J. (2001). *Teaching college students with learning disabilities.* ERIC Clearinghouse on Disabilities and Gifted Education.

Shaw, S. F., & Dukes, L. L. (2013). Transition to postsecondary education: A call for evidence-based practice. *Career Development and Transition for Exceptional Individuals, 36*(1), 51–57. https://doi.org/10.1177/2165143413476881

Shogren, K., Palmer, S., Wehmeyer, M., Williams-Diehm, K., & Little, T. (2012). Effect of intervention with the self-determined learning model of instruction on access and goal attainment. *Remedial and Special Education, 33*(5), 320–320. https://doi.org/10.1177/0741932511410072

Shogren, K., Wehmeyer, M., Palmer, S., Rifenbark, G., & Little, T. (2015). Relationships between self-determination and postschool outcomes for youth with disabilities. *The Journal of Special Education, 48*(4), 256–256. https://doi.org/10.1177/0022466913489733

Showers, A. H., & Kinsman, J. W. (2017). Factors that contribute to college success for students with learning disabilities. *Learning Disability Quarterly, 40*(2), 81–90.

Sparks, R., & Lovett, B. (2009). College students with learning disability diagnoses: Who are they and how do they perform? *Journal of Learning Disabilities, 42*(6), 494–510. https://doi.org/10.1177/0022219409338746

Test, D. W., Aspel, N. P., & Everson, J. M. (2007). *Transition methods for youth with disabilities.* Recording for the Blind & Dyslexic.

Theobald, R. J., Goldhaber, D. D., Gratz, T. M., & Holden, K. L. (2019). Career and technical education, inclusion, and postsecondary outcomes for students with learning disabilities. *Journal of Learning Disabilities*, 52(2), 109–119.

U.S. Department of Education. (2015). *Profile of undergraduate students: 2011-12.* https://nces.ed.gov/pubs2015/2015167.pdf

U.S. Department of Education. (2020). *Special education—Technical assistance on state data collection.* https://www2.ed.gov/programs/osepidea/618-data/state-level-data-files/index.html#bcc

U.S. Department of Education, National Center for Education Statistics. (2019). *Digest of education statistics.* https://nces.ed.gov/pubs2020/2020009.pdf

U.S. Department of Education, Office for Civil Rights. (2015). *Protecting students with disabilities.* https://www2.ed.gov/about/offices/list/ocr/504faq.html

U.S. Department of Health, Education, and Welfare. (1978). *Section 504 of the Rehabilitation Act of 1973: Fact sheet: Handicapped persons rights under federal law.* https://www.hhs.gov/sites/default/files/ocr/civilrights/resources/factsheets/504.pdf

U.S. Office of Personnel Management. (2017). *What is proof of disability documentation?* https://www.opm.gov/policy-data-oversight/disability-employment/faqs/

https://nces.ed.gov/pubs2020/2020009.pdfVettiyadan, M., Henna, F., & Shibymol, C. (2018). Academic self-concept and emotional maturity among students with learning disability. *Indian Journal of Health and Wellbeing, 9*(6), 845–848.

Wehmeyer, M. L., & Palmer, S. B. (2003). Adult outcomes for students with cognitive disabilities three-years after high school: The impact of self-determination. *Education and Training in Developmental Disabilities,* 38(2), 131–144.

Wehmeyer, M., Shogren, K., Toste, J., & Mahal, S. (2017). Self-determined learning to motivate struggling learners in reading and writing. *Intervention in School and Clinic,* 52(5), 295–303. https://doi.org/10.1177/1053451216676800

Weis, R., Dean, E. L., & Osborne, K. J. (2016). Accommodation decision making for postsecondary students with learning disabilities: Individually tailored or one size fits all? *Journal of Learning Disabilities,* 49(5), 484–498.

Weis, R., Sykes, L., & Unadkat, D. (2012). Qualitative differences in learning disabilities across postsecondary institutions. *Journal of Learning Disabilities,* 45(6), 491–502. https://doi.org/10.1177/0022219411400747

Yu, M., Novak, J., Lavery, M., & Matuga, J. (2018). Predicting college completion among students with learning disabilities. *Career Development and Transition for Exceptional Individuals,* 41(4), 234–244. https://doi.org/10.1177/2165143417750093

Chapter 8

Promoting Self-Advocacy in Students With Disabilities

Crystal M. Giddings, Shanju Vigasini, Antoinette C. Hollis, and Bridget Hollis-Staten

Introduction

The cornerstone of every school is to educate its students and thereby prepare them for lifelong success. For some students, this education can be difficult to achieve. Students with learning disabilities, or other developmental disabilities, usually struggle to get through high school to receive a diploma, which is seen as the basic employability credential. But in recent times, many initiatives have been implemented to work with students with disabilities, resulting in an increased emphasis on support at the elementary, middle, and high school levels and postsecondary school transition planning. Therefore, the number of students with disabilities completing high school and attending college or technical/trade schools is on the rise. Training and equipping students with disabilities to self-advocate remains a necessary component.

According to the U.S. Department of Labor (2014), only one third of individuals with disabilities are employed as opposed to two thirds of those without disabilities. The Institute for Community Inclusion conducted a national survey, which found that only 50% of students or youth with disabilities attend 4-year colleges/universities, while 40% attend 2-year colleges, and only 10% attend trade/technical schools (National Council on Disability, 2012). These results indicate the need to create strong, research-based transition plans geared toward improving the academic performance, socioemotional behavior and independent functioning of students with learning disabilities.

There is legislation that promotes self-advocacy for students with learning disabilities. Most any person can be an advocate for a student with a learning disability. However, to do so effectively, it is essential that one understands the required laws that govern programs and services for these students. The protection of the rights of these students is important, as is the continuation of these support programs and services. In the 1975 Education of All Handicapped Children Act, students with identified disabilities (special needs) were required to be educated in the least restrictive environment (LRE). In this way these students would be in a regular classroom with students rather than in a special needs classroom with only students with disabilities. Soon terms such as *mainstreaming, resource room*, and *inclusion* were used to describe various methods used to work with students with disabilities. In 2004, the *response to intervention* (RTI) process was introduced and incorporated in the 2004 reauthorization of the Individuals With Disabilities Act (IDEA). While it was not introduced as a part of the law, it did ask the legislators and the Office of Special Programs (OSEP) to write a statement requesting that school districts not rely on what is called the discrepancy model for identification of specific learning disabilities and consider using interventions tried within RTI. In practice, most school districts use RTI to intervene prior to special education referrals. For example, a student may receive an intervention recommended by the RTI team and then implemented by a teacher. If the student experienced success, the intervention is continued. A referral is may be made for testing and observation for students who do not improve with RTI (Berger, 2014; Special Education Guide, n.d.; Vernon & Schimmel, 2019).

Describing itself as *the* "Special Education Advocate newsletter," Wrightslaw is a popular organization where up-to-date information is available for parents, educators, advocates, and attorneys about special education law, education law, and advocacy for children with disabilities (Wrights & Wright, 2007). Wrights and Wright (2007) cite the Section 504 federal regulations which consists of three new sets of guidance regarding discrimination, restraint and seclusion. These provisions ensured that schools enforce federal civil rights law protecting the rights of students with disabilities. On December 2016 this mandate set forth clear rules from the U.S. Department of Education's Office for Civil Rights assisting states, districts, and schools (including magnet and charter schools, that reads, in part, as following:

> Guidance in recognizing, redressing, and preventing racial discrimination in special education in violation of the Federal civil rights laws. This Guidance explains the Title VI requirement that students of all races, colors, and national origins have equitable access to general education interventions and to a timely referral for an evaluation under the IDEA or Section 504 and requires students of all races and national origins to be treated equitably in the evaluation process, in the quality of special education services and supports they receive, and in the degree of restrictiveness of their educational environment. (Wright & Wright, 2007, para. 3)

This type of information is most useful in positioning for effective advocacy as it lays the groundwork for promoting advocacy for those who are unable to advocate for themselves and especially for those who are ready for self-advocacy (Wright & Wright, 2007).

Over 80% of all students with learning and attention difficulties receive instruction and interventions in the general education classroom setting (Maccini et al., 2002). According to the National Center for Learning Disabilities (2015), 1 in 5 children in the United States have learning and attention issues, but only very few of them are formally identified as having a disability in school. Only 1 in 16 of the school-aged children have an individual education plan (IEP) for specific learning disabilities (SLD), such as dyslexia and the disability category that covers ADHD and dyspraxia. One out of every fifty students going to public schools receives accommodations through a 504 plan. This report also unraveled survey results where 33% of the educators believe that learning or attention issues are just laziness. Forty-three percent of parents surveyed said that they didn't want to reveal their child's learning disability to others. These biases and prejudices play a strong role in creating an uncertainty in the minds of students with learning disabilities and an embarrassment about being identified as a student with a learning disability. Still, students with SLD represent 39% of the largest category of students with special needs that required special education services in 2015–2016.

The Every Student Succeeds Act (ESSA) provides funding to develop this decision-making framework, using data from the frequent progress monitoring to provide targeted instruction and support. Universal screening, which is an essential component of the multitiered system of support (MTSS), helps in assessing all students, not just the struggling students. Also, Section 504 of the Rehabilitation Act of 1973, one of the earliest disability rights legislations, is implemented through the Office of Civil Rights (OCR). It mandates all organizations that receive federal funding to provide equal opportunities and benefits for students with disabilities (Zeisler, n.d.).

The previous version of the law, the No Child Left Behind (NCLB) Act, which was enacted in 2002, revealed where students were making progress and where they needed additional support, irrespective of race, income, disability, home language, or background. The Research Excellence and Advancements for Dyslexia (READ) Act, that was signed into law in 2016, provides funding for training educators, developing curriculum and tools to implement successful models of dyslexia intervention. The act requires the NSF (National Science Foundation) to spend a minimum of $5 million per year toward research in the field of SLD in general and dyslexia in particular. Though children with SLD have average/above average intelligence, a survey of the 2013 National Assessment of Educational Progress (NAEP) scores points to a wide achievement gap between students with and without disabilities. So, the goal in working with students with SLD is to provide them the appropriate support and thereby bridge their achievement gaps (Horowitz et al., 2017).

In the 2017 executive summary of the U.S. Department of Education, IDEA Section 618, 7 out of 10 students (nationwide) who are identified as students with SLD and other health impairments (OHI) were spending 80% or more of their school day in the general education classroom setting during 2015–2016 school year. The concern here is that student success hinges on the skill set of the general education teachers. So, there is may be a need for some teachers to be provided with professional development to improve or enhance their instructional pedagogy. Also, additional resources may be needed to help meet students' learning challenges. Inclusion is a practice that can yield great results. However, creative and positive solutions should be explored and implemented.

High School to College Transition

With the introduction of the Common Core state standards, most states are striving to make all their students "college and career ready." These standards are designed to help students graduate with the skills needed to succeed in college and, subsequently, in the workforce. Millions of dollars are being spent to support Common Core. IDEA requires that teachers use research-based strategies for improving in school and postschool experiences of students with disabilities. The initiative to make students college and career ready implies that schools prepare students for success in college and in careers of their choice (U.S. Department of Education, 2010).

When a student reaches the age of 13 in South Carolina, teachers administer at least two transition assessments that include a student interview and another transition assessment that is specified in the Indicator 13 Checklist to help students to discover their areas of career interests and choices. Then, the student's special education teacher discusses the student's areas of strengths and weaknesses to map the results with selected career aspirations. The goal at this point is to determine a set of realistic postsecondary goals for the student. At the spring of each year, the school's team is reconvened and the student's transition plan, plus the IEP, is reviewed. Here, the student's annual progress and present levels of academic and functional performance (PLAAFP) are presented and discussed in detail. A student may continue with the same educational goals at the high school or college level. Or, new educational goals may be established.

Addressing retention, graduation, and dropout rates at high school level has been an important topic for decades. In the National Center for Learning Disabilities (NCLD) report (2015), students with IEPs have an 85% likelihood of repeating a grade whereas students with 504s have a 110% likelihood of repeating a grade, in comparison to their nondisabled peers with disabilities in a report of 2013–2014. This increased rate of retention leads to feelings of frustration and desperation, thereby increasing the risk of dropping out of high school.

The graduation data show that only 70.8% of students with learning disabilities and 72.1% of students with OHI have graduated with a regular high school diploma, 10 percentage points less than the national average. The dropout rate report shows that almost 1 in 5 students (19%) with IEPs miss 3 or more weeks of school as compared to 1 in 8 students (13%) without an IEP. School aversion and continued absenteeism lead to higher levels of dropout (Horowitz et al., 2017).

The state of learning disabilities is critical and demonstrates the need for a deep understanding. Consider that 1 in 5 students with special needs are more than twice as likely to be suspended from school as their nondisabled peers, which often leads to loss of instructional time in the classroom, creates intermittent gaps in knowledge, and can lead to an increased risk of dropout. Reports for 2013–2014 show that nearly 18.1% of students with SLD and 17.6% students with OHI dropped out of high school. One must realize that high rates of dropout tend to lead to incarceration and recidivism (Horowitz et al., 2017).

College Students With Learning Disabilities

When it comes to college or the workplace, individuals can receive accommodations only if they disclose their disabilities. But the major reason for the discrepancy is that many students do not have the necessary awareness about their strengths and weaknesses and lack self-confidence, self-advocacy skills, and self-efficacy.

The barrier of low self-esteem, social stigma, peer pressure, bullying, and fear of biased predisposition are all factors that affect the entry of students with disabilities into 2- or 4-year college programs. Though students with LD are just as smart as their peers, they enroll at only half the rate of their nondisabled peers. Not understanding the importance of accommodations in facilitating their academic success and ignorance about the paperwork needed to access special services in colleges can lead to low rates of enrollment and of success in college.

According to the National Longitudinal Transition Study-2 (NLTS-2), which followed more than 11,000 students for 10 years, only 24% of students with LD informed their college about their learning disability; 7% did not inform their college though they thought that they still had learning disability, whereas 69% believed that they no longer had a learning disability.

It becomes critical that students with disabilities know about their strengths, weaknesses, and required accommodations and are also able to explain to others what they need to succeed in college, including ways to establish their social and emotional well-being. Transition planning hence prepares students by specifying accommodations for college and postsecondary supports as early as possible. The Respond, Innovate, Succeed, and Empower Act (RISE Act), introduced in December 2016, removes barriers to receive accommodations as well as opportunities in both college and work. Students who seek academic support in colleges and insist on receiving accommodations have a higher likelihood of graduating in college (Horowitz et al., 2017). This study also found that 29% had completed higher education at a 4-year college as compared to 42% of the general population. The good news is that the success of the population with disabilities in 2-year community colleges was at 30% when compared to 14% of the general population. A comparison of data between NLTS-1 and NLTS-2, from 1990 to 2005, the rate of general population going to colleges grew from 26% to 45%, which presents a very progressive picture for the future (Morris, 2004).

The Need for Self-Advocacy

Advocacy is often described as an act or process of supporting a cause or an issue deemed worthy to a person, a group of persons, or an event or organization (Merriam-Webster, n.d.). Supporters of Susan B. Anthony Cancer Research and Black Lives Matter are good examples of advocacy causes. Self-advocacy refers to a person seeking support for themselves to receive the assistance they feel is needed for them to succeed in performing a specific task such as reading or playing a musical instrument. In the school system, parents are often the first advocate for their children, whereas school counselors and teachers are usually the school personnel who advocate for students. Specifically, teachers implement alternate strategies to help students overcome a learning disability or a barrier to learning. But it is usually the school counselor who works with students who have a learning disability to advocate for themselves (McGinley & Trolley, 2016).

Learning Disabilities Association of America (LDA), a nonprofit organization, provides information for the advocacy for children and adults with learning disabilities. Learning disabilities are often viewed as neurologically based processing problems. These processing problems can interfere with learning basic skills such as reading, writing, and/or math. They can also interfere with higher-level skills such as organization, time planning, abstract reasoning, long- or short-term memory, and attention. A child's ability to learn can affect their social development as well. Therefore, it essential that students with disabilities learn how to seek help and determine who in their school can help them reach their full potential (Berger, 2014; Learning Disabilities Association of America, 2020).

As children become older students, they can and should begin to advocate for themselves. Students with self-esteem usually have no problem asking for what they need, from a schedule change to tutorial service. However, those students with low-self-esteem may need a parent, counselor, or teacher to advocate for them. Helping students to seek help on their own volition can result in students having acquired a life skill that can be beneficial as they move into adulthood and beyond. The school counselor is trained in working with students with disabilities and is usually the key school personnel to links the student and parents with the additional support needed. Group counseling is offered to empower students to first understand their disability, their feelings about their disability, coping skills tried, and then discussions on what students think is needed to help them to experience school success (McGinley & Trolley, 2016; Vernon & Schimmel, 2019).

The Need for Self-Efficacy

According to Luman (2011), self-efficacy can also influence one's motivation, behavior, and social environment. It influences both goal setting and goal attainment. People with higher levels of self-efficacy can learn and achieve more than people with low self-efficacy, even if their ability levels are the same (Ormrod, 2008). Ackerman (2019) suggests a way to measure one's self-efficacy. The self-efficacy questionnaire, developed by the Research Collaboration in 2015, consists of 13 items and is helpful in measuring the self-efficacy of middle and high school students. In 2001, Chen et al. developed the New General Self-Efficacy scale (NGSE), while a similar tool, the Generalized Self-Efficacy scale (GSE), was developed by Schwarzer and Jerusalem in 1995. Still, Margolis and McCabe (2006), and others cited in Ackerman (2019) suggest many easy-to-follow solutions to help improve one's self-efficacy based on self-efficacy theory: (a) enactive mastery, the opportunity to accomplish small wins; (b) vicarious experiences, observing peer models who have accomplished success; and (c) verbal persuasion, offering words of encouragement and motivation. Ackerman (2019) believes that higher self-efficacy and self-regulation can be developed through modeling and also contribute to achievement of set goals. Mayer (2010) states than an individual's level of motivation to learn and their progress get boosted even when experiencing small successes. In other words, students with high self-efficacy tend to have more confidence and experience more school success.

Self-Efficacy and Learning Disabilities

Students with learning disabilities who also have positive and accurate self-accuracy beliefs are more likely to engage in challenging and difficult academic content with increased effort in learning tasks, take ownership for their learning processes and access the required supports and accommodations to experience success in academics (Bandura, 1997; Firth et al., 2008; Gretzel, 2008; Klassen, 2007). Klassen (2007) also wrote about the calibration of self-efficacy and purports that self-efficacy perceptions influence choice of activity, task perseverance, level of effort expanded, and, ultimately, degree of success achieved. So, the tenets of self-efficacy play an important role in academic choice, development of academic skills, and graduation completion rates for students with learning disabilities.

According to the National Center for Education Statistics, in the United States 88% of 2- and 4-year degree colleges and other postsecondary institutions enrolled students who self-disclosed that they were students with disabilities in the 2008–2009 academic year. Out of this 88%, 31% were identified as having learning disabilities (Kimberley & Laurie, 2011). However, individuals with learning disabilities are less likely to complete postsecondary education than their nondisabled peers (Gretzel, 2008; Mamisheshville & Koch, 2012), possibly due to lower self-efficacy beliefs (Klassen, 2007), lower self-advocacy skills affecting access to available accommodations and supports (Klassen & Lynch, 2007), increased levels of risk for school disengagement, fewer interpersonal relationships, and lower levels of hopefulness (Margalit & Lackay, 2008).

Elizabeth Hopper (2019) sees self-efficacy as it was originally developed by Albert Bandura in 1977, that is, as a concept that determines whether a person will succeed in a chosen task. There are two factors that Bandura believed influenced the involvement of an individual in a task: one's judgement of ability levels (self-efficacy) and one's expectation that the task will lead to good results (outcome expectancy).

Self-efficacy affects the amount of effort an individual puts forth toward a task. A person with high levels of self-efficacy continues to persevere in the face of setbacks, whereas individuals with low levels of self-efficacy avoid challenging tasks. For example, any student who has lower levels of self-efficacy in writing will avoid signing up for advanced language classes. However, an increased level of self-efficacy in one domain, such as the cognitive domain, does not necessarily mean that the person has increased levels of self-efficacy in other domains such as the affection or psychomotor domains (Hopper, 2019). Bandura believed that high levels of self-efficacy were strong predictors of one's goal progress. However, research found that there was a significant two-way interaction between self-efficacy and goal importance, which revealed that self-efficacy had higher impact on goal progress only when the individual perceives that goal to be important (Lord & Kernan, 1990). The finding also supports the fact that in the within-person effect, self-efficacy predicted a significant variance based on previous accomplishments. But this effect occurred only when goal importance was high and not for less important goals (Beattie et al., 2015).

How Self-Efficacy Leads to Self-Advocacy for Students With Learning Disabilities

As students engage in experiences that empower them to believe in themselves, an increase in their self-esteem may be noticed. While self-esteem if often known as one's sense of self-worth and value, self-efficacy is having the belief in your own abilities to get the job done. So, students at all school levels (i.e., elementary and middle schools and secondary and postsecondary schools) should be encouraged to believe in their ability to meet challenges and to seek help when needed. In other words, self-esteem helps students to focus on "being" and self-efficacy helps students to focus on "doing" something. Many students will then begin to advocate for themselves (Ackerman, 2019). It is critical that students learn to believe in their own capacity to achieve and that significant others show that they too believe in the students' capacity to achieve.

One example of a school's effort to work with students with LD is the Churchill Center and School. The Churchill Center and School, noted as a national leader in learning disabilities, stresses that for students to advocate for themselves they should be able to first articulate their disabilities to themselves and then others by expressing their strengths, weakness and strategies. See the following example:

Strengths: "I'm great at math facts."
Weakness: "I have trouble reading because I have dyslexia."
Strategies to help: "Books on tape." (Churchill Center and School, n.d.b., para. 1)

The use of literature is recommended by the Churchill Center and School as a useful strategy in that it can be used with students as early as kindergarten. This school emphasizes teaching self-advocacy from kindergarten through ninth grade. Also, they purport the following four steps to self-advocacy for high school students:

1. Know your **strengths**.
2. Be aware of your **weaknesses**.
3. Identify **strategies** to overcome those weaknesses.
4. Effectively **communicate** those needs to others. (Churchill Center and School, n.d.a., para. 3)

High School Strategies for Self-Advocacy

During the high school experience, students with disabilities still need continued support from school counselors, teachers, coaches, social workers, administrators, and other stakeholders. Similar to the elementary and middle school teachers, high school teachers provide the most continuous direct support to students as they work with students 7 to 8 hours daily, and even in extracurriculars. These teachers are instrumental in organizing and implementing and modification and accommodations that have been included in their individual education plan (IEP) for students with disabilities. Modifications refer to *what* a student learns, and accommodations refer to *how* a student learns. Though there are many strategies for high school students to engage in to promote self-advocacy, much guidance is needed for them to become able to self-advocate. School counselors and teachers continue to be the key school agents in helping students with disabilities. In fact, one of the roles of most school counselors is to close the achievement gap by addressing the needs of all students, especially those students with special needs. Therefore, high school students should work closely with their counselor (Hamlet, 2017; Holcomb-McCoy, 2007). They should become familiar with the special education faculty and realize that the school counselor is commonly the liaison between special education faculty and the regular education teacher. All these supporters are aware of students' need for counseling, organizational support, and postsecondary planning (Holcomb-McCoy, 2007).

In conjunction with the Connecticut State Department of Education, Bureau of Special Education, and Transition Consulting, LLC, the Connecticut Parent Advocacy Center offers many useful strategies for high schoolers' self-advocacy, which is an educational journey from self-discovery to advocacy. This organization begins with using journals where students write their feelings about their daily challenges and successes in dealing with their disability and any self-advocacy initiatives. A second strategy offered is the development of a personal self-advocacy plan that is modified as needed. Then there is a suggestion for students to simply request academic accommodations that they would like to try, such as recorded lectures or visual learning aids (Connecticut Parent Advocacy Center, 2013).

Perhaps the most important strategy for a high school student is deciding when and how to disclose information about their disability and how to use written information to support their advocacy goals (Wright & Wright, 2007). This is important because of the identity issues common to adolescents through early adulthood, including identity issues where adolescents are unsure of themselves and may not have explored how they want to live or what type of occupation they want. No doubt the school counselor can help students with disabilities think about, develop, and explore life transitions as student move through their life span (Berger, 2014; Erford & Tucker, 2017).

A great resource to help students with LD comes from the U.S. Department of Education's (2018) Office for Civil Rights (OCR) in the form of a very informative pamphlet entitled "Students With Disabilities Preparing for Postsecondary Education: Know Your Rights and Responsibilities." This pamphlet has typical questions a high schooler might want to know. Each question is given an expansive response that is easily understood and applicable in preparing for college. For instance, high schoolers need to know that the responsibilities they have as a student with disabilities will be different. Some of the responses let students know that they cannot be denied acceptance to a college because of their disability. Additional aspects to consider in preparing individuals with disabilities for higher education include: who pays for a new evaluation, do students have to disclose their disability and what steps to take if they think they are being discriminated against (U.S. Department of Education, 2018).

College/University Strategies for Self-Advocacy

Since 1985, there has been an increase in the number of students entering a postsecondary school with self-reported disabilities. The enrollment numbers for these students nearly doubled, from 15 to 32%. Clearly self-advocacy is a necessary tool for students with disabilities who want to attend a vocational 2-year or 4-year college or university. These students need to understand the difference in their school options as well as the needed support services (Barr et al., 1995).

The National Center for Education Statistics reports that of 2,563,000 undergraduate students in the United States, approximately 11% of all undergraduates enrolled had a disability in the 2011–2012 school years. BestColleges references these statistics in its overview of college resources for students with disabilities. This report states that college students need to first know their legal rights. Students should find out what is available on the college campus, confer with student services and disability coordinators, and seek academic advisement or academic services for assistance. This is important since many campuses already have addressed issues such as accessibility, accommodation, and assistive technology. Students should know that in addition to the campus-based resources, students with disabilities are protected by the state, federal, and local laws. For example, schools are prohibited from discrimination and require equal access to academic service, environments, and resources. BestColleges (2019) provides a list of sites, apps and software resources specifically designed to aid students with specific types of disabilities.

Barr et al. (1995) offer several strategies for college students' self-advocacy. First there is having documentation of your disability and having a transition plan before leaving high school. Know admissions requirements of the selected school(s). Seek help, usually from an academic advisor, for course selection and accommodative services within the department or school at large. Then there are compensatory strategies, which include allowing more time to complete tests, papers, and other projects; listening to audio tapes of textbooks while reading; and making up works to remind yourself to use the knowledge you already have. Here's area a few examples:

FOIL (First Outer Inner Last) to remember the sequence of steps in solving algebra problems when in school

PAL (Practice Alert Listening) when talking with friends and family, at work, and in school

USE (Use Strategies Every day)

Also, the authors suggest that students with disabilities understand their rights to the privacy of their records protected by the Family Educational Rights and Privacy Act (FERPA), known as the Buckley Amendment, after Senator Buckley of New York who first introduced the act.

Self-advocacy is a right that all students have, including those students with learning disabilities. There are many local, state, and federal legislations that protect the rights of students with special needs. This critical legislation offers funding which helps to provide the necessary funds, such as the Title I funding for disadvantaged children in the United States. Even though parents and educators advocate for students, enabling students with disabilities to self-advocate empowers these students to ensure they get what they need to experience school success, whether in high school or beyond. The ADA National Network Disability Law Handbook provides resources and current information on disability rights and legal issues. This information may be beneficial to those interested in disability and advocacy, including helping students with disabilities to advocate for themselves (Brennan, 2020).

In the case of blind/visually impaired students, long white canes, Braille, audio recordings, electronic text, or a computer screen reader called Jaws from Freedom Scientific may be used. For people with speech and hearing impairments, sign language interpreters and sound amplification aids are useful. In the context of the physically handicapped, a fully accessible barrier-free college environment may be helpful.

A student with a learning disability should not be discriminated against based on their disability. However, in the event of discrimination or suspected discrimination, a student with a disability needs to approach the 504 coordinator, ADA coordinator, or disability services coordinator. These offices are responsible for implementing 504, Title II, or both, compliance. This information should be most beneficial to self-advocating students with a disability. Students need to be aware that as a first step the grievance process can be initiated at the high school level. If the results or proceedings from the grievance process are not satisfactory, then a lawsuit can be filed in a court or with an OCR (officer of civil rights) (U.S. Department of Education, 2018). This is important since postsecondary institutions can provide accommodations based on an IEP from high school. Finally, requesting accommodations and other needed services falls under the Americans With Disabilities Act (ADA). Students attending public colleges are protected against discrimination based on disability by Title II, applicable for state and local government entities. Title III protections apply to public academic institutions. It should be noted that the U.S. Department of Justice is responsible for enforcing Titles II and III (Zeisler, n.d.).

Perhaps self-advocacy can best be achieved when the student with LD understands the process for requesting accommodations and needed services at the postsecondary level, because if a postsecondary school receives state or federal funds, they must comply with the legislation and laws aforementioned. In fact, state-supported institutions are eligible to receive grants for purchasing assistive technology. The Association of Assistive Technology Act Programs (ATAP) database provides a list of AT-funded institutions by State (Zeisler, n.d.).

IDEA defines as SLD as a disorder in one or more of the basic psychological processes involved in understanding or in using language, spoken or written, that may manifest itself in the imperfect ability to listen, think, speak, read, write, spell, or do mathematical calculations.

According to the National Dissemination Center for Children With Learning Disabilities (NICHCY), specific learning disabilities commonly affect skills in the following areas:

- Reading (called dyslexia)
- Writing (called dysgraphia)
- Listening
- Speaking
- Reasoning
- Math (called dyscalculia) (Special Education Guide, n.d.)

Due to their SLD these students face a lot of challenges in their learning processes. Many accommodations and modifications will be useful to increase students' school success, retention, and graduation rates. There are three common types of accommodations: general accommodations, classroom accommodations, and testing accommodations. To make school transition easier, The University of Texas at Austin (2016) has listed several accommodations for students with learning disabilities on their website.

After a person with disabilities is accepted and enrolled into a college of their choice, they will need to contact the appropriate office to apply for accommodations. At Clark Atlanta University this office is the Office of Counseling and Disability Services. Other schools may have a similar name. Accessing disability services is not part of the general college application process. Simply providing a copy of the IEP and evaluation results may not ensure the provision of accommodations and other related services. Under ADA, college admission offices are not allowed to request any information about a student's disabilities. Requesting accommodations is a separate process that may start after the student is officially accepted into the school. First, the student must register as a student with disabilities with the Disability Services Office. An appointment will mostly likely be needed and prior school records presented. Some information about this process may be available on the school's website. There will be additional forms to complete, and someone from the office will do a one-on-one intake, during which accommodations and support services can be requested. Should accommodations be granted, usually a letter for each of the student's teachers is provided. This is a confidential letter that tells each instructor what accommodations are needed. Also, the accommodation letter does not disclose the student's disability for protection of privacy. Finally, a high school transcript and a copy of the most recent IEP and SOP (summary of performance) may be required.

Questions/Considerations

1. Define self-advocacy.
2. What are some statistics related to employment and persons with disabilities?
3. What is the Education of All Handicapped Children Act?
4. What is Wright's law?
5. What are the Every Student Succeeds Act (ESSA), No Child Left Behind Act (NCLB), and Research Excellence/Advancements for Dyslexia (READ) Act?

Recommendations

The following recommendations may be useful in advocating for students and for students to feel empowered to advocate for themselves through self-efficacy. Therefore, the student advocate and/or the student may need to do the following:

1. **Know about multitiered system of supports** (**MTSS**): Multitiered system of supports, formerly called RTI (response to intervention), focuses on early identification and intervention. MTSS works on the premise of providing additional support to students with learning and behavioral problems by providing them with a variety of interventions based on the levels of need—namely tier1, tier 2, and tier 3.
2. **Know about positive behavior interventions and supports** (**PBIS**): These evidence and data-based centers were first initiated in the year 1997 and have been supported for the past 20 years by the Office of Special Education Programs. As of August 2017, the PBIS center and its national network support 26,316 schools comprising 13,896,697 students.
3. **Know about the Every Student Succeeds Act** (**ESSA**) (Department of Education, n.d.): This act was signed into law on December 10, 2015, includes provisions to bring about equity for America's disadvantaged and high-need students. ESSA also mandates that all students in America be taught to high academic standards to prepare them for success in college and careers.
4. **Know there are scholarships available for students with learning disabilities, such as the following** (BestColleges, 2019):
   a. Dyslexic Advantage-Karina Eide Memorial College scholarship
   b. Google-Google Lime Scholarship program
   c. Incight-Incight scholarship program
   d. National Center for Learning Disabilities, Allegra Ford Thomas scholarship
   e. P. Buckley Moss Society, P. Buckley Moss Endowed scholarship

5. **Know there are general accommodations for students with learning disabilities, such as the following:**
   a. Have access to PowerPoint presentations
   b. Utilize alternative textbook (The University of Texas at Austin, 2016)
   c. Make copies of class notes
   d. Ask for a course load reduction
   e. Secure exam accommodations
   f. Request permission for extended time
   g. Gain consent to audio record classes (lectures)
   h. Seek permission to leave or move about in class
   i. Request preferential seating
   j. Ask for priority registration (The University of Texas at Austin, 2016)
   k. Having access to readers for exams
   l. Reduced distraction environment
   m. Select separate room for testing
   n. Use assistive technology
   o. Use laptop
   p. Use a calculator for exams
   q. Use a computer for essay answers
   r. Use a laptop for taking notes
   s. Use spell check for exams

6. **Know the most common learning disabilities:**
   a. Dyslexia: A reading disorder
   b. Dyscalculia: A mathematical disability
   c. Dysgraphia: A writing disability

7. **Consider holding disability awareness meetings/sessions to the general public:**
   a. Local schools
   b. Local churches
   c. PTA meetings
   d. Blog group

8. **Consider forming peer-to-peer mentoring groups:** These groups reinforces positive role modeling and offer a consistent and reassuring presence through right match activities to build a strong foundation that fosters the mentees strengths.

9. **Know colleges that specialize in working with students with disabilities:**
   a. Beacon College
   b. Landmark College
   c. Hofstra University

d. Adelphi University

e. University of North Carolina at Chapel Hill

f. Marshall University

g. University of Arizona

h. University of the Ozarks

10. **Know about scholarships for students with disabilities.** Here's a partial list:

Attention Deficit Disorder:

- Michael Yasick ADHS scholarship

- Rise Scholarship Foundation, Inc.

- Autism Delaware

- Avonte Oquendo Memorial scholarship

- Kelly Law Team Autism scholarship

- KFM: Making a Difference

- Organization for Autism Research

General Disabilities

- 1-800 Wheelchair scholarship

- AAHD Frederick J. Krause Scholarship on Health and Disability

- American Speech-Language-Hearing Foundation

- Baer Reintegration scholarship

- Bella Soul scholarships

- BMO Capital Markets Lime Connect Equity Through Education scholarship

- Google Lime Scholarship for Students With Disabilities

- Hydrocephalus Association Scholarship program

- Incight Scholars

- Injury Lawyer News Annual Disability scholarship

- Lorraine Nelson Herrick scholarship

- Louise J. Snow Endowed Scholarship Fund for Disabled Students

- Microsoft DisAbility scholarship

- Newcombe Scholarships for Students With Disabilities

- Ralph G. Norman scholarship

- Science Graduate Student Grant Fund

Hearing impairment
- AG Bell College Scholarship program
- Anders Tjellstrom scholarship
- Graeme Clark scholarship
- Linda Cowden Memorial scholarship
- Sertoma Scholarship for the Hard of Hearing of Deaf
- Learning & Cognitive Disabilities
- Agee Memorial Dyslexia Scholarship Fund
- Allegra Ford Thomas scholarship
- Allina Health Scholarship for People With Disabilities
- Anne Ford scholarship
- Bennett A. Brown scholarship
- DREAM Institute's Higher Education Assistance Program (HEAP)
- The HEAP Scholar Award Scholarship Landmark College scholarships
- Landmark College scholarships
- Learning Disabilities Association of Iowa
- Liff Family Foundation scholarship
- P. Buckley Moss Endowed scholarship
- AmeriGlide Achiever scholarship
- Chair Scholars Foundation-Students attending Edinboro University of Pennsylvania or University of Tampa are eligible for this award
- Craig H. Nielsen Scholarship Fund for Students With Disabilities
- Ethel Louise Armstrong Foundation scholarship
- Keaton K. Walker Scholarship Fund
- Michigan Cerebral Palsy Attorneys

Speech disorders:
- American Speech-Language-Hearing Foundation
- National Stuttering Association scholarship

Visual disabilities:

- American Foundation for the Blind
- Lighthouse Guild
- Mary P. Oenslager Scholastic Achievement awards
- National Federation of the Blind

Conclusion

No doubt, students with learning disabilities benefit greatly from receiving accommodations to increase their school success. Unfortunately, many students do not disclose their disabilities because they don't want to be treated differently or stereotyped. It then becomes incumbent that school personnel seek to render needed services, as prescribed and required by law, to ensure that these students have the instructional support to maximize their full potential. Disclosure of one's learning disability should be viewed as a gateway to many opportunities to achieve preset goals.

Like secondary schools, support services are available for students at the postsecondary level. The chief difference is that there is no interdisciplinary team. Rather, students will need to seek such services on their own. It may be important that as part of the students' transition from high school to college emphasis be placed on contacting the appropriate office and personnel during the pre-application process. In this way, students can explore what services a school offers and then use this information to determine if this is the school they wish to attend. Visiting a college while still in high school would be a great way to gather needed information too.

Self-confidence, self-esteem, and self-awareness are critical elements for the student with learning disabilities. This triple threat may prove to be useful in helping students with any possible social stigma and peer pressure. Also, a heightened sense of self-efficacy may be observed. Yet, many students with learning disabilities may need parents, counselors, and teachers to help them to effectively communicate their needs and to the appropriated personnel. Then these students' self-advocacy can be appreciated. Perhaps the key here is the removal of unnecessary barriers to learning for all students, especially those with specific learning disabilities.

Teacher training, and in some cases parent training, may be necessary to provide continuous progress for students. Going beyond the accommodations would benefit the students and all stakeholders. To do anything less than this may result in social and educational injustice and multiple inequity issues.

References

Ackerman, C. (2019, March 7). *What is self-efficacy theory in psychology?* PositivePsychology. https://positivepsychology.com/self-efficacy/

Americans With Disabilities Act National Network. (n.d.). *What is the Americans With Disabilities Act (ADA)?* https://adata.org/learn-about-ada

Bandura, A. (1997). *Self-efficacy: The exercise of control.* W. H. Freeman and Company.

Barr, V. M., Hartman, R. C., & Spillane, S. A. (1995). *Getting ready for college: Advising high school students with learning disabilities.* http://www.ldonline.org/article/6132/

Batsche, G., Elliott, J., Graden, J., Grimes, J., Kovaleski, J., & Prasse, D. (2005). *Response to intervention: Policy considerations and implementation.* National Association of State Directors of Special Education. https://www.nasdse.org

Beattie, S., Hardy, L., & Woodman, T. (2015). A longitudinal examination of the interactive effects of goal importance and self-efficacy upon multiple life goal progress. *Canadian Journal of Behavioural Science, 47*(3), 201–206. https://doi.org/10.1037/a0039022

Berger, K. (2014). Children with special needs. In T. Churchill, L. Samuelson, T. Kuehn, & L. Kinne (Eds.), *The developing person through childhood and adolescence* (9th ed.) (pp. 341–346). Worth Publishers.

BestColleges. (2019). *College guide for students with learning disabilities.* https://www.bestcolleges.com/resources/college-planning-with-learning-disabilities/

Brennan, J. (2020). *The ADA national network disability law handbook.* The ADA National Network: Information, Guidance, and Training on the Americans with Disabilities Act.

Brinckerhoff, L. C., Shaw S. F., & McGuire, J. M. (1993). *Promoting postsecondary education for students with learning disabilities: A handbook for practitioner.* PRO-ED.

Cameto, R. (2005). The transition planning process. *National Longitudinal Transition Study-2, 4*(1). National Center on Secondary Education and Transition, University of Minnesota. http://www.ncset.org

Carey, M. P., & Forsyth, A. D. (n.d.). *Teaching tip sheet: Self-efficacy.* American Psychological Association. https://www.apa.org/pi/aids/resources/education/self-efficacy

Churchill Center and School. (n.d.a). *Self-advocacy and learning disabilities.* https://www.churchillstl.org/learning-disability-resources/self-advocacy/

Churchill Center and School. (n.d.b). Teaching self-advocacy: Kindergarten through fourth grade. https://www.churchillstl.org/learning-disability-resources/self-advocacy/

Connecticut Parent Advocacy Center (2013). *Stepping forward: A self-advocacy guide for middle and high school students.* The Connecticut State Department of Education, Bureau of Special Education, and Transition Consulting.

Connecticut State Department of Education, Bureau of Special Education (2013). *Connecticut assistive technology guidelines. https://www.birth23.org/files/SGsPlus/at_executive_summary.pdf*

Erford, B. T., & Tucker, I. B. (2017). The adolescent years: Emotional, identity, and social development. In A. Vernon (Ed.), *An advanced lifespan odyssey for counseling professionals* (pp. 270–271). Cengage Learning.

Family Educational Rights and Privacy Act of 1974, 20 U.S.C. § 1232g (1974).

Firth, N., Frydenburg, E., & Greaves, D. (2008). Perceived control and adaptive coping: Programs for adolescent students who have learning disabilities. *Learning Disability Quarterly, 31*(3), 151–165. https://www.doi.org/10.2307/25474645

Gretzel, E. E., & Thoma, C. A. (2008). Experiences of college students with disabilities and the importance of self-determination in higher education settings. *Career Development for Exceptional Individuals, 31*(2), 77–84. https://doi.org/10.1177/0885728808317658

Hamlet, H. S. (2017). The role of the school counselor in special education. In N. Davidson (Ed.), *School counseling practicum and internship: 30 essential lessons* (pp. 307–312). SAGE.

Holcomb-McCoy, C. (2007). The achievement gap: Our ultimate challenge. In S. Wagner, J. Coelho, V. Stapleton, & E. Meidenbauer (Eds.), *School counseling to close the achievement gap: A social justice framework for success* (pp. 1–14). Corwin.

Hopper, E. (2019, January 13). *Understanding self-efficacy*. ThoughtCo. https://www.thoughtco.com/self-efficacy-4177970

Horowitz, S., Rawe, J., & Whittaker, M. (2017). *The state of learning disabilities: Understanding the 1 in 5*. National Center for Learning Disabilities.

Kimberley, R., & Laurie, L. (2011). *Students with disabilities at degree-granting postsecondary institutions*. National Center for Education Statistics. https://nces.ed.gov/pubsearch/pubsinfo.asp?pubid=2011018

Klassen, R. (2002). A question of calibration: A review of the self-efficacy beliefs of students with learning disabilities. *Learning Disability Quarterly, 25*(2), 88–102. https://doi.org/10.2307/1511276

Klassen, R. (2007). Using predictions to learn about the self-efficacy of early adolescents with and without learning disabilities. *Contemporary Educational Psychology, 32*(2), 173–187. https://doi.org/10.1016/j.cedpsych.2006.10.001

Klassen, R., & Chiu, M. (2010). Effects on teachers' self-efficacy and job satisfaction: Teacher gender, years of experience, and job stress. *Journal of Educational Psychology, 102*(3), 741–756. https://doi.org/10.1037/a0019237

Klassen, R. M., & Lynch, S. L. (2007). Self-efficacy from the perspective of adolescents with LD and their specialist teachers. *Journal of Learning Disabilities, 40*(6), 494–507. https://doi.org/10.1177/00222194070400060201

Learning Disabilities Association of America (October, 2020). Retrieved from https://ldaamerica.org

Lord, R. G., & Kernan, M. C. (1990). Effects of valence, expectancies, and goal-performance discrepancies in single and multiple goal environments. *Journal of Applied Psychology, 75*(2), 194–203. https://doi.org/10.1037/0021-9010.75.2.194

Luman, S. (2011, April 17). Importance of self-efficacy. *Self-efficacy.* http://sbluman2.blogspot.com/p/importance-of-self-efficacy.html

Maccini, P., Gagnon, J., & Hughes, C. (2002). Technology-based practices for secondary students with learning disabilities. *Learning Disability Quarterly, 25*(4), 247–261. https://doi.org/10.2307/1511356

Mamiseishvili, K., & Koch, L. C. (2012). Students with disabilities at 2-year institutions in the United States: Factors related to success. *Community College Review, 40*(4), 320–339. https://doi.org/10.1177/0091552112456281

Margalit, M., & Lackaye, T. (2008). Self-efficacy, loneliness, effort and hope: Developmental differences in the experiences of students with learning disabilities and their non-learning disabled peers at two age groups. *Learning Disabilities: A Contemporary Journal, 6*(2), 1–20.

Margolis, P. and McCabe, H., (2006). Improving self-efficacy and motivation: What to do, what to say. *Intervention in School and Clinic, 41* (4), 218–227.

Mayer, R. E. (2010, July 20). Motivation based on self- efficacy. *Learning and instruction,* pp. 504–510.

Mazzetti, V. L., & Rowe, D. A. (2015). Meeting the transition needs to students in the 21st century. *Teaching Exceptional Children, 47*(6), 298–300. https://doi.org/10.1177/0040059915587695

Merriam-Webster. (n.d.). Advocacy. In *Merriam-Webster.com dictionary.* Retrieved from https://www.merriam-webster.com/dictionary/advocacy

McGinley. V. A., & Trolley, B. C. (2016). Working with assessment and evaluations and plan. In V. McGinley (Ed.), *Working with students with disabilities: Preparing school counselors counseling and professional identity* (pp. 103–105). SAGE.

Morris, C. (2014, September 11). Beacon for learning disabled. *Diverse,* 14–15. https://diverseeducation.com/article/66907/

National Center for Learning Disabilities. (2015). *Student voices executive summary.* https://www.ncld.org/wp-content/uploads/2015/08/Student-Voices-Executive-Summary.pdf

National Council on Disability. (2012, April 22). *SECTION 2: Cross-system focus to improve outcomes across the lifespan for people with ID/DD.* National Council on Disability. https://ncd.gov/publications/2012/apr222012/section2

Ormrod, J. E. (2008). *Human learning* (5th ed.). Pearson Education.

PACER Center. (2015). Prepare your child for age of majority and transfer of rights. PACER's National Parent Center on Transition and Employment, 1–2.

Parent Center Hub. (2015, June 16). *Learning disabilities (LD).* https://www.parentcenterhub.org/ld/

Schwarzer, R., & Jerusalem, M. (1995). Generalized Self-Efficacy scale. In J. Weinman, S. Wright, & M. Johnston, Measures in health psychology: A user's portfolio. Causal and control beliefs (pp. 35–37). NFER-NELSON.

Shea, M., Dahir, C. & Stone, C. (2015). *Working with students with disabilities: Preparing school counselors*. SAGE.

Special Education Guide. (n.d.). *Specific learning disabilities*. https://www.specialeducationguide.com/disability-profiles/specific-learning-disabilities/

The Understood Team. (n.d.). *7 things to know about college disability services*. https://www.understood.org/en/school-learning/choosing-starting-school/leaving-high-school/7-things-to-know-about-college-disability-services

United Way. (n.d.). *About us*. https://www.unitedway.org/our-impact/focus/education/out-of-school-time/data/ewrs#

The University of Texas at Austin (2016). *Accommodations and services. Division of diversity and student engagement*. https://diversity.utexas.edu/disability/accommodations-and-services/

U.S. Department of Education. (n.d.). *Every Student Succeeds Act* (ESSA). https://www.ed.gov/essa

U.S. Department of Education. (2010, March). *A blueprint for reform: The reauthorization of the Elementary and Secondary Education Act*. https://www2.ed.gov/policy/elsec/leg/blueprint/blueprint.pdf

U.S. Department of Education. (2011). *Students with disabilities preparing for postsecondary education: Know your rights and responsibilities*. https://www2.ed.gov/about/offices/list/ocr/transition.html

U.S. Department of Labor. (2014). *Economic picture of the disability community project: Key points on disability and occupational projections tables*. https://www.dol.gov/agencies/odep/publications/statistics

U.S. Department of Education. (2018a, September 25). *How to file a discrimination complaint with the Office for Civil Rights*. https://www2.ed.gov/about/offices/list/ocr/docs/howto.html

Vernon, A., & Schimmel, C. J. (2019). Counseling children and adolescents with exceptionalities. In T. Stone & P. Brott (Eds.), *Counseling children and adolescents* (pp. 323–331). Cognella.

Wright, P., & Wright, P. (2007). *Paper trails, letter writing & documentation*. http://www.wrightslaw.com/info/ltrs.index.htm

Zeisler, A. (n.d.). *Overview of college resources for students with disabilities*. BestColleges. https://www.bestcolleges.com/resources/students-with-disabilities/

Chapter 9

Library Resources
Working With Students with Disabilities

Terrilyn Battle, Caleb Cuthbertson, Ebrahim Mansaray, and Glacia Ethridge

Introduction

What are library resources? Why is knowledge regarding library resources beneficial for me to know? How can library resources be utilized to help me be successful in my academic career? How can library resources be made accessible for individuals with physical, mental, and/or intellectual disabilities? These are questions that may come to mind for students needing to identify library resources and services as they navigate their academic endeavors.

As we assess the resources provided to all individuals, regardless of ability, it is important to recognize the specific role libraries plays in the transition, inclusion, and success of individuals with disabilities.

> Libraries work as service organizations which facilitate all their users without discrimination, including persons with special needs. According to disability prevalence, it is emerging as the largest marginal group in the world. The global disability prevalence was 10% in 1970s which has increased day by day. World Health Organization and The World Bank (2011) state that 15% of the total world population is suffering from some kind of special needs. (Bashir et al., 2017, p. 216).

The library serves as a central location aiding numerous purposes for the student body. The inclusion of all individuals has been a focus of library faculty as they create an environment that supports learning on campus, virtually and through their Web presence. This chapter explores various research relevant to individuals with disabilities and the resources provided by libraries and universities to support students' academic endeavors and technological needs in postsecondary education.

Purpose

There is no refuting students with disabilities who endure hardships when accessing various supports. While there have been many advances in providing services regarding library resources for the general population, students with disabilities may be more likely to encounter difficulties navigating supports regardless of various settings (secondary schooling and postsecondary endeavors such as undergraduate education and graduate studies). The purpose of this chapter is to provide information to students and educators regarding library resources for students with disabilities. In doing so, this chapter will focus on providing information regarding students with disabilities and their utilization of library supports. Additionally, this chapter will provide background information on library resources and identify potential supports one may access to be academically successful.

Limiting Discriminatory Actions for Individuals With Disabilities

Individuals with disabilities compose the largest minority group in the United States (Wentz et al., 2015). The Americans With Disabilities Act (ADA) reflects the prohibition of discriminatory actions within the workplace, state and local governmental settings, public accommodations, commercial facilities, transportation, and telecommunication efforts (Graves & German, 2018; U.S. Department of Justice, 2020). To be protected by the ADA, an individual must have a disability or direct association with an individual with a disability (U.S. Department of Justice, 2020). An individual with a disability, as defined by ADA, is an individual who has a physical or mental impairment that yields limitations in one or more major activities of daily living (ADA National Network, 2020; U.S. Department of Justice, 2020). These activities include but are not limited to actions such as walking, talking, taking care of bodily functions, and/or being independent of an aid or caregiver.

The Rehabilitation Act of 1973, in conjunction to the ADA, aims to prohibit discrimination based on disability in programs administered by federal agencies and programs receiving financial and employment supports (Graves & German, 2018; U.S. Department of Justice, 2020). Identifying discrimination under the Rehabilitation Act poses the same constructs used in Title I of the ADA; however, in association with the Rehabilitation Act, these standards are reflected as Section 501, Section 503, Section 504, and Section 508 (U.S. Department of Justice, 2020). Specifically, Section 504 identifies "no qualified individuals with a disability in the United States shall be excluded from, denied the benefits of, or be subjected to discrimination under any program or activity that either receives Federal financial assistance or is conducted by any Executive agency or the United States Postal Service" (U.S. Department of Justice, 2020, Section 504, para. 1).

The Office for Civil Rights (OCR) enforces a responsibility to eliminate discrimination against students with disabilities (U.S. Department of Education, 2020). Additionally, the OCR supports Section 504 in programs and activities receiving federal financial assistance from the Department of Education; "this includes public school districts, institutions of higher education, and other state and local education agencies" (U.S. Department of Education, 2020, Introduction, para. 3). While each agency is responsible for enforcing its own set of Section 504 regulations (U.S. Department of Justice, 2020), the American Library Association (ALA, 2019) implies the notion to minimize barriers within library settings, stating the mission "to provide leadership for the development, promotion and improvement of library and information services and the profession of librarianship in order to enhance learning and ensure access to information for all" (Policy Manual Section A, p. 8). In 2001, the ALA authorized the Library Services for People With Disabilities policy, which directed libraries to provide comprehensive programming and services for users regardless of their status of disability (Graves & German, 2018).

Background

In 1998, Congress amended the Rehabilitation Act of 1973, mandating "federal agencies to make their electronic and information technology (EIT) accessible to people with disabilities." Section 508 of the legislation specifically states, "Agencies must give disabled employees and members of the public access to information comparable to the access available to others" (U.S. General Services Administration, 2020, para. 1). Since the amendment there has been a rise in lawsuits against Title IV institutions or those involved in federal student loan programs (Carlson, 2018). In these legal instances, people have claimed Title IV institutions have violated Section 508 of the Rehabilitation Act of 1973 and that these institutions possess inaccessible electronic information on their websites. Breach of Section 508 has also been cited in institutions as being unable to offer suitable learning software for students who are blind and/or visually impaired, the absence of closed captioning of institutionally published videos, college application and financial aid processes that are inaccessible or difficult to navigate, and lack of Web-accessible textbooks and course materials (Carlson, 2018). With the most recent amendment of Section 508, all Title IV participating U.S. institutions of higher education are required to abide by Web content accessibility guidelines (WCAG) 2.0, level A and AA standards (Taylor, 2019; U.S. Access Board, 2018).

With more and more individuals with disabilities enrolling in colleges and universities, the awareness of library accessibility has become more imperative. The literature on this topic has largely focused on physical accessibility (building standards, restroom accessibility, classroom, and/or shelf accessibility, etc.) and Web accessibility, specifically for students with learning and physical disabilities navigating online library databases (Brannen et al., 2017). In terms of Web accessibility, Taylor (2019) notes an observation made by Hackett and Parmanto in which they infer that as internet technology advances it has become difficult for institutional websites to keep up and become accessible, thus making it increasingly inaccessible for those with disabilities. Advancement of internet technology is why the U.S. Congress has continuously amended Section 508 to reflect rapidly changing technologies and their minoritizing impact on students with disabilities (Taylor, 2019).

WCAG 2.0 was created by the World Wide Web Consortium and became the standard for Web accessibility when the U.S. Congress incorporated WCAG 2.0 standards as an amendment of Section 508 (Taylor, 2019). WCAG 2.0 assesses Web accessibility conformance at three levels: level A, level AA, and level AAA. Level A is the lowest level of compliance and standards defined by WCAG, such as captioning for those who are hard of hearing (W3C, 2018a). Level AA is the standard level of conformance Title IV–participating institutional websites are required to abide by per the ADA (U.S. Access Board, 2018). Level AA standards include all level A standards, in addition to another layer of compliance. Examples of standards reflect the utilization of color-contrast minimums and using distinct labels to assist students in recognizing Web pages (W3C, 2018a). Level AAA is the highest level of compliance an institution can have, following both level A and level AA standards (W3C, 2018a). It is not necessary for institutions who receive federal aid to meet level AAA standards at present. "It is not recommended that Level AAA conformance be required as a general policy for entire sites because it is not possible to satisfy all Level AAA Success Criteria for some content" (Taylor, 2019, p. 453).

Staff Awareness

Staff awareness training is often discussed when addressing accessibility. This reflects the need of library personnel being familiar with available resources for people with disabilities and dependable supports in the library, university, or community for students to access services. Such services are beneficial for library staff to gain training from professionals working with individuals with disabilities. With training, staff are likely to increase awareness of how to serve individuals with disabilities, how to facilitate an atmosphere of inclusion to aid equitable opportunities to students, and how to advance the likelihood of students meeting their desired academic goals. Two primary techniques libraries utilize to facilitate staff training are arranging for live training sessions and using Web training modules. To avoid instances of having unprepared staff and a level of service that is not up to par, outreach programs have been utilized to introduce services to underserved groups and to encourage more interaction, a genuine relationship between library personnel and students. These outreach activities, especially when conducted periodically, assist in addressing important learning and information services. Research notes the benefits of collaborative efforts among individuals with disabilities and library personnel to teach and facilitate disability outreach programs (Brannen et al., 2017; Lewis, 2013). Having representation in the form of volunteers or paid staff allows for individuals with disabilities to more readily participate in events that facilitate relationship building between the library and the community as well as familiarity with services the library offers.

The manual affiliated with the American Library Association (2019) contains a section devoted to serving people with disabilities. Subsection B.9.3.2 "Library Services for People with Disabilities" of Section B.9 "Library Personnel Practices" contains outreach information at the national level (Brannen et al., 2017). This subsection allows for continued communication with support organizations in the community, including entities that serve people with disabilities. This interaction will allow the library to provide current and accurate information and have an attentive ear directed toward issues as well as events and programs taking place. Furthermore, this facilitates a strong bond between the library and support and organizations.

Additional goals for the enhancement of staff awareness include increasing the number of librarians in charge of services and programs to individuals with disabilities, encouraging efforts of training for library staff to aid awareness of resources available to individuals with disabilities, and access to specialized assistance to ensure the quality of services provided are equitable to all students regardless of ability. Additionally, training staff and making them more proactive to addressing the needs of students and/or hiring staff who may have disabilities could foster an atmosphere that is amiable and inclusive. These suggestions could help ensure a commitment to excellence for the community (Brannen et al., 2017).

Library Resources for Students With Disabilities

Educational institutions have identified practices for reasonable accommodations for an array of learning needs (Graves & German, 2018). Libraries are called to promote access of services to individuals with diverse needs and a range of both abilities and disabilities (Graves & German, 2018). Promoting and providing equitable services to individuals with disabilities accessing library facilities and services is required by Section 504 of the Rehabilitation Act of 1973, applicable state and local regulations, and the ADA of 1990 (American Library Association, 2019; WebJunction, 2019). "Libraries are one of the important segments of any academic institution that work as the center of information resources and services" (Bashir et al., 2017, p. 216). Oftentimes, when inquiring of library supports, print resources are thought to be the standard. Resources such as books, journals, conference papers, and secondary publications (e.g., catalogues, indexes, bibliographies, and reviews) are typically the resources in which library users seek to access and inquire knowledge (Okezie, 2016). Bashir et al. (2017) say that libraries are service organizations that facilitate all their users without discrimination, including individuals with special needs. The ALA's (2019) Office for Literacy and Outreach Services (OLOS) offers resources to library and information workers providing services to individuals from traditionally underrepresented groups.

Students With Visual Impairments

According to the National Federation for the Blind (2019), roughly 15% of people with visual impairments who enroll in college (schools where they may be the minority) have been found to graduate with a bachelor's degree or higher. A factor believed to contribute to this number is the lack of confidence young students may have when entering college. College may be observed as a moment where students with visual impairments confront the level of independence or lack therefore that was previously experienced. College for students, both those without disabilities and those with disabilities, is a time where young individuals learn to become autonomous. A level of responsibility not had before is placed on their shoulders; this may be true in terms of students who are visually impaired. Students with visual impairments are expected to have a level of responsibility and autonomy in their academic progress. The availability of applications/resources to assist in forming the confidence and independence among students with visual impairments to promote successful progress through their postsecondary education is necessary.

Job Access With Speech

There is an array of assistive technologies currently present in libraries that encourage us to think about not only accessibility but usability. Job Access With Speech (JAWS) is an application that serves as a screen reader equipped with voice synthesis. It assists individuals with visual impairments in their ability to access computer screens, and when used in conjunction with an internet browser JAWS provides a comprehensive description of the Web page. The user has the option of either listening to the entire description or only pertinent portions of it. JAWS also provides detailed contextual facts on control elements like drop-down menus, specifically making the user aware of necessary operational functions and available options. The student utilizes particular keystrokes to navigate JAWS and the Web page. Difficulties in using JAWS are that one must be trained in the program and each new version requires more training. JAWS typically reads pages horizontally and from top to bottom, which can make navigating more complex Web pages difficult. Additionally, it has been observed that if too many tabs are present at one time, an excessive number of links or pages that are long make navigating Web pages with JAWS time consuming (Schiff, 2009).

ZoomText

ZoomText is a screen magnification software that also uses voice synthesis and assists with visually amplifying text and graphics. Text can be magnified up to 36 times, in flexible steps. Through keyboard commands or positioning the mouse over text the student using the app dictates reading the Web page. The student can also display the screen in a multitude of ways: full, with overlays, or split screen. Other features include scrolling through the contents, zooming in and out, and changing screen colors, among other tasks. An area of concern in utilizing this application is that it does not help students who are experiencing progressive deterioration of visual capability. Individuals with more advanced visual impairment are advised to use JAWS, but the transition from one application to the other may be difficult (Schiff, 2009). If assistive applications are difficult to use for students with disabilities, it brings to question the equity these students have in not only using library resources but also in pursuing their education.

ReadPlease

ReadPlease is a text-to-speech application that transforms text on a Web page into audio. When using this application, the individual copies and pastes text into ReadPlease and an audio of the text is produced. ReadPlease gives users the opportunity to change the pace of the recording in addition to the ability to adjust the font size of text. There are different versions of the application; however, the paid version of ReadPlease offers more functions for the user to choose from. It should be noted this application does not help with reading e-books (Vernon, 2010).

Optical Character Recognition

Optical character recognition (OCR) allows students to make images or scanned pages into electronic text format like a word-processor file. This application allows users to obtain scanned Web page images and export text output to Microsoft Word. It can also be used to upload images to be converted into text. Two identifiable concerns of this application are that images are converted into a plain text document and only 10 pages can be converted in 1 hour (Vernon, 2010).

Students With Hearing Impairments

It is the belief that because libraries largely contain visual information students with hearing impairments may not have issues with navigating libraries. Literature pertaining to students with disabilities and the accessibility of libraries to individuals with hearing impairments primarily focuses on students who have a visual impairment or issues with reading print (Gett & Stewart, 2018). This does not come as a surprise since instinctively when associating thought to a library, books are typically the picture we envision. However, this leaves out other services the library provides and other students who have different disabilities that need to be accommodated.

Dragon Dictation

Dragon Dictation is a speech recognition software that allows a person to transform their speech into text or e-mails. It is easy to master and makes typing optional. It is available for desktops as well as laptops, tablets, and mobile devices. It allows individuals to perform tasks accurately and efficiently, which may, at times, pose issues for some comparable assistive technologies. This application may help in performing a task a person may not be able to perform otherwise (Alkhalifa & Al-Razgan, 2018).

Closed Caption

Closed caption is software that assists users in interacting well with visual content. It allows students the option to change settings on visual content to read information provided by written modes instead of having to listen. Text appears on screen, usually near the bottom. This application allows for equal access to visual content that would otherwise be difficult for students with hearing impairments to utilize. Concerns with closed captioning may reflect possible errors that may make it difficult to understand visual content. Library personnel must allocate time to make appropriate edits to these captions. Transcripts that come with closed captions would be helpful for users since it allows them to review the visual content the information provides at their own pace. It is also important that captions do not block important visual content and that captions incorporate accurate audio descriptions (Getts & Stewart, 2018). The YouTube captioning function is often used by many libraries. Other software programs are Amara, Magpie, and Subtitle Workshop (Getts & Stewart, 2018).

Kanopy

Libraries have also worked to make their databases accessible by working with media vendors possessing content that have text alternatives. Kanopy is a media vendor that has accessible services and documents. In their (public) accessibility statement it is noted that their media player is accessible to those with auditory disabilities. Although not all the visual content within Kanopy has closed captioning, it has a quick and easy way for users to request the addition of closed captioning in visual content that may not already have it. It is important to the level of accessibility for students with hearing impairments that libraries partner with vendors that hold accessibility of their content as a priority (Getts & Stewart, 2018).

Real-Time Text

Real-time text (RTT) services have been used in place of teletype (TTY) services. RTT usage has been encouraged to replace TTY services since 2016 by the Federal Communication Division (FCD). RTT interactions, in comparison to TTY, emulate person-to-person conversation. Those who use RTT have their texts sent automatically without hitting "send" as opposed to TTY, where one would have a 60-word per minute limit. These services help students who may be taking distance learning courses or who are not on campus but can still have reliable access to library staff (Getts & Stewart, 2018).

Students With Intellectual Disabilities

Historically, adult individuals with intellectual disabilities have been limited to skill training, work programs, and day programs that allow the caregiver to fulfill their personal duties (Gallinger, 2013). However, according to Gallinger (2013), opportunities for higher education are increasing at institutions throughout the country. Opportunities for individuals with intellectual disabilities have been segregated and focused in supportive employment and vocational rehabilitation, but most recently a shift for inclusion in other opportunities has transpired. Postsecondary education opportunities for intellectual disabilities have revealed many inconsistencies in program options, services rendered, and university collaborations, hindering the opportunity for postsecondary education (Davidson, 2018).

With the expansion of postsecondary education opportunities for individuals with intellectual disabilities, it is imperative that policies and resources be implemented at institutions of higher education related to support services. Research relevant to how the library does and can support these initiatives is needed. Individuals at postsecondary institutions found independence through academic support (Gallinger, 2013). As students are integrated into general education courses, resources such as the library, academic support center, and more will be beneficial and necessary for their success. However, because students with intellectual disabilities are considered "non-degree seeking" it presents challenges on the services that can be provided to them (Adams, 2017). Faculty have been noted as receptive and eager to welcome students into their courses, but barriers are presented as other support services are explored, including library resources (Adams, 2017).

Students With Physical Disabilities

Students with physical disabilities often encounter hardships navigating school activities (Pamatani et al., 2019). Additionally, students experiencing physical limitations may require support pertaining to their physical needs and conditions (Pamatani et al., 2019). Physical disabilities and impairments reflect but may not be limited to an individual who possesses an impairment that inhibits individual activities as a result of damage to the bones, muscles, joint, and nervous system due to disease, viruses, and/or accidents that occurred either before birth, at birth, or after birth (Pamatani et al., 2019).

In attempts to explore information availability and services administered to physically challenged students or students with mobility limitations accessing library resources, Lawal-Solarin (2012) sought to identify problems students encountered. While identifying information needs of physically challenged students, Lawal-Solarin (2012) noted the work of Adesina regarding information needs of the physically challenged:

a. Information for educational development: This is of paramount importance. As a student, additional information would be needed to build on what was taught in the classroom.
b. Information for social and personal development: Information is needed on assistive devices that could aid mobility.
c. Information for recreational purposes: These may include materials for light reading. (p. 2)

As a public institution, libraries are commonly at the forefront of working with the public (Pionke, 2017). While serving a conglomerate of individuals, libraries are noted to lag in their support to individuals with disabilities (Pionke, 2017). Specific to individuals with physical disabilities, the ADA was intended to create accessibility to buildings and services for all individuals (Pionke, 2017). Under the ADA, 12 categories have been identified to reflect public accommodations to remove barriers (Institute for Human Centered Design, 2016):

1. Places of lodging (e.g., inns, hotels, motels, except for owner-occupied establishments renting fewer than six rooms)
2. Establishments serving food or drink (e.g., restaurants and bars)
3. Places of exhibition or entertainment (e.g., motion picture houses, theaters, concert halls, stadiums)
4. Places of public gathering (e.g., auditoriums, convention centers, lecture halls)
5. Sales or rental establishments (e.g., bakeries, grocery stores, hardware stores, shopping centers)
6. Service establishments (e.g., laundromats, dry-cleaners, banks, barber shops, beauty shops, travel services, shoe repair services, funeral parlors, gas stations, offices of accountants or lawyers, pharmacies, insurance offices, professional offices of health care providers, hospitals)
7. Public transportation terminals, depots, or stations (not including facilities relating to air transportation)
8. Places of public display or collection (e.g., museum, libraries, galleries)

9. Places of recreation (e.g., parks, zoos, amusement parks)
10. Place of education (e.g., nursery schools, elementary, secondary, undergraduate, or postgraduate private schools)
11. Social service center establishments (e.g., daycare centers, senior citizen centers, homeless shelters, food banks, adoption agencies)
12. Places of exercise or recreation (e.g., gymnasiums, health spas, bowling alleys, golf courses) (p. 5)

Similar to the 12 categories to remove barriers to individuals with disabilities, the ADA standards for accessible design reflect four priorities: (a) accessible approach and entrance, (b) access to goods and services, (c) access to public toilet rooms, and (d) access to other items such as water fountains and public telephones (Institute for Human Centered Design, 2016). Considerations for accommodations among individuals with disabilities accessing library settings reflects the need of an accessible route from site arrival points and an accessible entrance for all individuals (Institute for Human Centered Design, 2016). Furthermore, considerations of accessible layouts of buildings allowing individuals with disabilities to obtain goods and services, partake of activities without assistance, as well as feasible accessibility to public toilet rooms should be made. Additionally, supports should be made for individuals accessing amenities and public telephones within buildings and facilities (Institute for Human Centered Design, 2016).

Accommodations specific to individuals with physical disabilities should reflect but are not limited to the acknowledgement of slip-resistant flooring, widened spaces, and asphalt surfaces instead of gravel (Institute for Human Centered Design, 2016). Curb ramps and/or handrails are to be installed, regraded, and/or reconfigured to meet the accessibility requirements for individuals who may use wheelchairs or need such supports to aid mobility. To encourage the use of support, signs should be displayed to inform individuals of accessible resources. Additionally, the entrance should offer direct access to the main floor of the library, the lobby, and elevator (Institute for Human Centered Design, 2016).

Virtual Learning

As technological and educational efforts continue to be ever changing, virtual learning and remote collaboration have become impactful in learning efforts. Video conferencing systems have become increasingly popular in telehealth services, as well as classroom instruction. Allowing the accessibility for individuals to attend and participate in class instruction via virtual learning offers flexibility and creativity in the learning process.

Zoom

Video chat applications have been present for a long time, allowing individuals to see one another while communicating online (Crookes, 2020). Zoom, a free video conferencing application, was developed in 2013 for the primary utilization of business users. Sutterlin (2018) identifies the benefits of utilizing Zoom video conferencing within the classroom and proposes allowing individuals to complete introduction discussion forms via offering short introductory videos rather than implementing the standard discussion post responses. Additionally, Sutterlin (2018) notes the utilization of live meetings for instruction as it offers the flexibility of usage by computer or mobile device. The accessibility of Zoom reflects capabilities of typing closed captioning if a participant is assigned to caption a live meeting. Users also have access to auto-generated transcripts that can be used and disseminated to students to aid learning.

Webex

Much like Zoom, Cisco Webex is a video conferencing system that is often used for educational and/or health care purposes. With the concept of working together remotely, Webex offers modes of accessibility in which individuals who are deaf and hard of hearing are able to enable closed captioning resources and pin an interpreter's video for utilization when a presenter shares their content (Cisco, 2020). Furthermore, like Zoom, hosts of Webex can access transcripts from the recordings based on their settings and website preferences. Participants are able to utilize screen share to provide access to attendees to view different documents and applications throughout their usage of the application (Cisco, 2020).

Learning Management Platforms

Most college campuses use some form of a learning management system (LMS) to further aid the learning process. While there are many options of LMS, among the most common are Canvas, Blackboard, and Moodle. As focus for inclusion and accessibility become more prevalent on college campuses, the use and accessibility of LMS is a necessity.

Canvas

Canvas provides several resources to ensure that faculty are providing accessible content to their students. This includes compatibility with screen readers and browsers, font sizing, testing and quizzes, and third-party resources to provide feedback on course accessibility (Sasaki, 2020). According to Sasaki, Canvas is compatible with VoiceOver, JAWS, and NVDA when using Safari and Firefox Web browsers. Additionally, students who require extended time on assessments or multiple attempts can be provided this opportunity through individualized settings created through Canvas (2020). Faculty members are often able to identify feedback on the course's accessibility through the Universal Design Online Content Inspection Tool (UDOIT). UDOIT will verify that accessibility features such as alternative text for images, descriptive link text, and captions for videos are used. Additionally, the UDOIT tool looks for errors in accessibility and provides an individualized report of suggestions to the faculty member (Bates & Sato, 2019).

Moodle

Moodle (2020) takes the stance that "there should be no barriers for people regardless of disabilities, assistive technologies that are used, different screen sizes and different input devices (para. 1)." Like Canvas, Moodle provides support to individuals with disabilities by providing coding standards, external resources, and accessibility tools. In comparison to Canvas and Blackboard, Moodle has accessibility features that are compatible with Google Chrome. Moodle has established a relationship with an external auditor to maintain compliance with accessibility regulations. Furthermore, Moodle has also created a collaborative group that dedicates time monthly to developing and assessing the accessibility of Moodle services.

Blackboard Collaborate

Blackboard's (n.d.) learning management system provides several resources for various disabilities. Similarly, Canvas, Moodle, and Blackboard abide by the Web content accessibility guidelines (WCAG). The services provided by Blackboard meet the guidelines set to ensure accessibility across this platform. Services provided include accommodations for individuals with vision and hearing impairments and mobility challenges. Features of Blackboard include text size formatting for notes and conversations, auditory notifications, and keyboard shortcuts. Blackboard also features visual notifications, closed captioning, and adjustable camera and microphone settings. Blackboard aims to make sure the product and services provided are usable by all abilities.

Future Directions

Future research should include both qualitative and quantitative designs. The experience of individuals with disabilities is imperative in guiding administrators, faculty, and library staff in navigating services provided at universities, community colleges, and local libraries. Qualitative research will assist in guiding the implications of the necessity of resources specific to individuals with disabilities. Data and narratives will guide the implementation of vital and beneficial services for students.

Literature and research reveal further knowledge needed in the following areas related to library resources for individuals with disabilities:

- The usefulness of screen reading software provided by libraries while navigating online databases (Dermody & Majekodunmi, 2011)

- Comparative research of resources and technological services provided at predominately White institutions versus historically Black colleges and universities (Taylor, 2019)

- Resources and services provided to individuals with physical and intellectual disabilities

- The benefit of specifically employed library staff to assist individuals with disabilities (Lawal-Solarin, 2012)

Most research conducted on individuals with disabilities and library resources is outdated. It is important that new trends be explored as higher education and knowledge on disability is ever changing. The fact that many universities have an office dedicated to accessibility and inclusion may imply why research has not been conducted related to the services provided by the library. While there is overlap in services provided by the library and an office dedicated to accessibility and resources and services of individuals with disabilities, it is imperative that libraries be at the forefront as a pillar in student success. This is especially imperative as campus enrollment growth includes individuals with disabilities.

Implications

Suggestions in improving accessibility of library resources among students with disabilities are creating, improving, and investing in support services. Moreover, ensuring the level of services provided to those with disabilities and individuals without disabilities are equitable, and the implementation of regular training of library personnel to interact with students with disabilities in a proactive, friendly, and welcoming manner may deem beneficial in enhancing library supports for individuals with disabilities. Encouraging collaborative efforts of individuals with disabilities among library staff in impactful roles; hiring librarians and staff with background, training, and skills in serving individuals with disabilities; actively advertising library resources and services; and gathering, learning and acting on the experiences of students with disabilities from regularly surveying (collecting feedback from students on services) them would also be beneficial in strengthening supports for students with disabilities accessing library resources. Additional suggestions reflect the reinforcement of the importance of accessibility to vendors of e-resources and other media so that incoming products/services cater to those with disabilities (Brannen et al., 2017).

By recognizing the cultural aspect of disability, consideration of how to foster inclusion and make the issue of accessibility for students with disabilities is a more important one.

Library personnel should address accessibility issues and address multiculturalism and acceptance within the college community. Having outreach and other social programs in libraries that discuss topics such as learning about the culture of individuals who are deaf and/or hard of hearing or culture found among individuals with blind and/or visual impairments may allow those in service or of influence on campuses to also be aware of the needs of these communities . Barriers to inclusion and students with disabilities succeeding should be observed as this allows parallels to be made pertaining to the efforts made by various institutions to support students who belong to different racial, religious, sexual, and gender minority identities and more. There may be some value in viewing this topic similarly to how we view inclusion of other social minority groups.

Issues with Web accessibility may leave minority postsecondary students with disabilities disproportionately behind, preventing them from accessing higher education due to their disability and not being accommodated. Minority students typically face systematic factors that limit their enrollment in higher education. Future studies should continue to consider websites of predominantly White institutions (PWIs) and how accessible they have become for students with disabilities. Studies could compare websites of PWI, historically Black colleges and universities (HBCUs), Asian American and Native American Pacific Islander–serving institutions, (AANAPISI) and Hispanic-serving institutions (his) to shed light on how (or to what extent) racial and ethnic minority students with disabilities could be facing obstacles in having access to higher education due to poor Web accessibility. Additionally, future research could also address the ever-changing and technological nature of the modern U.S. college experience (Taylor, 2019).

Educational researchers, HBCU leaders, and communication professionals can learn from the results of previous studies of different types of institutions and websites' accessibility to improve Web accessibility. HBCU leaders and communication professionals must make themselves aware of Web accessibility guidelines and methods of website accessibility auditing to fix errors that may be present, for instance, providing context and including important metadata to Web pages to prevent missing information on the purpose and use of certain hyperlinks or buttons with unknown destinations or tasks/purposes. Providing knowledge to users pertaining to the use of certain features and their function may deem beneficial (where do they lead the user when accessed?). "Perhaps web accessibility professional development can be the remedy for the many web accessibility errors" (Taylor, 2019, p. 463). Focusing on Web accessibility is a way of increasing accessibility to a broader array of potential students and diversifying campus communities.

Conclusion

"Laws, policies, and guidelines that protect and advocate for persons with disabilities are salient in higher education" (Graves & German, 2018, p. 561). While assistive supports are available for students with disabilities, the context in which these services are accessed or utilized may be continuously debatable. Library resources have been and will continue to be essential in the advancement and successful navigation of knowledge. However, individuals with disabilities are oftentimes challenged with their resources to access services. Through acknowledgment of library resources, their use, and the need of students, educators can provide guidance to an array of individuals needing supports to aid student success in postsecondary endeavors, as well as higher education.

Questions/Considerations

1. In what ways could accessibility influence the quality of a transition to an online learning environment?
2. What are some of the barriers to accessibility that will impact students with disabilities to engage in online course instruction?
3. What types of training should library staff engage in to better serve students with disabilities on campus?

References

ADA National Network. (2020). *What is the definition of disability under the ADA?* https://adata.org/faq/what-definition-disability-under-ada

Adams, C. M. (2017). *Inclusive post-secondary education and quality of life: A case study* [Unpublished master's thesis, University of Regina].

Alkhalifa, S., & Al-Razgan, M. (2018). Enssat: Wearable technology application for the deaf and hard of hearing. *Multimedia Tools and Applications, 77*(17), 22007–22031. https://doi.org/10.1007/s11042-018-5860-5

American Library Association. (2019, January). *ALA policy manual section A: Organization and organizational policies.* http://www.ala.org/aboutala/sites/ala.org.aboutala/files/content/Section%20A%20New%20Policy%22Manual-1%20%28final%204-20-2020%29%20with%20TOC%29.pdf

American Library Association. (2019, June). *ALA policy manual section B: Positions and public policy statements.* http://www.ala.org/aboutala/sites/ala.org.aboutala/files/content/Section%20B%20New%20Policy%20Manual-1%20%28REVISED%2011_25_2019%29.pdf

American Library Association. (2019, January). *Library services to persons with disabilities: Home.* https://libguides.ala.org/libservice-disability

Bashir, R., Fatima, G., Malik, M. Y., & Ali, I. (2017). Library resources for persons with special needs: A quantitative analysis. *Bulletin of Education and Research, 39*(2), 215–224.

Bates, J., & Sato, C. (2019, October 15). *UDOIT information.* https://community.canvaslms.com/docs/DOC-6504-udoit-information

Blackboard. (n.d.). *Accessibility in Blackboard Collaborate with the Ultra Experience.* https://help.blackboard.com/Collaborate/Ultra/Administrator/Accessibility

Brannen, M. H., Milewski, S., & Mack, T. (2017). Providing staff training and programming to support people with disabilities: An academic library case study. *Public Services Quarterly, 13*(2), 61–77. https://doi.org/10.1080/15228959.2017.1298491

Canvas (2020, September). *Once I publish a timed quiz, how can I give my students extra time?* https://community.canvaslms.com/t5/Instructor-Guide/Once-I-publish-a-timed-quiz-how-can-I-give-my-students-extra/ta-p/999#:~:text=Add%20Extra%20Time%20on%20Current,quiz%2C%20click%20the%20clock%20icon.

Carlson, L. L. (2018). *Higher ed accessibility lawsuits, complaints, and settlements.* http://www.d.umn.edu/~lcarlson/atteam/lawsuits.html

Cassidy, B., & Shahtalimasehi, S. (2010). The impact of modern library services on the rehabilitation of people with disabilities. *International Journal on Disability and Human Development, 9*(4), 301–306. https://doi.org/10.1515/IJDHD.2010.038

Cisco (2020). *Meetings that work for everyone.* https://www.webex.com/accessibility.html

Crookes, D. (2020). Our guide to Zoom. *Web User,* 38-39.

Davidson, B. (2018). Promoting equity in education: Understanding the secondary lived experiences that propelled intellectually disabled students to continue their education in college.

Dermody, K., & Majekodunmi, N. (2011). Online databases and the research experience for university students with print disabilities. *Library Hi Tech, 29*(1), 149–160.

Edwards-Johnson, A. (2009). Library media specialists and assisted technology. *School Library Media Activities, 25*(10), 22–24.

Gallinger, K. R. (2013). *Inclusive post-secondary education: Stories of seven students with intellectual disabilities attending college in Ontario, Canada* [Unpublished doctoral dissertation, Queen's University].

Getts, E., & Stewart, K. (2018). Accessibility of distance library services for deaf and hard of hearing users. *Reference Services Review, 46*(3), 439–448. https://doi.org/10.1108/RSR-03-2018-0032

Graves, S. J., & German, E. (2018). Evidence of our values: Disability inclusion on library instruction websites. *Portal: Libraries and the Academy, 18*(3), 559–574.

Holmes, A., & Silvestri, R. (2011). *Employment experience of Ontario's postsecondary graduates with disabilities.* Higher Education Quality Council of Ontario.

Institute for Human Centered Design. (2016). *ADA checklist for existing facilities.* https://www.ada-checklist.org/doc/fullchecklist/ada-checklist.pdf

Lawal-Solarin, E. O. (2012). A survey of library and information services to physically-challenged students in academic libraries in Ogun state, Nigeria. *Library Philosophy and Practice*.

Lewis, J. (2013). Information equality for individuals with disabilities: Does it exist? *Library Quarterly, 83*(3), 229–235.

Mabawonku, I. (2005). The information needs of Artisans: Case study of Artisans in Ibadan, Nigeria. *Lagos Journal of Library and Information Science, 3*(1), 61–76.

Moodle. (2020, June 12). *Accessibility*. https://docs.moodle.org/dev/Accessibility

Mulliken, A., & Atkins, A. (2009). Academic library services for users with developmental disabilities. *The Reference Librarian, 50*(3), 276–287. https://doi.org/10.1080/02763870902873461

National Center for Education Statistics (NCES). (2020, May). *Students with disabilities*. https://nces.ed.gov/programs/coe/indicator_cgg.asp

National Federation for the Blind. (2019). *Blindness statistics*. https://www.nfb.org/resources/blindness-statistics

Okezie, C. A. (2016). Types of library and information science publications available in selected academic libraries in Nigeria. *Journal of Library and Information Sciences, 4*(1), 63–72.

Pamatani, S. L., Himawanto, D. A., & Widyastono, H. (2019). Availability of supporting facilities for students with physical disabilities who use wheelchairs in special schools. *Social Science and Humanities Journal, 3*(12), 1675–1680.

Pionke, J. J. (2017). Beyond ADA compliance: The library as a place for all. *Urban Library Journal, 23*(1), 1–17.

Sasaki, D. (2020, March 2). *Accessibility within Canvas*. https://community.canvaslms.com/docs/DOC-2061-accessibility-within-canvas

Schiff, R. A. (2009). Information literacy and blind and visually impaired students. *Urban Library Journal, 15*(2). https://academicworks.cuny.edu/ulj/vol15/iss2/5

Stella, J., & Corry, M. (2017). A capability approach for online primary and secondary students with disabilities. *British Journal of Special Education, 44*(4), 448–464.

Stewart, J. M., Schwartz, S., Bilodeau, P.-L., & Hanin Frédéric. (2018). Equal education, unequal jobs: College and university students with disabilities. *Relations Industrielles, 73*(2), 369–394. https://doi.org/10.7202/1048575ar

Sutterlin, J. (2018, December). *Learning is social with zoom video conferencing in your classroom*. https://elearnmag.acm.org/archive.cfm?aid=3236697&doi=10.1145%2F3302261.3236697

Taylor, Z. W. (2019). HBCUs online: Can students with disabilities access historically Black college and university websites? *Journal of Black Studies, 50*(5), 450–467. https://doi.org/10.1177/0021934719847373

U.S. Access Board. (2018). *Text of the standards and guidelines*. https://www.access-board.gov/guidelines-and-standards/communications-and-it/about-the-ict-refresh/final-rule/text-of-the-standards-and-guidelines

U.S. Department of Education. (2020). *Protecting students with disabilities.* https://www2.ed.gov/about/offices/list/ocr/504faq.html

U.S. Department of Justice. (2020, February). *A guide to disability rights law.* https://www.ada.gov/cguide.htm#anchor65610

U.S. General Services Administration. (2020). *IT accessibility laws and policies: Section 508 of the Rehabilitation Act of 1973.* https://www.section508.gov/manage/laws-and-policies

Vernon, R. (2010). Inexpensive accessibility options for your library. *Feliciter, 3*(56), 98–99.

W3C. (2018a). *Web content accessibility guidelines (WCAG) overview.* https://www.w3.org/WAI/standards-guidelines/wcag/

W3C. (2018b). *Understanding success criterion 1.1.1.* https://www.w3.org/TR/UNDERSTANDING-WCAG20/text-equiv-all.html

Wentz, B., Jaeger, P. T., & Bertot, J. C. (2015). *Accessibility, inclusion, and the roles of libraries.* https://www.researchgate.net/publication/290211686_Accessibility_Inclusion_and_the_Roles_of_Libraries

Chapter 10

Leading the Next Generation of Students

Cassandra Sligh Conway, Noel A. Ysasi, and David Staten

T HE CHAPTERS PRESENTED IN THIS TEXTBOOK have enlightened educators and students about the resources required to assist students with disabilities in various environments. In Chapter 1 the authors presented a historical review of the definition of disability, types of disabilities, and some select literature on students with disabilities. Proceeding chapters discussed topics such as cultural pedagogy, universal design in instruction, learning disabilities, certain laws/policies/ACTS, reasonable accommodations, library resources, cultural aspects to consider in working with students with disabilities, specific issues to consider when working with students with specific disabilities, and personal testimonies. The overall aim of each chapter was as follows: (a) Professionals who work or who have experiences in the helping professions provided the reader with resources to consider using with students with disabilities; (b) questions were provided at the end of chapters that can assist students in understanding the chapter information and be applied in their profession or in their day-to-day interactions with persons with disabilities. Each topic was interconnected and weaved together the importance of the continued work that is necessary to meet the needs of the next generation of students with disabilities.

The next section provides some considerations and recommendations that can be utilized globally with students with disabilities.

Transitioning Into Postsecondary Institutions

The process for entering postsecondary education can often be quite daunting for the applicant; individuals must complete a college application, which requires submitting standardized test scores (e.g., SAT and/or ACT), writing a college essay, submitting letters of recommendation, paying an application fee, and completing a Free Application for Federal Student Aid (FASFA) form. Oftentimes, the student who is finally accepted becomes primarily focused on registering for classes as deadlines are fast approaching and class availability becomes limited. Additionally, new admissions for fall and spring can be overwhelming for the academic advisor with a significantly high caseload. As a result, academic advisors must solely direct their attention toward class registration for students they see. When this occurs, students in need of specific services are left without receiving information on the available campus resources (e.g., veteran resources, disability accommodations, etc.). It should be noted that although students are often given a packet detailing the services provided within their respective institution, many fail to thoroughly review the information, may be overwhelmed by the entire process, are often clouded by the excitement of starting college, and feel as though receiving a course schedule is the final step. Consequently, students will fail to complete, submit, and/or register for additional services needed to successfully integrate into college. The aforementioned discussion of entering a postsecondary institution serves as a reminder of the overwhelming admissions process that each new student must endure. For a student with a disability, an array of emotions can take place, but even more so when they are uncertain about any additional steps that must be taken to ensure a smooth and successful transition into college. When comparing K–12 and postsecondary institutions, schools are responsible for identifying students with disabilities, testing those students, and providing accommodations and modifications to their educational instruction. Conversely, students at the college level are responsible for locating the office that provides services for students with disabilities, identifying themselves as having a disability, requesting accommodations, and providing the necessary documentation to support the need for accommodations. For college students who are able to successfully complete all the necessary requirements for receiving accommodations, postsecondary schools face challenges with being able to adequately and efficiently support students due to insufficient staffing and space, financial constraints, and lack of campus-wide coordination (Mamiseishvili & Koch, 2011).

Providing Effective Services for Students With Disabilities

In an effort to ameliorate the transitional difficulties experienced by students with disabilities entering a postsecondary institution while simultaneously enhancing services received, a comprehensive revision of the Higher Education and Opportunity Act of 2008 (HEOA) was enacted (U.S. Department of Education, 2019). The HEOA added new provisions to the Higher Education Act, with special attention toward addressing the needs of minority students. These amendments included (a) a focus on providing quality instruction through the use of scientifically based research on teaching and learning and implementation of classroom technology and mentor programs; (b) increasing post-baccalaureate opportunities for Hispanic and low-income students at predominately Hispanic-serving institutions; (c) supporting institutions that primarily serve minorities; and (d) increasing financial assistance. Despite these legislative efforts, an array of complex issues remain. As HEOA (2008) made significant strides to address the needs of minority college students with disabilities, they nonetheless have poorer academic performance and higher dropout rates in comparison to other students (Dennis et al., 2005). A study conducted by Terenzini et al. (1996) found minority students are often less equipped for college due to the following: (a) poor academic preparation from high school; (b) insufficient college preparation (e.g., mentoring, guidance, and support from high school teachers and guidance counselors); (c) a lack in both personal skills and social supports, which generally contribute to positive academic outcomes; and (d) lower critical thinking scores prior to college.

We briefly turn our attention to minority and nonminority students with a disability. Overall, students with disabilities will often experience discrimination; lack of understanding and cooperation from administrators, faculty, staff, and other students; and inaccessibility of building facilities and grounds (Walker, 2008). College students with disabilities often experience academic challenges due to a lack of appropriate and necessary accommodations; this often occurs when students are no longer able to receive similar accommodations and modifications (e.g., reduction in work assignment) as they once did during their K–12 schooling; an institution's disability services (DS) office has limited support staff and/or operates under a one-size-fits-all approach. For instance, let us consider two college students diagnosed with attention deficit hyperactivity disorder (ADHD). Both have been approved for extended time and a reduced distraction site for exams, but one individual is a low-income minority student unable to afford the cost of prescription medication used to treat ADHD and is experiencing a heightened level of anxiety as a result. Additionally, the student has begun to exhibit signs and symptoms of depression due to the transitional difficulties commonly experienced by minority students when understanding and cooperation is lacking from faculty and staff. In order to provide effective services for both minority and nonminority students with disabilities, institutions must increase DS support staff, preferably with a rehabilitation counseling background, as they are trained to appropriately screen and identify whether further diagnostic testing is needed. Furthermore, all students should be informed of the health services generally covered on campus, but DS staff should provide this for each new applicant seeking accommodations as prescription medication may not be covered by postsecondary tuition and fees. To safeguard against poor academic achievement and improve educational services for minority and nonminority students with disabilities, additional recommendations are encouraged: (a) Trainings designed at providing disability awareness among administrators, faculty, and staff should be standard practice; (b) college applications should encourage students with disabilities to self-disclose and provide reassurance that doing so will not affect one's chance of being accepted; (c) academic advising centers working with new student registration should designate a minimum of one advisor for students with disabilities to provide guidance, mentoring, and information pertaining to various support services offered within their respective institution; and (d) require students with disabilities to register at their institutions' DS office prior to registering for classes and/or place an academic hold on students who identify as having a disability but fail to register with the DS office.

Considerations for Working With Students With Disabilities Post-COVID-19

Nationally, 707,000 students with disabilities are enrolled in a postsecondary institution (19.4% undergraduate; 11.9% graduate; U.S. Department of Education, 2019). The type of disability reported by institutions include specific learning disabilities (31%), ADHD (18%), mental illness or psychiatric conditions (15%), and health impairment or condition (e.g., visual and/or hearing impairment; 11%; U.S. Department of Education, 2019). As institutions of higher education and legislative efforts have aimed to ameliorate the challenges minority and nonminority students with disabilities experience when enrolled in a postsecondary institution, new and creative strategies undoubtably will be necessary to circumvent the issues faced as a result of the 2020 COVID-19 pandemic. As states began implementing stay-at-home orders and universities began to shift all face-to-face courses to distant learning, on-campus services quickly became interrupted and the method of delivery was impeded. Furthermore, the ability to seek an environment conducive to learning (e.g., libraries and study halls) was no longer available, inevitably affecting students diagnosed with a learning disability or ADHD as studying from home can be considerably distracting. For others, staying at home for extended periods of time without having the opportunity to socialize with their peers can exacerbate symptoms (e.g., depression) commonly found among individuals diagnosed with a mental health disorder. For students who are visually or hearing impaired, the ability to successfully complete coursework online may create more stress and heighten one's anxiety. As a case in point, an application known as JAWS (Jobs Access With Speech) is a screen reader application used by individuals with a visual impairment, yet Blackboard (an online learning management system) is not compatible with the software. When students have chosen to take a course with a face-to-face delivery method but are now having to learn and navigate through an unfamiliar learning platform, frustration, anxiety, and stress can set in, ultimately hindering their chances for successful course completion. Although it is not uncommon for universities to cancel class due to a natural disaster (e.g., hurricane), extreme weather conditions (e.g., blizzards), or crises (e.g., school shooting), rarely do they completely shift their method of instruction to online as power outages are common and/or low-income students may not have the resources to complete online schoolwork from home (e.g., no internet, computer, laptop, etc.). As a result, institutions must begin to reflect on the difficulties students with disabilities face during the global pandemic, develop new methods for ensuring all students have equal access to a quality education, and modify accommodations as appropriate for students with disabilities. Some examples can include but are not limited to (a) providing telehealth counseling services for students with mental health disorders or psychiatric conditions; (b) partnering with local libraries to allow college students with disabilities to have priority access to study rooms and/or areas with sound masking (e.g., noise reduction areas); (c) allowing students with disabilities to have access to buildings and rooms that are monitored off. site; (d) increasing funding for DS offices for assistive technology (AT) and hiring additional staff; (e) ensuring all learning platforms are compatible with AT used by students; (f) ensuring all instructional and supplemental videos have closed captioning capability; and (g) maintaining frequent communication with students regarding any issues or concerns they are experiencing.

In light of the global pandemic of COVID-19, it is hoped that the lessons learned globally about the need for remote platforms and reaching the distance education needs of students with disabilities will be a constant review at the secondary and postsecondary levels. No longer will the face-to-face classroom ever be the best platform for classroom delivery, especially in times of crisis. No one technique will work for every student, and there must be an open dialogue to include the views of various cultures. There is no room for discrimination, prejudice, racism, sexism, or any behavior that excludes or limits the access of students who need services and opportunities. Our world must continue to seek justice for diverse populations and be a voice for all, including students with disabilities.

References

Dennis, J. M., Phinney, J. S., & Chuateco, L. I. (2005). The role of motivation, parental support, and peer support in the academic success of ethnic minority first-generation college students. *Journal of college student development, 46*(3), 223–236.

U.S. Department of Education, National Center for Education Statistics. (2019). *Digest of Education Statistics, 2017* (2018–070). Higher Education Opportunity Act of 2008, Public Law 110–315. (2008).

Mamiseishvili, K., & Koch, L. C. (2011). First-to-second-year persistence of students with disabilities in postsecondary institutions in the United States. *Rehabilitation Counseling Bulletin, 54*(2), 93–105.

Terenzini, P. T., Springer, L., Yaeger, P. M., Pascarella, E. T., & Nora, A. (1996). First-generation college students: Characteristics, experiences, and cognitive development. *Research in Higher education, 37*(1), 1–22.

Walker, D. K. (2008). *Minority and non-minority students with disabilities in higher education: Are current university policies meeting their needs?*. University of Illinois at Urbana-Champaign.

Afterword

COLLEGE STUDENTS WITH DISABILITIES DIFFER IN some ways from the average student. Although no student is the same, they all share some similarities, but it is those differences that this book addresses. This book was written to provide the reader with empirical and conceptual literature, essential statistics, model programs, value of resources, and strategies and recommendations helpful in working with students with disabilities in higher education. Students who progress to the post-secondary arena may still need some resources in order to have a fair chance at succeeding academically. It is the responsibility of those in higher education to ensure that those resources are available and provided. School officials, faculty, staff and students must be involved in a sharing of information.

The difference in services for students in k-12 and those in higher education is that students with disabilities in higher education have to inform the institution that they have a disability and need services, the student must also provide documentation to the institution's coordinator of disabilities, or Disability Service Officer. More and more high school students with disabilities are planning to continue their education in post-secondary schools, including vocational and career schools, two- and four-year colleges, and universities. Unlike high school, however, postsecondary schools are not required to provide FAPE (free appropriate public education). Rather, they are required to provide appropriate academic adjustments as necessary to ensure that it does not discriminate on the basis of disability. However, disclosure of a disability is always voluntary (UDOE, OCR, 2011, https://www.disabled-world.com/disability/education/student-disability-rights.php).

This book was written to provide information to students and educators related to resources for working with students with disabilities in higher education. Often times only that faculty who work in the education department have taken one or more courses in working with students with disabilities, because it is a requirement. However, those who are outside of the field of education have not had any experience or taken any course in working with students with disabilities. Therefore, faculty, staff, and students need to be informed on ways to help students with disabilities so the needs of the whole student can be addressed, not just the academic needs. Students may need accommodations to be involved in social activities as well. Therefore, this book can be useful to the entire college community (including student services, food services, custodial staff, housing, financial aid and business services etc.) and external agencies because more and more students with disabilities are pursuing higher education and transitioning to diverse jobs/careers.

As the goal should be to ensure that students with disabilities who go on to higher education institutions be successful and have a positive experience, it is of the utmost importance that persons working with these students have an understanding of their disabilities., utilize best practice and proven strategies. Working with Students with Disabilities: Utilizing Resources in the Helping Professions is a contemporary book that provides that information. This book was written for general educators, counselors, special educators, lay persons, students, researchers, agencies, and administrators who work with individuals with disabilities. The contributing authors all have worked with persons with disabilities, are from diverse backgrounds and areas of concentration, and each of them brought a wealth of experiences and knowledge to the writing of this useful, relevant, and informative book. I applaud Dr. Cassandra Sligh Conway for bringing us all together for such a time as this, i.e., sharing of resources from multiple institutions and agencies.

Gloria Hayes, Ph.D.
Dean of Fundamental Studies
Miles College

Reference

Disabled World (2011). Students with Disabilities Preparing for Postsecondary Education: Know Your Rights and Responsibilities. Retrieved on June 10, 2020, https://www.disabled- world.com/disability/education/student-disability-rights.php.

About the Editors

Dr. Cassandra Sligh Conway is a tenured professor at South Carolina State University. She has earned over 1.5 million dollars in grant awards. She has several publications in journals, book chapters, and has authored an academic book entitled *Faculty Mentorship at HBCUS*.

David Staten, Ph.D, LPC-S, LPC, CRC is a professor in the rehabilitation counseling program at South Carolina State University. He is a Licensed Professional Counselor-Supervisor and Certified Rehabilitation Counselor. Dr. Staten received his Ph.D in rehabilitation counselor education from the University of Iowa, M.A. in rehabilitation, and B.S. in criminal justice from SCSU in 1992. His primary areas of research includes racial identity development of minorities with disabilities, health orientations of African American college students, and health disparities of minorities with disabilities.

Dr. Staten has been employed by South Carolina State University as a rehabilitation counselor educator for the past 19 years. He is currently the president of the SC State University Faculty Senate. He is also the editor of the *HBCU Times Magazine*. Additionally, he has over 15 years of administrative experience as the program director of the rehabilitation counseling program and several years of experience serving as department chair. He has successfully managed several million dollars of external grant funds from agencies such as Rehabilitation Services Administration (RSA), National Institute for Disability Related Research (NIDRR), and the United States Department of Agriculture.

Dr. Mable Scott is a retired public school physical education teacher and is now an associate professor in the Health Sciences Department at South Carolina State University. She has written several book chapters including "Motivating Students to stay Focused in College" (2013) and "Mentorship of Faculty at HBCUs and the Role in Motivating Students" (2017).

About the Contributors

John Bates has a Master of Rehabilitation Counseling degree from South Carolina State University and is a certified rehabilitation counselor. He currently works with the South Carolina Department of Vocational Rehabilitation as a training center manager.

Dr. Terrilyn Battle is an Assistant Professor in the Master of Arts in Counseling program at Stockton University. Dr. Battle's research agenda reflects exploring employability among underrepresented populations, the awareness of Imposter Phenomenon and implications of mentorship, and cultural immersion among counselors-in-training to enhance multicultural competency.

Freddie Boan, MPA, MRC, directs an office that oversees rehabilitation services in South Carolina. Mr. Boan has spent a large part of his professional career as an advocate for individuals with disabilities. He has appeared before the U.S. Congress and State of South Carolina Congress as an advocate for the National MS Society. Freddie is a proud graduate of Samford University and received his Master's of Public Administration degree from Augusta University and a Master of Rehabilitation Counseling from South Carolina State University. In addition to his experience in rehabilitation services Freddie serves on the CPI Advisory Board at Voorhees College, the Rehabilitation Counseling Advisory Board at South Carolina State University, and the Community Advisor Board at Denmark Technical College. Mr. Boan's passion for second chances and working with offenders led to his collaboration with Mr. Stephen Patterson on the publication of *Six Steps to Employment*, a guide to help offenders secure and maintain work.

Dr. Cynthia Bryant was born in Roxboro, North Carolina. Her family lived in Florida before moving to Orangeburg, South Carolina. She attended South Carolina State University where she received her undergraduate and graduate degrees. She continued her studies at the University of Alabama where she obtained her Doctor of Education degree. Dr. Bryant has taught in the public schools of North Carolina and South Carolina as well as in higher education. She has taught at Virginia Commonwealth University, the University of North Carolina at Chapel Hill, the University of North Carolina at Wilmington, North Carolina Central University, the College of Charleston, and Columbia College. She is presently employed at South Carolina State University. Dr. Bryant has taught courses in early childhood special education, diversity, intellectual disabilities, emotional disabilities, learning disabilities, education, and gifted education. Her licenses are in the areas of cross-categorial, emotional disabilities, intellectual disabilities, and learning disabilities.

Wanda Copeland is committed to educating students, colleagues, families, and the community through understanding and establishing strong relationships. She's an educator and Diversity, Including, and Belonging facilitator with over 20 years of public and higher education experience. Wanda firmly believes in equity and establishing a sense of belonging for student success.

Caleb Cuthbertson is a 2nd-year student in the Mental Health-Rehabilitation Counseling program at North Carolina Agricultural and Technical State University. His research interest area is masculinity and trauma. He serves as the student representative for the National Association for Multicultural Rehabilitation Concerns (NAMRC).

Dr. Glacia Ethridge is an associate professor in the Department of Counseling at North Carolina Agricultural and Technical State University. She is the program coordinator for the Mental Health-Rehabilitation Counseling program. She is a licensed clinical mental health counselor associate, a licensed clinical addiction specialist, a national certified counselor, and a certified rehabilitation counselor. Her research interests include career barriers for persons with psychiatric disabilities, social justice, addictions, and ex-offenders.

Dr. Crystal M. Giddings is department chair and associate tenured professor in the Department of Counselor Education at Clark Atlanta University. She is a retired teacher/school counselor of 38 years, has authored two books, book chapters, and professional articles, and is colead on the $1.8 million grant HBCU CARES.

Gloria Hayes, Ed.S., Ph.D. holds an Ed.S. in Special Education and a Ph.D. in Secondary Education with an emphasis in Higher Ed. Administration. She has taught special education in middle school, high school, and at the college level. She has been a special education director, a high school administrator, and college administrator. She is currently an Associate Professor of Education, Director of Jump Start Academic Readiness bridge program, and Interim Director of Student Support at Miles College in Birmingham, Alabama.

Antoinette C. Hollis, EdD, LPC, NCC is an assistant professor in counselor education at South Carolina State University in Orangeburg, South Carolina. She received her doctorate in counseling psychology from Argosy University. She is the principal investigator for a $500,000 1890 research grant to study "The Effects of Horticultural Therapy on At-Risk Youth Living in a Rural Community."

Dr. Bridget Hollis Staten is a tenured full professor in rehabilitation counseling at South Carolina State University in Orangeburg, South Carolina. She is a licensed professional counselor, licensed professional counselor-supervisor and certified rehabilitation counselor. She received her doctorate in rehabilitation counseling and administration from Southern Illinois University Carbondale, Illinois.

Ebrahim Mansaray is a 2nd-year student in the Mental Health-Rehabilitation Counseling program at North Carolina Agricultural and Technical State University. His research interests include studying the resiliency of sexual and gender minorities, immigrants, and first- and second-generation Americans who live with disabilities.

Dr. Cherilyn T. Minniefield earned her Bachelor of Arts degree in Psychology from Bennett College. She completed both her master's and doctoral degrees in clinical psychology from Bowling Green State University in Ohio. Dr. Minniefield is a licensed clinical psychologist who began her career at the University of Virginia's Center for Counseling and Psychological Services, where she spent 3 years providing mental health care to UVA's graduate and undergraduate student population. She spent 3 years as the director of counseling and wellness services at Presbyterian College in Clinton, South Carolina. Additionally, Dr. Minniefield has taught psychology at both the undergraduate and graduate levels as an adjunct professor at colleges and universities in the Midwest and the Southeast. For the past 11 years, she has served as the director of counseling, testing, and student disability services at South Carolina State University.

Bernace Murray is a retired blind Braille instructor who contracted glaucoma, the silent blindness disease. He resides in Columbia, South Carolina, where he occasionally writes and does public speaking engagements to audiences of all ages. His favorite quote is "A man who does not read is no better off than a man who is blind."

Stephen Patterson, MEd is a professional trainer, speaker, and consultant. Steve specializes in ways to incorporate humor into your professional and personal life. His love for humor led to his writing his first book *Better Living Through Laughter: An Attitude to Live By* (2009). Since its publication he has written two additional novels *The King's Last Ride* (2017) and the soon to be released *Let's Go if You're Going*. Steve is a proud graduate of Elon University and received his Master's of Education from the University of South Carolina. For over 30 years Steve has designed programs and training opportunities for a variety of industries, from health care to banking. Steve began his career as a counselor specializing in personal development through self-awareness while working in psychiatry. Now Steve helps direct a prerelease program for offenders reentering society and specializes in creating hope for those with a criminal background. His work with offenders has led to the publication *Six Steps to Employment*, a guide to help offenders secure and maintain work.

Dr. Rose Skepple serves as the school of teacher education coordinator in the College of Education at Florida State University. Her research interest is culturally responsive assessment and evaluation of teacher education programs. Her other interests include school culture, equity, and student academic performance in urban and rural schools.

Dr. Tammara P. Thomas studied rehabilitation counseling education at the University of Iowa. Dr. Tammara Thomas is an associate professor at Winston-Salem State University's School of Education. She teaches in the Department of Rehabilitation Counseling/Rehabilitation and Human Services Undergraduate program.

Her teaching and research activities have focused on issues of rehabilitation counseling, mental health counseling and cooccurring disorders, gender-specific treatment, program development and supervision, evaluation and management, ethics, and vocational counseling and evaluation.

Dr. Thomas has served as a vocational rehabilitation counselor for the Department of Veteran Affairs, providing counseling and career development for both veterans and soldiers.

Dr. Thomas's professional activities are extensive as a rehabilitation counselor, counselor educator, practitioner, and administrator. Dr. Thomas has served as trainer, speaker, instructor, program developer, manager and evaluator, grant writer/reviewer, curriculum developer, and community liaison. Dr. Thomas has provided myriad services aimed to help individuals achieve a better quality of life for over 2 decades.

Shanju Vigasini is a special education teacher in Greenville county schools. She holds degrees in rehabilitation science, counseling psychology, and special education. She is currently pursuing her doctoral research on intervention strategies for ADHD and learning disabilities. She has worked in multiple capacities in the school system and in the resource, inclusion, and self-contained settings.

Dr. Quiteya Walker is an Associate Professor in Rehabilitation Counseling at Winston-Salem State University. Dr. Walker is a graduate of South Carolina State University with both her Bachelor's and Master's degrees in Criminal Justice and Rehabilitation Counseling, respectively. She received her Master's Degree in Clinical Mental Health Counseling from Walden University and Doctorate in Counseling, Rehabilitation, and Student Development from The University of Iowa. She is a Licensed Clinical Mental Health Counselor Associate (LCMHCA) in the State of North Carolina, a Certified Rehabilitation Counselor (CRC), and a National Certified Counselor (NCC). Dr. Walker has over a decade of experience as a counselor educator and experience providing services to individuals with disabilities in the postsecondary settings and community agencies.

Courtney Ward-Sutton, PhD, CRC, is a post-doctoral research fellow at the Advanced Rehabilitation Research and Training (ARRT) program, situated within the Rehabilitation Research and Training Center (RRTC) on Research and Capacity Building for Minority Entities at Langston University.

Dr. Sheila Witherspoon is the program coordinator and associate professor in the Counselor Education program at South Carolina State University in the Department of Human Services. Dr. Witherspoon received her doctorate in counselor education and supervision from the University of South Carolina and her master and bachelor degrees from South Carolina State University. She is currently a learner in the MS Ed. in Instructional Design for Online Learning at Capella University and has been an online doctoral educator for over 10 years in the areas of counseling, psychology, human services, and organizational psychology. Her expertise in higher education in both academic (master's and doctoral) and college student affairs (admissions counselor, recruiter, and academic advisor) as well as K–12 education (school counseling) spans over 30 years. The qualitative action researcher studies culturally responsive instructional design in online learning—particularly in courses designed to enhance cultural competence through the examination of microaggressions and undiagnosed PTSD in African Americans. She gives back to her community by participating in counseling, distance education, and civic organizations such as the American Counseling Association, Black Doctoral Network, Inc., Online Learning Consortium–Affordable Learning Summit, Southern Regional Education Board, Association of Counselor Educators and Supervisors, Palmetto State School Counseling Association (South Carolina), South Carolina Counseling Association, Association of Counselor Educators and Supervisors, Southern Association of Counselor Educators and Supervisors, New Brunswick Education Foundation (New Jersey), and Alpha Kappa Alpha Sorority, Inc.

Noel A. Ysasi, PhD, CRC, is an assistant professor in the Department of Addictions and Rehabilitation Studies and serves as coordinator for the Certificate in Military and Trauma Counseling. Dr. Ysasi has 12 years of teaching in higher education and has published 26 book chapters and journal articles. Dr. Ysasi's area of research includes the veteran and military population and culture, psychosocial adjustment to disability, perceptions of people with disabilities, and forensic rehabilitation. Dr. Ysasi is past president for the American Rehabilitation Counseling Association and past at-large director for the Commission on Rehabilitation Counselor Certification (CRCC).

CPSIA information can be obtained
at www.ICGtesting.com
Printed in the USA
LVHW100409110221
678960LV00003B/20